IT'S NO ACCIDENT

HOW CORPORATIONS SELL DANGEROUS BABY PRODUCTS

E. Marla Felcher

Common Courage Press

Monroe, ME
Philadelphia, PA

Library of Congress Cataloguing in Publications Data

Felcher, E. Marla, 1957-
        It's no accident: How corporations sell dangerous baby prod-
            ucts/ by E. Marla Felcher
                p. cm.
        Includes bibliographical references and index.
        ISBN 1-56751-205-4 (cloth)—ISBN 1-56751-204-6 (pbk.)
            1. Products liability—Infants' supplies—United States.
            2. Product recall—Law and legislation—United States. 3.
            Graco (Firm)—Trials, litigation, etc. 4. U.S. Consumer
            Product Safety Commission. I. Title.
            KF1297.I54 F45 2001
            346.7303'8—dc21

Common Courage Press
P.O. Box 702
Monroe, Maine 04951
207-525-0900; fax: 207-525-3068
orders-info@commoncouragepress.com

www.commoncouragepress.com

First Printing

In memory of Danny Keysar,
December 31, 1996–May 12, 1998,

In gratitude to my sister, Adrienne B. Bannon, for her
frequent doses of encouragement, and
for listening when she'd already heard enough,

With love to my husband, Max H. Bazerman, the most
tolerant human on the planet.

Contents

Author's Note:

One morning a few years ago, when I had just started to work on this book, I received a telephone call from a former student, seeking career advice. She had taken my Marketing Management class, as an undergraduate at Northwestern University. Now, she told me, she was working as an intern at a major television network, and had been assigned to a prime time "news magazine" show. I congratulated her, impressed that she had gotten a job that most of her cohorts would have deemed ideal. She told me she hated it. Why, I asked. "All I do is chase down grieving parents whose children have died in some horrible way. I can't stand it." She wanted to know if I could help get her a job in marketing. I told her that I had recently decided to make the opposite career switch she was envisioning for herself: I had left marketing for journalism. I don't imagine that the advice I gave her was very useful.

Shortly after this call, I began to receive files I had requested from the U.S. government, documenting the stories of children who had been killed by baby products. Many of these files identified the dead children by name, and even included their families' addresses and telephone numbers, making it easy for me to track them down. But I couldn't get myself to call them. My friends, Linda and Boaz, were one of these families, and I had watched, firsthand, as the press had hounded them the days following their son Danny's death. I didn't want to become, in the words of my ex-student, a journalist who "chased down grieving parents whose children died in some horrible way." For this reason, I have changed the names of all the victims I write about in this book. There are a couple of exceptions, people I have spoken with extensively, and who want their stories to be told, in the hopes that other parents will be spared the pain they have experienced: my friends, Linda Ginzel, Boaz, and Ely Keysar; Portia Moore (Chapter 4), whose son was injured when he fell out of his infant carrier (he has recovered), and Ruthann Scarlatella (Chapter 4), whose daughter was caught in the rails of a toddler bed (she was not injured).

If your child has been injured by a baby product, I urge you to come forward and report the incident to the government and the manufacturer (See Chapter 6).

Introduction

As I was finishing research on this book, I attended a product-safety conference in Orlando, where I listened for three days to manufacturers, defense lawyers, government regulators, and consumer advocates debate the legal, medical, and public policy issues surrounding consumer product safety. By the second day, I was exhausted. Every key player relevant to this book was there, and I scurried between sessions and interviews at a frenetic pace. An afternoon session of the second day was called "Parents as Advocates." Three parents bravely told the death stories of their children—all of them killed by products that were unsafe. The room was packed. Halfway through the session, a conference organizer ran out of the room in search of a hotel employee. "Please," she asked a woman who was refilling the coffee urn, "can you get me a couple of boxes of tissue, fast?" The roomful of conference attendees, dressed in business attire, had no place to wipe their tears.

That night, at a post-meeting cocktail party, I spotted a high-level Consumer Product Safety Commission (CPSC) regulator I'd wanted to talk to. The CPSC is the federal regulatory agency that oversees the safety of infant products. I had interviewed him six months before, and had been pleasantly surprised by his candor. In the time since, I'd had a tough time getting anyone from the federal agency to "open up," and there were a few nagging questions I was certain this man could answer. Approaching him, I extended my hand and asked what he'd thought of the day's sessions. He looked uneasy, his eyes darting over my head. Shaking my hand, his eyes, wary and uncertain, finally settled on mine. "Well, do you still hate me?" he said.

I'm not easy to catch off-guard, but he'd done it. I'd thought we had an agreeable, albeit cautious, relationship. He, at least, was one of the few people at the CPSC who returned my calls. Hate? Clearly, I'd misjudged. I mumbled a confused denial, made small talk I can no longer remember, and was grateful when someone else caught his attention.

That night, I reflected back on that initial interview. What I remembered was this: Though, at that point, I had been working on this book for a year, the profound difficulty of the job of CPSC regulator only became clear to me that day. This man read horrible stories, all day long, about how people—many of them children—were injured and killed by products that should never have been on the market in the first place. His agency could nip at the heels of industry, but rarely could it take a satisfying bite. Driving away from his office, I'd wondered, "How does this man deal with what has to be one of the most frustrating jobs in the universe?" But at the cocktail party six months later, I learned that while I was admiring his commitment to public safety, he was wondering why I hated him. What had I said?

As soon as I got home to Boston, I pulled up my notes of that interview. It took me only a couple of minutes to figure out the puzzle: I had asked him tough questions that day, ones that burrowed deep to the core of his agency's vulnerability. At the time I didn't know this, which made asking the questions easy. I had been on a mission: My friends' seventeen-month-old son Danny had recently been killed by a Playskool portable crib, and I was looking for the culprit. At the time, the CPSC was a leading suspect. The CPSC is responsible for protecting children from dangerous products, and yet somehow Danny had been killed by a crib the CPSC was well aware was deadly. My friends, both University of Chicago professors, read all the right parenting books, child proofed their home, and interviewed daycare providers as if they were seeking a corporate C.E.O.—

yet they had not known the crib had been recalled. How had this happened?

Talking with the regulator in his office, I didn't understand that Danny's death was not the CPSC's fault. I only figured this out a few weeks later, when a lawyer who had been closely following the CPSC since its inception in 1972 told me, "The agency is small and vulnerable and easy to ridicule. That's one of the reasons they get worried about the press—they are easy to criticize." More recently, when I complained to another source that the two CPSC regulators I've most wanted to talk with have refused, for two years, to grant me an interview, the person attributed their behavior to "typical CPSC paranoia."

Organizations, like individuals, don't like to be criticized. When the organization is a federally funded regulatory agency subject to the political whims of the president and Congress, the stakes are ratcheted up another notch. For the past thirty years, the CPSC, one of the smallest government agencies, has been fighting for funding, power, and at times for its life. Anything said publicly about the agency can be used against it by politicians who would like to let industry operate unencumbered by government intervention. This was precisely the fear of the CPSC regulator: that anything he revealed to me would one day be used by his adversaries as evidence that the CPSC should be abolished. Sometimes, the paranoid really *are* being stalked.

"You can't underestimate how worked up [some people] can get on product safety issues," a long-time CPSC fan told me. "They go on about how stupid people who get injured are, how they take advantage of the system." Maybe. But my friends aren't stupid. They are smart, they have always been obsessed with safety, and they have always taken necessary precautions. Yet their baby was killed.

Whose fault is it that Danny never lived to see his second birthday? To me, the answer is simple. Kolcraft Industries, the Chicago company that manufactured the crib, and Hasbro, the

Rhode Island corporation that leased its Playskool brand name to Kolcraft, are to blame. Eventually, the courts will decide if I'm right. The tougher, more complex question is, "Why did Danny die?" This is the question I address in this book.

When 11,600 parents bought the Playskool Travel-Lite crib, they entered into an implicit agreement with Hasbro and Kolcraft: We will give you money, and in exchange, you will give us a product that will not injure or kill our child. Both Kolcraft and Hasbro violated this agreement six times—each time the Travel-Lite collapsed and killed a baby. The CPSC does not have the authority to test the safety of products before they reach the marketplace. This was the responsibility of Kolcraft and Hasbro, and both companies shirked it. The CPSC recalled the Playskool crib after it killed three children, but the agency does not have the authority or budget to make sure that consumers get rid of hazardous products. This was the responsibility of Kolcraft and Hasbro, and both companies shirked it.

✳ ✳ ✳

Every consumer product has a certain level of risk associated with it. Through carelessness or poor judgment, humans will figure out ways of being injured by such seemingly innocuous products as artificial plants and VCRs. But the issue is bigger than the random death of one or two children in a crib, high chair, or cradle. Rather, the issue is how a regulatory system allowed more than a dozen infants to be killed by a Graco cradle (Chapter 1), sixty–six children to die in bath seats (Chapter 2), and six children to die in a Playskool portable crib (Chapter 3). These deaths were not random, and they were not completely unforeseen. Manufacturers who failed to adequately test their products and a government agency that has been stripped of the authority and budget it needs were responsible for these deaths. The deaths were not accidents. And until Congress gives the CPSC the budget and authority it needs to carry out its original mandate—*to protect the public against unreasonable risk of injury and death*—these tragedies will occur again and again and again.

    E. Marla Felcher, August 2000
    Cambridge, MA

Prologue

How Danny Died, and How We Found Out

I was standing on the porch of my Boston townhouse, fumbling for the front door key, when I heard the phone ring inside. My two border collies watched through the window, barking, "Hurry up! Hurry up!" I made it to the phone just as the answering machine was about to click on. It was my friend Dedre, calling from Chicago.

"Marla," she said gravely, then stopped. "Have you heard?" The dogs scratched at my legs for attention. Cupping the phone between my neck and shoulder, I knelt down on the kitchen floor to calm them.

"What's up?" I asked, looking at my watch. A chronic workaholic, Dedre rarely called during work hours. It was 11:10 a.m.

"Have you heard?" she asked again, then paused. "About Boaz? Have you heard what happened to Linda and… and… Boaz?" Her voice was soft and deep, the words syncopated in a way that suggested something was terribly wrong. Worried, I stood up and reached into the cabinet for treats to occupy the dogs.

"Are they okay? What happened?" I asked. Boaz was from Israel, and he and his wife Linda often visited his family there. Suddenly, I thought: Bomb.

"No, it's not them," Dedre said. "It's their baby, Danny." She took a deep breath, then exhaled loudly into the phone. "He's dead."

Nothing in one's life prepares a person for a sentence like that. Standing there, I stared out my kitchen window at the azalea, its magenta flowers in full bloom. I decided I'd misunderstood.

"Danny?" I asked. "Their baby, Danny?"

"He's dead," Dedre said.

How, I asked Dedre, could our friends' healthy seventeen–month–old baby be dead? She didn't know. But I couldn't stop asking questions.

"Was it a car crash?"

"No."

"Had he been ill?"

"Not that anyone knew."

"What happened?" I pleaded.

"I don't know," Dedre repeated in a whisper. "No one has any idea."

I remember little else about the next few hours, other than my frantic attempts to find out what had occurred. By the time I reached my husband at work, he had already gotten an email with the news of Danny's death. I called Linda and Boaz, but their phone was permanently busy—we later learned they had taken it off the hook when reporters started calling, one after another. From Boston, I was able to piece together bits and pieces of news, snippets of information that raised more questions than they answered. One friend said she'd heard Danny had been asleep at his baby-sitter's house when "the accident" occurred, but she wasn't sure exactly what "the accident" was. Another said Danny had been killed by a crib.

"A crib?" I asked. "How could a baby be killed by a crib?"

She didn't know.

By the end of the day, I was certain of only one thing: Danny's funeral had been set for the next day—May 14, 1998.

* * *

Danny had indeed been killed by his crib. On the afternoon of May 12, Danny's daycare provider, Anna, put the seventeen–month–old baby down for a nap in a portable Playskool Travel-Lite crib. When she checked on him a little later, Anna found that the crib had collapsed with Danny in it, trapping his neck in the "V"-shaped wedge of its folded rails. He was no longer breathing. Apparently, Danny had grabbed the crib's top rails and tried to stand. Though the toddler weighed only twenty-five pounds, the rails collapsed under his weight, folding shut at the center hinge.

Gathered under a hot afternoon sun at the cemetery, Linda and Boaz's family and friends stood shoulder-to-shoulder in a tight semi-circle around Danny's open grave. Shooting furtive glances at the tiny mahogany coffin, we didn't want to look, yet were unable to look away. We were grateful when Linda stood and faced the crowd, signaling the funeral was to begin.

"I want to tell you about Danny," Linda said in her take-charge teaching voice. Boaz and Danny's four-year-old brother Ely sat slumped in metal folding chairs, their backs to the crowd, their heads bowed identically. "Because he was only seventeen months old, most of you never had the opportunity to know him," Linda continued. She was wearing baggy clothes and an enormous navy blue scarf, tied under her chin in a loose knot. The scarf covered most of her face, but I could still see her eyes, sunken and exhausted. She looked like a refugee.

"What can I tell you Danny liked to do?" Linda asked the mourners. "He loved to flush the toilet. He always wanted to brush his teeth and hair, but would sometimes confuse the separate functions of a hairbrush and a toothbrush. He loved to shut doors, but then couldn't turn the knob to open the door once he had shut it, and so we would often hear his muffled voice behind the closed door calling, 'MAHHHHH?' We'd open the door, he'd smile at his rescuer and then grab the knob and shut it again." Linda's voice didn't waver as she spoke for ten minutes about her son, a toddler who never tired of humming "Twinkle, Twinkle, Little Star," who preferred to eat his crayons rather than draw with them, and whose favorite book was *Lila Tov Yareach*, the Hebrew version of *Goodnight Moon*.

When the funeral was over, we filed back to our cars in silence, stunned. As we drove out of the cemetery I asked my husband what it had felt like to be a pallbearer, lifting the coffin from the hearse, placing it beside the waiting grave.

"Light," he said, staring straight ahead at the mid-afternoon traffic, his voice parched, like mine, from standing too long in the sun. "All that was going through my head was how light a solid wood box could feel."

❖ ❖ ❖

Linda and Boaz did not blame Anna for their son's death. Anna had been caring for the child in her Sweet Tots daycare home for ten months, and she loved Danny, Linda told us again and again, as if he were her own son. As a licensed daycare provider, Sweet Tots was required to undergo periodic safety inspections. State inspectors had been to the home just eight days before the accident and had noted nothing unusual about the crib.

"It was a freak accident, a fluke," became Linda's mantra during the few days following Danny's death. "It could have happened to anyone." Sometimes when she said this, though, her voice would crack, her eyes would fill with tears, and she'd look straight up, as if addressing God. "But why," she'd ask, "why did it have to happen to my sweet Danny?"

In the days following Danny's funeral, as they began to piece together information about their son's death, Linda and Boaz's acceptance turned to horror. A newspaper reporter preparing an article on Danny's death had discovered that it had not been an isolated incident. The Playskool Travel-Lite portable crib that had strangled Danny had killed four other infants. The crib was so dangerous that the government had ordered it off store shelves five years earlier.

The Playskool Travel-Lite was not the only dangerous portable crib on the market. Between 1990 and 1997, more than 1.5 million portable cribs manufactured by Evenflo, Draco, Century Products, and Baby Trend had a similar faulty design, a center hinge on the top rails. Eleven–month–old Anthony Gonzales of Los Angeles was the first baby to die in a portable crib, in 1991, and Danny was the twelfth. The cribs' marketers, corporations whose names parents equate with safe products for children, knew that more than one million recalled cribs could still have been in circulation, being used in homes and daycare centers—yet they did very little to warn their customers of the danger of injury or death.

Within a week of Danny's death, Linda and Boaz no longer described the incident as a "freak accident, a fluke." They now blamed manufacturer Kolcraft Industries and Hasbro, the three–billion dollar corporation whose Playskool brand name was stamped on the crib's side.

"We realized that the crib was a time bomb," Boaz started telling the press, "and that it would kill again." He turned out to be right. Three months after Danny died, ten–month–old William Conahan of New Jersey became the thirteenth child to be killed by a portable crib, the sixth to be killed by a Playskool Travel-Lite. The statistics are staggering: One out of every two thousand Playskool Travel-Lite cribs sold has killed a child. And yet, to this date, no one knows how many cribs are still in use.

In 1999 alone, parents, grandparents, and caregivers spent $4.9 billion on infant products such as cribs, cradles, baby carriers, car seats, high chairs, and strollers. Today's parents, many of them older, dual income, with more money than time, are demanding product features that were unheard of fifteen or twenty years ago: portable cribs that weigh only a few pounds and easily collapse for storage, car seats that double as infant carriers, oversized strollers designed for parents who jog. Products, it turns out, that are too often inadequately tested and ultimately unsafe. In 1999, more than 65,000 children were rushed to emergency rooms for injuries associated with infant products and hundreds died. Yet most parents are no more aware of these products' dangers than Linda, Boaz, Anna, and the state daycare inspectors were before Danny died.

CHAPTER 1

The Graco Converta-Cradle:

A Deadly New Product Disaster

No infant product conjures images of old-fashioned simplicity like a cradle: A mother places her snugly bundled baby, belly full of milk, in a homemade, heavy wooden cradle. She rocks the cradle gently, lulling the infant to sleep.

Perhaps this is the image Rose and Jon Malden of West Bridgewater, Massachusetts had when they bought a Graco Converta-Cradle for their newborn son Alex in August 1991. The cradle was motorized, so Alex could be rocked even when his parents left the room or when they fell asleep, as exhausted new parents are bound to do.

On the night of November 10, 1991, Jon Malden placed his son in the cradle, wound it a couple of times, then sat down on the sofa and fell asleep. When Jon woke up less than two hours later, the cradle had stopped rocking, it was resting at an unusual angle, and Alex, sleeping on his stomach, had slid from the middle of the cradle into the corner. Unable to breathe, the infant had suffocated.

"I knew he was gone as soon as I looked at him," said Alex's mother, who is an emergency room nurse. "I've seen enough dead bodies to know. He was gone." The coroner believed Alex was a victim of Sudden Infant Death Syndrome (SIDS), but from the start the Maldens suspected the cradle's angle and rocking motion were to blame.[1]

In the weeks before her first grandchild was born, Margaret Forrester spent hours browsing in stores like Toys R' Us. When she spotted the Graco Converta-Cradle, Margaret knew it would be the perfect gift for her daughter's first child. Remembering how much her own babies had loved to be rocked, she wished the product had existed thirty years ago.[2]

Margaret was right—her granddaughter Lucy loved the cradle. Whenever the infant grew fussy, her mother wound the cradle's motor and the child calmed down almost instantly. Sometimes Lucy would shift from the cradle's center toward one side, but her mother would simply move the child back to the center. Lucy used the cradle for the first few months of her life. When she outgrew it, her parents stored it in the basement.

Two years later, when their son Connor was born in October 1991, Lucy's parents dusted off her Converta-Cradle. Connor, too, seemed to love the cradle's rocking motion. Like his sister, Connor sometimes shifted from the center of the cradle into a corner, but his mother figured out a way to keep the infant in place: She rolled up a baby blanket, bent it in a horseshoe shape, and tucked it around his head. This seemed to work.

The morning of November 25, 1991, Connor's mother gave the six–week–old baby his bottle, put him down for a nap in the cradle, and covered him with a homemade quilt. Connor quickly fell asleep. A few minutes later, a neighbor stopped by for a visit, and the two women sat at the dining room table drinking coffee and talking, with Connor in full view. Over the next hour and a half, Connor's mom got up to rewind the cradle four times. Each time she did this, Connor appeared to be sleeping.

When the neighbor went home, Connor's mom checked on him again, thinking it was time for him to eat. The cradle was still swinging, so she stopped it. This is when she noticed that Connor had drifted toward the head of the cradle, and his complexion seemed to match his yellow blanket. When she lifted the baby out of the cradle, his body was limp and he didn't respond to her touch. His lips were very blue. Holding the infant, Connor's now frantic mother ran to the front door and yelled to her neighbor, who was crossing the driveway. "Help!"

she screamed. "It's Connor! Help! Quick, call 911!" Clutching the child tightly, she ran back into the house and started CPR, knowing in her heart that it was too late. When the paramedics arrived fifteen minutes later, they were unable to revive the baby. Connor's death certificate looked hauntingly similar to that of Alex Malden, the Massachusetts infant who had died two weeks earlier. Under "cause of death," Connor's death certificate said SIDS. Occurring two thousand miles apart—Connor had spent all of his short life in rural Washington—no one noted the similarities of the two boys' deaths.

Malika Thomas, a single mother, lived with her seven children, ages thirteen, eleven, nine (twins), seven, four, and two months, in the Blue Plains Road Housing Project in the Bronx.[3] On December 8, 1991, Malika needed to go to the store to buy groceries. Before leaving, she carried two–month–old Christian from the bedroom she shared with him into the living room, where his brothers and sisters were playing. She put the baby in his brand-new Converta-Cradle, adjusted the speed to "slow," told her thirteen–year–old son to watch his younger siblings, and left the apartment.

When Malika returned from the store, she checked on Christian and found that he was "crowded into the bottom corner" of the cradle, his face pressed against the bumper. He wasn't breathing. Lifting the baby out of the cradle, Malika started CPR, then ran out of the apartment with Christian in her arms, screaming for help. A neighbor responded quickly, taking over mouth-to-mouth resuscitation while Malika called 911. But it was too late: Christian was pronounced dead at the Bronx Medical Center emergency room.

Like Alex's and Connor's parents, Malika, too, suspected that the Graco cradle was to blame for her son's death. She insisted to investigators that Christian died as a result of his face being pressed against the cradle's bumper. But the New York Police Department's Prosecutor's Office wasn't convinced.

Confiscating the cradle as evidence to be used in a "possible criminal case," they suggested Christian's death had been Malika's fault.[4] A month later, Malika was charged with child neglect, and child welfare officials took four of her children away from her. The children were put into foster care.[5]

When the New York Police Department charged Malika with negligence, they were missing an important piece of information: Like Malika, the Graco Converta-Cradle was under investigation. Three months before Christian died, regulators at the Consumer Product Safety Commission (CPSC), the federal regulatory agency responsible for recalling dangerous children's products, had sent a letter to Graco company president Derial Sanders, informing him that the agency had received "two incident reports" involving Graco Converta-Cradles. One baby had been found in his cradle "turning purple" with his nose bleeding. He was saved, but a second baby had died. In both cases, the Converta-Cradle had been tilted downward. CPSC regulator Marc Schoem's letter asked Graco to forward to the CPSC information on the cradle's testing, performance, assembly instructions, and warranty claims. By law, Graco had ten days to respond to the request.[6] Once the data was in, the CPSC would determine whether or not the product was dangerous enough to recall.

On September 13, 1991, three days after receiving the CPSC's recall investigation letter, Graco stopped production of the Converta-Cradle.[7] However, it did nothing about the cradles sitting on store shelves or being used in homes and daycare centers. For the next four months, while the CPSC carried out its investigation, stores continued to sell Converta-Cradles, unaware of the danger, and parents and caregivers continued to put babies to sleep in them. It's no accident that during this time, four more babies died in their cradles: Alex, Connor, Christian, and thirteen–week–old Michael Hecht of Cayugha Falls, Ohio.[8]

By the time the CPSC convinced Graco to recall the Converta-Cradle, in February 1992, the company had sold 160,000 units. The recall notice mentioned two deaths and two "near" deaths.[9] In fact, the death and injury toll was far higher. Two years later, in the summer of 1994, *Boston Globe* reporter Kevin Cullen launched his own investigation of the Converta-Cradle. Cullen uncovered a total of twelve infant deaths and at least twenty–one injuries (breathing problems) or near-misses.[10] Seven months later, NBC's *Dateline* reported fourteen deaths associated with the Converta-Cradle.[11] The infant fatalities uncovered by these journalists tell the horrifying story of a company so focused on its profitability and reputation that it continually denied overwhelming evidence that its product was deadly.

Three–week–old Shane Slayton of Tulsa, Oklahoma, was the Converta-Cradle's first known victim.[12] He died on August 4, 1990, less than a year after the new product had hit store shelves. Two–month–old Chrissie Smithberg of Brooklyn Park, Minnesota died in her Converta-Cradle a few months later, in October.[13] In November, nine–week–old Patrick Morse of Dayton died in his Converta-Cradle.[14] In December, ten–week–old Eliza Hastings of New Orleans became the Converta-Cradle's fourth victim.[15] Two New England babies died in their Converta-Cradles on June 7, 1991: seven–week–old Glenn Farland of Madison, Connecticut and five–month–old Matthew Solomon of Framingham, Massachusetts.[16] The Converta-Cradle's seventh victim, eleven–week–old Andrew Doherty of Sweeny, Texas, died two weeks later.[17] Three–month–old Pamela Rowe of Mt. Holly, New Jersey, died in her cradle in July 1991.[18] Three–week–old Steven Kaiser died in his Converta-Cradle in Crest Hill, Illinois a month later, becoming the cradle's ninth victim.[19] At this point, CPSC regulator Marc Schoem informed Graco president Sanders that the agency knew of "two incidents." (Schoem's letter did not identify which two.) Michael Hecht, Alex Malden, Connor Forrester, and Christian Thomas died after Schoem sent this letter, in the months leading up to the Converta-Cradle recall.

Why did so many deaths go undetected by the U. S. government, slipping one by one through the CPSC's surveillance system? Because coroners and medical examiners across the country had classified each death as SIDS, the diagnosis used to describe an infant's death that cannot be explained by any discernable cause. While parents voiced their concerns about the cradle—many eventually had the SIDS rulings overturned by courts—it was years before anyone admitted they were right.[20] Graco headed off the growing suspicion of parents and reporters by denying culpability and blaming the children's parents themselves for the deaths. On *Dateline*, Graco attorney Richard Bethea, Jr. explained that caregivers were expected to "supervise" infants as they slept in a Converta-Cradle; a parent who fell asleep beside his or her child's cradle was being negligent. In the same interview, Bethea blamed the deaths on SIDS. "This is a real tragedy," he said. "I mean, it's so difficult for us to accept that there's a phenomenon out there known as Sudden Infant Death Syndrome, where an otherwise normal and healthy baby suddenly dies, but that's what's happened. The Graco Converta-Cradle is in no way responsible, or—or in no way contributed to those unfortunate deaths."[21]

Every major manufacturer of baby equipment—Evenflo, Hasbro (Playskool), Century Products, Baby Björn, Cosco, Safety 1st, Mattel (Fisher-Price), and Kolcraft—has in recent years recalled a product after babies have been seriously injured and/or killed. Yet even in an industry marked by widespread corporate malfeasance, Graco's behavior is unprecedented. Ignoring the safety warnings of its own engineers, the company rushed an inadequately tested product to market.[22] Refusing to take responsibility for the mounting death toll, the company chose to blame SIDS and caregivers.[23] Ten years after the product was launched, Graco still refuses to divulge how many babies the Converta-Cradle killed. Whether the final death toll is thirteen, fourteen, or higher, no infant product to this date is known to have killed so many infants in so little time.

How an Inadequately Tested Cradle Hit the Market

Graco product engineers developed an innovative design for the Converta-Cradle: The product rocked a child from head-to-toe, unlike traditional cradles, which rock side-to-side. Parents valued this feature, Graco's market research indicated, because a cradle that rocked head-to-toe was smaller and took up less space.[24] But what kind of testing did the cradle undergo before it was put on the market? Citing "trade secrets," Graco refused to provide details to the press, or even to the lawyer of one of the families who sued the company for the wrongful death of their son. In July 1994, attorney Mark Fortier, who was representing the parents of Connor Forrester, requested pre-market testing records from Graco as part of the discovery process. The company refused to turn over the documents. "Much of this information," wrote Graco attorney Bethea, "would fall in the category of proprietary or confidential business records, the unnecessary or unrestricted disclosure of which could be detrimental to Graco."[25]

Lawyer Richard Bethea did reveal one alarming fact about the Converta-Cradle testing process: Graco's own employees tried out the product. "Graco people test their products on their own children," said Bethea. "They put them in the homes of their employees who have small children. There were never any problems."[26]

Relying on employees to provide honest feedback on a new product is a dangerous practice, warn the CPSC and consumer advocates. By the time an employee is handed a product to test, it has been in development for years. The employee is acutely aware that colleagues and friends have a lot riding on a timely product launch. "By relying entirely on inside personnel, rather than recruiting outsiders to participate in a use-safety audit," says human factors safety researcher E. Patrick McGuire, "a corporation automatically becomes a hostage to its own corporate culture. Moreover, by the time these questions are asked a product may be virtually on the precipice of being introduced. Company careers may be at stake if the product's launch is delayed. Investments in tooling, planned promotions, and the like create significant pressures to dismiss foreseeable use considerations and get the product to market."[27]

Daniel Leonard, the lawyer the Maldens hired to sue Graco for Alex's wrongful death, was more successful than the Forresters' lawyer in getting pre-market testing documents from Graco. It was Leonard who discovered that Graco's own research and development department had identified the Converta-Cradle's fatal design flaw: The cradle's head-to-toe swinging motion could shift a child into a corner. The engineers had identified this hazard as early as April 1989, seven months before the product was put on the market. Subsequent testing confirmed that there was indeed a problem. Internal documents dated November 1989 revealed that Graco testing engineers jotted down questions such as, "Head in corner—excessive pressure on neck?" and "What if baby spits up? Suffocation?" One engineer noted, "problem of tilted cradle when baby is off-center, head-down." The engineers proposed adding a restraint belt to keep infants in place. But, according to lawyers for the dead children's families, Graco tested the restraint belt with consumers, who didn't like the idea of strapping down an infant. In the end, the engineers' safety warnings were ignored.[28]

Why would the government allow a company to bring such a potentially problematic product to market? Because, while the CPSC has the authority to recall the cradle from stores once it was determined to have caused injuries and deaths, the agency has virtually no control over the product's pre-market testing. Why? In 1981, Congress decided mandatory federal testing and safety standards were unnecessary for most consumer products.[29] Since then, the only infant products that are required to meet government safety standards are car seats, pacifiers, rattles, and cribs.[30] Each manufacturer decides independently how they will design and test their cradles, strollers, high chairs, and so on, with little or no input from the government. Nothing the CPSC does prevents Graco—or any other manufacturer—from putting a baby product as dangerous as the Converta-Cradle on the market today.

News of the Converta-Cradle Recall
Fails to Reach Parents

Graco was required by law to notify the CPSC within twenty–four hours of learning of the first Converta-Cradle death.[31] This should have occurred soon after three–week–old Shane Slayton died in his Converta-Cradle in August 1990.[32] But Graco insists the company hadn't heard about Shane's death, or about the eight Converta-Cradle-related deaths that followed over the next year. Graco lawyer Richard Bethea claimed the company did not know about any of the deaths or injuries until the CPSC contacted them in September 1991.[33]

It took so long for Graco to learn of the infants' deaths because in each case, the medical examiner ruled the cause of death as SIDS, which absolved the product—and Graco—of any responsibility. Why the CPSC didn't hear of the problem until after so many infants had died is another issue, and one that highlights one of many shortfalls in the agency's recall system. Operating on a skeleton budget, the CPSC lacks the resources to adequately monitor product-related injuries and deaths. Incidents can go undetected for months, during which time a company continues to pump hazardous products through the retail pipeline.

In February 1992, Graco and the CPSC jointly sent the Converta-Cradle recall press release to the media and asked for it to be reported as news.[34] But there was no guarantee that anyone would pick up the story. And even if the story was reported, there were no guarantees that owners of the cradle would be watching the TV news that night, or spot the story buried deep inside the newspaper.

As is the protocol today, Graco was given the opportunity to wrangle with the CPSC over the language and tone of the recall press release. Announcing that the recall was "voluntary" and that only the cradle portion of the swing was being recalled, the Converta-Cradle notification gave little indication of the magnitude of the product's dangers. "The company offers," the press release said, "in exchange for proof of the destruction of the cradle, a choice of one of several Graco products or a refund of $25.00 for the value of the cradle portion of the swing." The Converta-Cradle had retailed for $99.00. The word "death" was avoided.[35]

In addition to the press release, Graco took additional steps to spread the word about the recall: It mailed "safety alert" posters to children's stores and pediatricians and sent 90,000 notices to consumers who were "likely to have bought children's products."[36] But these efforts were sure to slip past the radar screen of at least some Converta-Cradle owners, because Graco did not maintain up-to-date customer files, so it had little idea who had bought the cradle and where to find them. How many of the 90,000 consumers who were 'likely to have bought children's products' owned a Converta-Cradle? Lacking complete customer files, Graco had no way to know.

Graco also neglected to use one tried-and-true communication tactic that was sure to have reached more Converta-Cradle owners: paid advertising. Children outgrow cradles in a couple of months, so their parents often pass the product on to other family members or friends, or sell it in a garage sale. If a product is recalled, it is difficult for a manufacturer to reach these second-hand owners through direct mail. Advertising is the company's best way to reach them. Graco, like most infant product manufacturers today, did not advertise the cradle recall in newspapers or magazines specifically targeted to parents.[37]

One Graco customer who missed the recall news was Mary Hecht of Ohio. In September 1991, Mary's infant son Michael died while sleeping in his Converta-Cradle. Mary didn't learn that the cradle had been recalled until 1994, when her local newspaper reprinted the *Boston Globe's* Converta-Cradle story. "I couldn't believe it," said Hecht. "I guess I just assumed someone would have told me. The store, the manufacturer, the government." [38] Mary's response reflects the naiveté of many parents. If she hadn't filled out and returned a warranty or product registration card, and if she had paid for the cradle with cash (instead of a credit card), how could Graco or a retailer have known she owned the product? Mary should have gotten the news from the government, but because the CPSC doesn't have a budget to advertise, the government, too, let her down.

It is no accident that when an infant product is recalled, the company generally hears back from only 10–30 percent of the product's owners.[39] Why? There is no law that requires manufacturers or retailers to keep up-to-date records of who buys their products, so that owners can be contacted if the product is recalled. And there is no law that requires companies to advertise a product recall, or to demonstrate that recall news reaches product owners. Everyday, parents and caregivers strap children into baby equipment like cradles, high chairs, infant swings, cribs, strollers, and carriers, completely unaware that the product has been recalled.

Founders' Religious Beliefs Clash with an Abysmal Safety Record

Six months before the cradle claimed its first victim, the *Philadelphia Enquirer* profiled Pennsylvania-based Graco and its owners, the Cone family. Founded in the mid–1940's as a sheet-metal jobber, Graco became a family business in 1953. By 1989, under the leadership of brothers Ed and Robert Cone, Graco was boasting yearly revenues of about $150 million. The Cone brothers are independent Baptists who believe that the Bible "embodies God's literal word." Under their direction, the company gave Graco employees paid, mandatory breaks to participate in the company's "chapel program," which included activities such as Scripture readings and movies about Christian values. "We try to incorporate the Bible into everyday actions, like honesty and paying on time," said Cone, citing a principle from the Book of Proverbs.[40] Graco attorney Richard Bethea repeatedly referred to the Cones' religious beliefs throughout the company's defense of the Converta-Cradle. "These people—not just the Cone family but many of the people who work at Graco—are Christians who try to practice their beliefs in their business," he told *Globe* reporter Kevin Cullen. "They have a tremendous sense of responsibility... They didn't want anybody to suffer."[41] But while company rhetoric brimmed with references to "Christian values" and God, Graco's reaction to the Converta-Cradle deaths told quite a different story. And as it has turned out, the Converta-Cradle was just one in a long line of Graco baby products that proved to have decidedly un-Christian outcomes.

In October 1990—around the same time the Converta-Cradle's first victims died—Graco recalled seven models of strollers that had lacerated, broken, and amputated children's fingers.[42] In February 1991, Graco paid a $100,000 civil penalty to the CPSC for allegedly breaking the law by failing to report the stroller injuries to the agency in a timely fashion.[43] Also in 1991, Graco walkers were recalled for posing a "small-parts hazard"; children were able to remove a plastic piece from the tray, leading to multiple reports of choking.[44] In 1993, a year after the Converta-Cradle recall, Graco recalled over 200,000 infant swings following reports that babies had "pushed themselves up and over the back of the seat, resulting in falls, loss of consciousness, or restricted breathing."[45] In 1996, Graco recalled 133,000 play yards after toddlers unraveled the product's mesh sides and became entangled in them.[46] In 1997, Graco recalled 63,000 stationary entertainers after sharp edges on the product's seat injured at least four hundred children.[47] A few months later, the company recalled 564,000 infant carrier/swing seats after four infants fractured their skulls and two babies suffered concussions when the carrier's plastic handle unexpectedly unlocked, throwing them to the ground.[48] In 1998, Graco recalled its stationary entertainers for the second time after it was discovered that children were pulling out and eating the product's screws.[49] A few months later, Graco bedside cradles were recalled after fifty consumers reported that the cradles' legs had become loose or separated.[50] At the end of 1998, Graco recalled two million play yards after five children were fatally strangled by protruding rivets.[51] In April 2000, the company recalled seven million infant swings after 181 reports of falls, nine bone fractures and concussions, twenty-two reports of infants being caught at the neck or chest by the swings' restraining straps, and six deaths.[52] Two months later, Graco's walkers were found to be faulty, after they collapsed with children in them.[53]

The numbers are astounding: Between 1990 and 2000, Graco recalled thirteen products, accounting for more than ten million units, more than six hundred injuries, and over two dozen deaths (see Table 1–1). It is difficult to reconcile the Cones' espoused moral values with a track record like this.

Table 1-1: Graco Recalls, 1990–2000

Product	Date	Units	Incidents	Injuries	Deaths
Stroller	9/90	N/A	7	7	0
Baby walker	12/91	11,000	14	2	0
Converta-Cradle	2/92	169,000	20+	4+	14+
Carrier/swing	11/93	208,000	5	1	0
Mesh play yards	10/96	133,000	9	0	0
Stationary entertainer	5/97	63,000	400+	400+	0
Carrier/swings	12/97	564,000	45	6	0
Stationary entertainer	9/98	19,000	8	3	0
Play yard	11/98	2,000,000	N/A	N/A	5
Bedside cradles	11/98	1,800	50	0	0
Bath set	8/99	100,000	4	4	0
Infant swings	4/00	7,000,000	209	181	6
Infant walkers	6/00	31,000	27	27	0
TOTAL		10,299,800	798	635	25

Graco has a long history of selling products that turn out to be unsafe.

"We can't spoon-feed everyone everything," said CPSC Chairman Ann Brown when asked about the shortcomings of the Converta-Cradle recall. "Government has an obligation, but so do people, especially if you have kids, to get information and be informed."[54] But the case of the Graco Converta-Cradle shows just how difficult it is for even the most diligent parent to get the safety information they need.

In 1994, two–and–a–half years after the product recall, when *Boston Globe* reporter Kevin Cullen initiated his own investigation, his goal was to uncover exactly how many infants had been injured or died in the Converta-Cradle. Cullen met with industry and government secrecy that remains just as strong today. Manufacturers like Graco have been remarkably successful at making sure that a product's body count remains concealed. Under constant threat of expensive lawsuits, they routinely blame parents and caregivers for injuries and deaths and refuse to release any information that would suggest otherwise.

While manufacturers are required by law to report product-related injuries and deaths to the CPSC, a statute in the Consumer Product Safety Act prohibits the agency from releasing company-specific information (i.e., any document identifying Graco as the cradle's manufacturer) to the public without prior approval from the company.[55] The statute supersedes the Freedom of Information Act, which guarantees public access to safety information of this sort.[56] So, in 1994, when *Globe* reporter Cullen tried to tally exactly how many babies had died in a Converta-Cradle, the CPSC was of no help. "It's against the law for us to release that information at this time," CPSC Chairman Ann Brown told him. The figures would become available eventually, she assured him, but exactly when, she couldn't say.[57]

Eventually, after months of scouring death certificate files and interviewing medical examiners and grief-stricken parents, Cullen accounted for twelve infant deaths in the Converta-

Cradle, and "about 2 dozen" near-death suffocations—far more than the two deaths and two "partial suffocations" reported in the CPSC's recall press release.[58] Three days after Cullen's article ran, the law magazine *The Legal Intelligencer* reported, "Documents filed in conjunction with lawsuits against the company [Graco] show the government knew of at least twenty–seven deaths and injuries to children who slept in the Graco Converta-Cradle model."[59]

The CPSC is still prohibited from sharing all that it knows about the cradle injuries and deaths. A Freedom of Information Act (FOIA) request filed with the CPSC in 1999 put the count at nine deaths. Admitting the count is higher, the agency could report only that there were seven "additional complaints" for which they could release no information, as they had not yet "received confirmation of the accuracy" from Graco.[60]

"I'd just like to see the system get better," Rose Malden said in 1994 after she and her husband filed suit against Graco, "so something like this doesn't happen to someone else. No one should have to go through this."[61] Rose Malden has not gotten her wish. The Graco Converta-Cradle disaster is just as likely to occur today as it was ten years ago. Nothing has changed to prevent it. In fact, many argue, the situation has gotten worse over the past decade. During this time the market for baby equipment has nearly doubled from annual sales of $2.45 billion to $4.9 billion, while the CPSC's $50 million budget is close to where it was in 1981 ($42 million), and its staff of 480 is about half of what it was twenty years ago.[62] Chronically under-funded and prohibited from telling the public the whole truth about dangerous products, the CPSC has been no match for infant product manufacturers intent on fulfilling consumers' seemingly insatiable demand for stylish, cutting-edge products that promise to make life with baby easier and more convenient.

CHAPTER 2

Inadequately Tested Baby Products Hit the Market

Each year, consumer products injure about thirty million Americans and kill 22,000.[1] Since the 1960s and 1970s, when Congress enacted a slew of consumer protection laws, the number of product-related deaths has decreased by thirty percent—yet during the same time, product-related injuries have risen by fifty percent.[2] Among children under four years old, unintentional injuries such as drowning, suffocation, and choking are still the leading cause of death, each year killing more children than any disease.[3] Far too many of these deaths occur when a child has been placed in a product that is supposed to protect her from harm, such as a cradle, crib, or bath seat.

Why has the number of product-related injuries *increased* over the last thirty years, despite stronger consumer protection laws? Plausible explanations include a population increase, the proliferation of consumer products, and an increasingly litigious citizenry that is more likely to report injuries. But there is another important factor, one unrelated to societal trends: industry trade groups' increasingly tenacious efforts to undermine consumer protection. Over the last twenty years, organizations like the Juvenile Products Manufacturers Association (JPMA) have held tight to the notion that their member companies are entitled to market baby products, unencumbered by mandatory government safety standards.[4] And groups like the U. S. Chamber of Commerce have pushed for and won legislation that requires the government to censor product-related injury and death data from the public—information that would prevent parents from buying unsafe baby products.[5]

The main hindrance to industry's efforts to cut corners on safety has been the Consumer Product Safety Commission (CPSC), the federal regulatory agency responsible for overseeing the safety of most consumer products sold in the U.S. Over the years, as the agency has shifted more and more of its resources to protecting children, in particular, from dangerous products, manufacturers have worked ceaselessly to dilute the agency's efforts. At the same time, Congress has decimated the agency's budget and passed legislation that thwarts the CPSC from carrying out its original mandate: to protect the public against unreasonable risk of injury from consumer products.

The CPSC was born out of the consumer movement of the late 1960s and early 1970s. In 1972, against the wishes of President Richard Nixon, Congress enacted the Consumer Product Safety Act, establishing the CPSC as an independent federal regulatory agency.[6] The CPSC was imbued with broad powers: to create mandatory safety standards for consumer products, to collect and maintain a national database of product-related injuries and deaths, to recall hazardous products, and to ban products that could not be made safe by a standard. The Act stipulates the appointment of up to five CPSC commissioners, including one chairman, appointed by the president for staggered seven–year terms.[7]

Over its short life, the CPSC has been alternately lauded, accused of giving good intentions a bad name, subjected to an unrelenting stream of criticism from industry, consumer groups, and Congress, and nearly abolished by two presidents. In 1977, just five years after the agency got off the ground, a Government Accounting Office report sharply critiqued the CPSC's efforts.[8] The commission's first chairman, Richard Simpson, had vowed to decrease product-related injuries and deaths largely by promulgating mandatory safety standards. His initial goal had been to set standards for one hundred products within ten years. By 1977, however, the CPSC had issued only three mandatory standards, for swimming pool slides, architectural glass, and matchbook covers. With a track record like this, it was easy for conservatives to argue the agency was squandering federal money. Jimmy Carter, looking for a way to prove that Democrats could be as tough as Republicans on inefficient government agencies, strongly considered the recommendation of his advisers to abolish the agency altogether. Congressional Democrats saved the CPSC at the eleventh hour, and Carter eventually backed off. But the struggle was a clear signal that the "consumer decade" was over.

Congressional Democrats rescued the agency again in 1981, when President Ronald Reagan's Office of Management and Budget Director David Stockman declared war on the CPSC. Claiming the agency had "adventured too far" in its regulation, Stockman, who had what insiders described as a "visceral hatred" of the agency, tried but failed to do away with it.[9] Under Stockman's tutelage, President Reagan pushed for changes that damaged the agency so profoundly, his effect is still felt today. In one year, Congress cut the Commission's budget by twenty–five percent and eliminated more than two hundred jobs.[10] Emaciated, the agency's legal department no longer had the funds to enforce regulations, nor was there sufficient money to collect data on product-related injuries and deaths. "Reagan was very much of the attitude, 'If you eliminate the data, you eliminate the problem,'" says Andrew McGuire, executive director of the Trauma Foundation at San Francisco General Hospital, who during this time worked closely with the agency on household fire hazards.[11] When three of the five commissioners' terms were up, Reagan refused to replace them. Lacking enough votes for a quorum, much of the agency's work came to a complete halt.

Amendments added to the Consumer Product Safety Act in 1981 further restricted the agency's powers. Among the most damaging: The CPSC was prohibited from promulgating mandatory safety standards if industry agreed to set standards voluntarily.[12] Today, the only infant equipment regulated by mandatory government standards are car seats, rattles, pacifiers, and cribs.[13] Safety standards for all other baby equipment are *voluntary*.

Voluntary safety standards specify which hazards a manufacturer must address and how a product must be tested before it is put on the market. As the term implies, a manufacturer can decide to comply with a voluntary standard, or not. Some products, like front and back infant carriers, are not even covered by a voluntary standard.[14] A committee began work on a hard-handled carrier safety standard in November 1997; it was finished in July 2000. Most parents don't know this. Nor do they know that since 1996, over 2.5 million hard-handled infant carriers have been recalled.[15] Because products can be sold with no safety standard in place, manufacturers do not always have a strong incentive to rush their standard-setting work. Most standards are in development for years.[16] During this time, millions of products are sold, subject to no uniform safety standard. Standard-setting rarely keeps pace with product launches, so new product innovations are likely to be the least stringently tested according to a uniform standard. Focused on highly touted benefits such as convenience and styling, parents take safety for granted, and wrongly assume the product wouldn't be on the market unless it had passed rigorous government tests.

"Consumers have a sense that the product wouldn't be sold if it weren't safe, that the government is actively checking," says Consumer Federation of America general counsel Mary Ellen Fise, who has been tracking the industry for fifteen years. "This is simply not true."[17] A 1999 Coalition for Consumer Rights survey of Illinois voters found that seventy–five percent of adults believe, erroneously, that the government oversees the pre-market testing of baby products. Seventy–nine percent of adults mistakenly assume that manufacturers are required to test the safety of children's products before they are sold.[18]

The Draco All Our Kids portable crib underscores the danger of voluntary standards. Draco, a Taiwanese company that maintained a small office in California, sold 13,000 All Our Kids portable cribs between 1992 and 1995.[19] The CPSC was alerted to a problem in May 1994, when a Rhode Island mother reported that her toddler was standing in his crib, leaning on the top rail, and fell when the rail collapsed (see Appendix 2–1 for illustration).[20] The child sustained minor injuries. The CPSC launched an investigation: The Draco crib design was similar to that of the Playskool Travel-Lite, a portable crib that had been recalled in 1993, after three children were killed.

CPSC investigators asked Draco about the pre-market testing of its cribs. A Draco employee claimed that president Jerry Teng, along with his chief engineer "John" Wang, had supervised the All Our Kids' crib development and testing. But when the regulators asked for proof of this testing, the employee responded, "At the time of development in Taiwan, product development data was not recorded and notes of 'analyses,' 'evaluations,' and 'pre-market test and reports' were not kept, therefore, are unavailable."[21] Trying to assess the crib's durability, the CPSC asked Draco to estimate the expected life of the crib. The company replied that the crib would last, "the length of time the product will be used by one child and one child only."[22] Perhaps because the All Our Kids crib had not yet seriously injured or killed a child, the CPSC took no action against Draco.

By April 1996, two more children had been killed by top rail, center-hinge portable cribs, one in a Baby Trend crib and one in Evenflo's.[23] The Baby Trend crib had been recalled in 1995; now there were three brands of center-hinge cribs left on the market: Evenflo, Draco, and Century Products. CPSC engineers decided to run their own tests on multiple models of the Draco All Our Kids and Century Fold-N-Go cribs.[24] Multiple CPSC documents suggest that the two brands were both designed and manufactured by Draco, although Century Products' brand name appeared on the Fold-N-Go.[25]

Simulating a variety of use scenarios, CPSC engineers had no trouble making these cribs collapse. After testing the strength needed to collapse the hinges on one Century crib model, the engineers reported, "these values could well be within the strength capabilities of an occupant."[26] In other words, if a child standing in the crib were to grab its top rails, he could collapse it. Another Century model failed the engineers' "shaking" test: When the crib was shaken back and forth by its top rail, it collapsed.[27] Draco's All Our Kids crib fared even worse than the cribs the company produced for Century; it was the easiest for a child to collapse on his own, and failed the shaking test as well.[28] CPSC human factors psychologists, experts on how consumers use products in the real world, tested the cribs, too. In June 1996, CPSC regulator Zulma Soto called Century Products corporate counsel, Sharon Freimuth to give her the results of these tests: The Century Fold-N-Go model 10–810 was "difficult to set up and easy to collapse."[29] Ms. Freimuth informed Soto that Century was getting out of the play yard (portable crib) business, but the company was still selling the product, trying to use up its inventory.[30]

The CPSC now had plenty of evidence that the Draco-manufactured cribs were dangerous. Yet the agency didn't recall the All Our Kids and Century Fold-N-Go cribs until seven months later, in November 1996, after each brand had killed a child.[31] By then, Draco had declared bankruptcy, the California office had been vacated with no forwarding address, and president Teng had disappeared somewhere in Asia, presumably, Taiwan.[32]

By 1997, portable cribs designed with a center hinge on the top rails—marketed by Century Products, Draco, Evenflo,

Playskool, and Baby Trend, and varying in price from $50 to $130—were recalled, after collapsing and killing ten children.[33] The lesson? Choosing to buy top-of-the-line infant products manufactured by large companies does not ensure that a portable crib, high chair, or stroller will be more stringently tested than the cheapest knock-off on the market. Complicating the issue is the common practice of well-respected companies licensing their brand names to lesser known manufacturers. While the Fold-N-Go was stamped with the established Century brand name, the crib's real manufacturer, Draco, turned out to be a fly-by-night operation. And Kolcraft Industries manufactured the Playskool Travel-Lite—not Hasbro, the owner of the Playskool name.[34]

Most large manufacturers abide by voluntary safety standards when such standards exist. But voluntary standards require only minimum levels of performance and fail to address all hazards posed by a product.[35] It is extremely difficult, if not impossible, for a parent to know which hazards are addressed and which are not; this information appears nowhere on a product. The reason: The voluntary standard-setting process is dominated by manufacturers' engineers, whose job it is to balance the precarious trade-off between child safety and corporate profits.

How Manufacturers Set Safety Standards for Infant Products

Twice a year, product engineers from infant product companies—Graco, Cosco, Evenflo, Playskool, Safety 1st, Fisher-Price, Kolcraft, and Century Products—meet for four days to hash out voluntary safety design and testing standards for their products. In the summer they gather in Philadelphia, and in the winter they fly south to Orlando. The meetings are open to all manufacturers and consumer advocates, but typically only the big players show up; smaller companies and most non-profit consumer organizations can't afford the expense. The engineers are backed by a host of contracted service providers, engineers from testing labs and recall consultants who are on the manufacturers' payrolls.[36] The Juvenile Products Manufacturers Association's (JPMA) lawyer always shows up, as do a handful of consumer advocates (from *Consumer Reports*, the Consumer Federation of America, the Danny Foundation, etc.), and a couple of engineers and an occasional epidemiologist from the CPSC. The same 1981 Consumer Product Safety Act amendment that denied the CPSC the right to promulgate mandatory standards if industry agreed to set them "voluntarily," requires the agency to assist in the development of the voluntary standards.[37]

Safety standards for infant products are written under the auspices of the American Society of Testing and Materials (ASTM), which stipulates that all stakeholders (manufacturers, consumer advocates, and the CPSC) must participate in the standard-setting discussions.[38] One of the largest standards development organizations in the world, ASTM claims to provide a non-partisan forum for stakeholders with divergent interests to meet on common ground. ASTM does not maintain its own product testing labs, engage in technical research, send engineers to the standards meetings, or make any substantive contributions to safety standards. Rather, the organization merely specifies the process that the manufacturers, consumer advocates, and CPSC use to hash out voluntary standards for infant products. Then, once the standard is finished, ASTM publishes and distributes it.

ASTM claims that the standards it publishes are highly credible because its process provides "a balanced representation of interests at the standards-setting table."[39] It is true that representatives of all the stakeholders participate in the process. But the fact that the consumer advocates' safety concerns are often overshadowed by the manufacturers' objections suggests that the standard-setting process is less than "balanced."

Appendix 2–2 lists the names and affiliations of participants in a voluntary standard-setting meeting for hard-handled infant carriers held in February 2000. As is typical of these committee make-ups, twenty–eight manufacturers and their contracted service providers (product testing labs and recall consultants) faced off against seven consumer advocates and one CPSC regulator.[40] The committee's goal was to create the first voluntary standard for a product that had been associated with over 3,500 consumer-reported failures.[41] Over the previous few years, Kolcraft, Graco, Cosco, Evenflo, and Playskool had all recalled carriers, all for the same reason: The carriers' handles had unlatched unexpectedly, sometimes throwing infants to the ground. Hundreds of babies had sustained injuries, including skull fractures and concussions.[42] The manufacturers' engineers had all made the same design mistake, which reflected a failure to anticipate the "real world" use of the product. While they had adequately tested the up-and-down motion of the carrier's handle, they didn't consider its sideways motion, when a mother rested the carrier on her hip, usually when she opened a car door.[43] This is how many of the carrier failures occurred.

During the three–hour meeting, manufacturers' engineers discussed certain components of the proposed standard—static load tests and the wording of warning labels and consumer instructions—but deflected other issues raised by consumer advocates, most notably, the restraint systems used to secure infants into the carrier frame.[44] Why? The engineers insisted their first priority was to write a standard that addressed carrier *handles*—not the entire carrier. Throughout the first hour of the meeting, each time a safety issue was broached that addressed a component other than the handles, the committee chair suggested the issue be placed on the "memory sheet," deferring it for at least six more months, until the next meeting.[45]

Listening to the discussion, CPSC engineer Mark Kumagai became frustrated by the committee's lack of progress. The group had been meeting for two–and–a–half years, yet the standard was still in development and addressed only one issue—the handle.[46] "Washington will not be happy with this," he admonished the committee, indicating that the CPSC thought the industry had already taken too long to come up with a carrier standard.[47] "I want to go back to D.C. and say the standard has been revised," Kumagai said, "and it will be out for provisional ballot." He pushed the engineers to make discernible progress on the standard within the next few weeks. At his prodding, the group created a sub-committee to write the restraint-system section of the standard at a later date. Eventually, the restraint system sub-committee's recommendations will be integrated into the carrier standard, along with the handle and warning label specifications, and whatever else the group deems appropriate.[48] Then, as a final step, the group as a whole—the manufacturers' engineers, their testing labs and recall consultants, and the consumer advocates—will vote to accept or reject the new voluntary standard for carriers. Each organization gets one vote (i.e., each manufacturer, testing lab, consultant, and consumer group), except the CPSC; the agency is required to participate in the discussions but it is not allowed to vote.[49] Outnumbered by the manufacturers and their service providers, the consumer advocates—representing the interests of infants—rarely win.

The manufacturers' disregard for consumer input is evident throughout the standard-setting meetings. While attentive to each others' comments, the engineers often ignore the consumer advocates' pleas, or summarily dismiss them as impractical. During the August 1999 committee meeting on cribs, one consumer advocate suggested that the standard require manufacturers to mark all cribs with a manufacturing date. His goal was to help consumers assess the safety of hand-me-down cribs (i.e., whether a crib had been recalled, and what standards were in effect when it was manufactured).[50] The manufacturers refused his request, one adding in a stage whisper: "Oh, he's such a pain."[51]

This industry dismissal of consumer input is reinforced each time the official meeting notes are released, a few weeks after each standard-setting meeting. ASTM, in conjunction with the industry trade group, JPMA, distributes the minutes to all attendees. The "official" record is as carefully sanitized as a corporate press release, all traces of negative emotion and contention erased from the picture. Three-hour discussions—like the infant carrier meeting—are edited down to a couple of pages.[52] Consumer advocates' pleas for more stringent standards and greater safeguards often disappear without a trace. Although CPSC engineer Kumagai spoke throughout the carrier meeting, urging the engineers again and again to pick up the pace, not one of his comments was reported in the minutes. In fact, the only indication that a CPSC engineer even attended the meeting was the presence of Kumagai's name on the attendance roster. Why are the notes so cryptic? Acutely aware of the litigious nature of the products under discussion, the JPMA makes sure that there is no record of comments that could one day be used against a manufacturer in court.

Setting the Standard for Infant Bath Seats: A Case Study

Bath seats, a product designed for bathing an infant in a regular bathtub, illustrate just how inadequate the industry's voluntary standard-setting process can be. The baby sits on a plastic seat, which is affixed to the bottom of the tub with plastic suction cups. His legs straddle a plastic post attached to a chest-level plastic ring that surrounds him; the baby can hold onto the ring for support. The product retails for under $20, and is frequently found in second-hand stores for less than $10, making it affordable for most families. The CPSC estimates U.S. bath seat sales to be about one million per year, or one for every four live births.[53]

Bath seats hit the U.S. market in 1981 with no voluntary safety standard in place. The CPSC learned of the first bath seat drowning in 1983.[54] By the end of 1994, with the body count up to eighteen, the Commission asked the industry to begin work on a voluntary bath seat standard. In a 1997 article in the journal *Pediatrics*, CPSC researcher Renae Rauchschwalbe explained her agency's interest in the product:

> Drowning is the third leading cause of unintentional-injury death among children in the United States... Since the 1970s drowning rates have decreased markedly in most age groups with the exception of toddlers, where rates have remained fairly stable, and infants, where rates may have actually increased... In contrast to toddlers, who are likely to drown in residential swimming pools, more than 50% of unintentional infant drowning deaths occur in the bathtub. As part of our ongoing investigation of infant and toddler drownings, we became aware of a number of incidents in which a bath seat or bath ring was in use at the time of the drowning event.[55]

Manufacturers elected Paul Ware, vice president of quality assurance for Safety 1st, to chair the standard-setting committee. There was a lot at stake for Ware: His company is the dominant player in the bath seat market. In 1999, Ware estimated gross sales of the product to be, "on the order of four to five million dollars."[56] New safety standards may have required Safety 1st to redesign its top-selling product.

The CPSC believed two features of bath seats were contributing to the majority of deaths: the size of the leg openings, and suction cups that were coming off. Straddling the bath seat's plastic bar, infants could fit both legs through one leg opening, then slip through and drown—a phenomenon called "submarining." The agency pushed Ware's committee to prevent such incidents by adding a maximum leg-opening dimension to the standard. Suction cups were problematic for two reasons: They came off too easily, and when a bathtub was covered with an anti-skid strip or appliqué, the suction cups didn't always stick to the bottom of the tub. Without adequate suction, the bath seat was more likely to tip over with the infant in it. The CPSC asked Ware's committee to address these issues in its new safety standard.[57]

In April 1999, following five years of work, during which time forty–three more infants drowned (about half of them associated with the Safety 1st bath seat), Ware and his committee finally approved their new safety standard. Their years of work had culminated in a standard that called for no significant structural product changes: the leg openings are just as wide, and the suction cups just as likely to detach. In other words, the committee completely disregarded the CPSC's requests, the arguments of consumer advocates, and the continuing bath seat death toll.[58] It's no accident that as of February 2000, sixty–six infants had died in the U.S. while using bath seats (see Appendix 2–3 for the list of fatalities).[59] Quite predictably, the voluntary standard has done nothing to slow the bath seat mortality rate, which has held steady at about eight infant deaths per year.

How can engineers refuse to accept responsibility for improving a product as deadly as bath seats? Easily enough: They foist the blame onto parents. "You can't replace common sense with all the instructions in the world," said one manufacturer after a discussion of bath seat warning labels. "It's like letting your child play in the street… Parents simply need to use common sense."[60] (Consumer advocates compare industry arguments against tighter safety standards to the National Rifle Association's popular argument against gun control: Poorly designed bath seats don't kill babies, inattentive parents do.) One fact remains undisputed by manufacturers and consumer advocates alike: Children don't die in bath seats when their caregivers are with them. As the descriptions of infant drownings in Appendix 2–3 illustrate, parents too often leave their child unattended in a bathtub. A mother leaves her baby securely sitting up in a bath seat, and when she returns, the child has drowned.[61] In over ninety percent of bath seat drownings, reports the 1997 *Pediatrics* study, "there was a reported lapse of adult supervision."

Most parents will tell you they would never *willfully* leave an infant unattended in a bathtub. Yet bath seat drowning data indicates that, willful or not, too many parents and caregivers do engage in this risky behavior, with tragic consequences. In March 2000, addressing the National Congress on Childhood Emergencies, professor Clay Mann of the Intermountain Injury Control Research Center at the University of Utah Medical School, presented research findings that clarify this discrepancy between what parents say they will do and what they actually do, given the demands of daily life. The study, which compared thirty–two bath seat drownings with thirty–two infant drownings that did not involve a bath seat, goes far toward implicating bath seats in infant drowning deaths. Dr. Mann found two significant differences between the groups: caregivers filled the bathtub with more water when they used a bath seat (median depth 7 inches with bath seats, versus 4.5 inches without), and they were more likely to make a *willful* decision to leave a child unattended in the tub when a bath seat was being used.[62] "Willful decisions" were defined as being premeditated or thought-out in advance (e.g., to perform household chores), as opposed to "impulsive decisions" (e.g., to answer a telephone or respond to another child). Dr. Mann found that parents had made a willful decision to leave the child alone in 75 percent of the bath seat drowning incidents, compared to only 45 percent of the non-bath seat drownings. His conclusion: bath seats increase the probability that a caregiver will leave a child unattended in a bathtub. By fostering the belief that it is okay to leave a child alone "for just a minute," bath seats actually increase the likelihood that an infant will drown.

Defending their right to market the product, manufacturers ignore the role their product plays in infant drowning, opting instead to blame parents. In a 1999 deposition, Safety 1st vice president Paul Ware admitted he was well aware of the CPSC research demonstrating bath seats were likely to *encourage* parents to leave a baby unattended in the tub. Yet even after at least twenty babies had died while using this Safety 1st product, the company did little to act on this knowledge.[63]

Most large infant products manufacturers appear to be cognizant of these dangers, and have avoided the bath seat market altogether. Hasbro, Fisher-Price, Graco, and Century Products have either left the market, or never entered it. "Nothing that these guys can talk about here today will make bath seats safe," said a European manufacturer after listening to Paul Ware's bath seat committee report. "It's ridiculous. We would never make such a product." [64]

It is ironic, then, that a leading U.S. bath seat manufacturer is named Safety 1st. The CPSC finds this not so much ironic as problematic. "One provision CPSC got manufacturers to agree to is that they would never put on the outside of the box that it [bath seat] is a 'safety device,'" said one CPSC regulator. "But we couldn't do anything about the name Safety 1st... People look at their box and look at the name of the company and just assume it's a 'safety' product."[65]

Why Voluntary Safety Standards Don't Work for Infant Products

What is the purpose of voluntary safety standards? "Ideally, a standard should enable consumers to draw distinctions among products of differing safety, with products meeting the standard being viewed as of higher quality," writes Harvard University economist Kip Viscusi in his book *Regulating Product Safety*.[66] In other words, one purpose of voluntary standards is to help consumers sort through the confusing myriad of product offerings.

Standing in front of the stroller display at Babies R' Us, a parent intent on buying a safe product should be able to quickly narrow her choice set to only those strollers that comply with the standard. But because the pecuniary interests of manufacturers have usurped the standard-setting process, voluntary standards are no longer diagnostic. Do these standards adequately discriminate products that are safe from those that are not? That about one hundred children's products are recalled each year, many that comply with a voluntary standard, suggests the answer is a resounding "No." [67]

Voluntary Standards Do Not Require Products to Be Tested in the Field

The most flagrant, though easily surmountable shortcoming of voluntary safety standards is that they do not require manufacturers to test their products in the field with "real" product users—babies and their caregivers. Standards require products to be tested only in a controlled laboratory setting, where inert stuffed dummies, all the exact same height and weight, fill in for real babies. The engineers strap the dummies into products, then bang, drop, clamp, and rock them. Unlike "real world" caregivers, the engineers are not harried or exhausted, nor are they forced to abandon their dummies with a split second's notice, to answer a ringing doorbell, grab a diaper, or attend to a dummy's screaming sibling in the next room. The penalty for leaving a dummy unattended during a coffee break, or when their boss calls them into the next room—as product warning labels admonish caregivers never to do—is not very high. Dummies can't squiggle or squirm, dummies can't get injured, and dummies certainly can't die. Nonetheless, it is the engineers' job to simulate the chaotic, unpredictable world of babies and their caregivers. Some of the time they get it right. But too often, they get it wrong.

The case of the Baby Trend Home and Roam portable crib underscores the inadequacy of lab testing. A small, California-based manufacturer of strollers, high chairs, and baby walkers, Baby Trend launched one of the first portable cribs in 1992. The Baby Trend Home and Roam crib complied with the voluntary safety standard for portable cribs, ASTM F–406.[68] Nevertheless, the crib was recalled in 1995, after 65,000 units had been sold and two toddlers were killed.[69]

Jared Zalinski was a Baby Trend portable crib victim. On an August morning in 1994, Linda Zalinski, Jared's mother, put the eight–month–old baby in his crib, then proceeded to take a shower. Stepping out of the shower a few minutes later, Ms. Zalinski heard her four–year–old daughter screaming that Jared was having a problem. When Ms. Zalinski got to Jared's bedroom, she found that the portable crib had collapsed, trapping Jared at the chest in the "V" created by the folded top rails (see Appendix 2–1). He was not breathing. Ms. Zalinski tried to resuscitate her son, but he was pronounced dead on arrival at the hospital.[70]

The Baby Trend crib was designed with the top rail center-hinge flaw that allowed it to collapse with a child in it. To set up the crib properly, a caregiver had to securely lock the crib's hinges by rotating a pivot handle. If the pivot handle was not rotated completely, the crib could fold up and collapse at the top rail's center hinge, potentially strangling the child trapped inside. This is how Jared Zalinski died.

Jared Zalinski's parents sued Baby Trend for the wrongful death of their son. Baby Trend claimed the product was safe, and had collapsed only because Jared's parents had not followed the assembly instructions, which the company insisted were clear. When asked in a pre-trial deposition how the crib's assembly had been tested, Baby Trend manager of operations Jim Dodds said, "... there were girls in the office... in their first years of marriage... and we would have them basically take a look at all the products, including the play yard [Home and Roam portable crib]."[71] When Johnson asked how many women had tested the product, Dodds answered, "I really don't recall." And when asked more pointedly if the "girls in the office" had any difficulty rotating the crib's pivot handles, Dodds replied, "I don't know that we asked that question." Later, when asked if he had tested the crib with real children, Dodds replied, "I did on a very informal level." Dodds had given the product to a couple of his friends and watched "the reaction of the child with the product." In sum, Dodds' test subjects were a handful of his employees and friends.

Some large companies do subject their products to stringent laboratory tests, and some test their products in the field, as an extra precaution. And yet even these products are not immune to recalls resulting from shoddy workmanship, poor quality control, or faulty design. The Playskool 1–2–3 high chair, launched with much fanfare in May 1994, was one of the most expensive high chairs on store shelves, and complied with the industry voluntary standard, ASTM F–404.[72] Yet it was recalled a year–and–a–half later, after thousands of consumers called Hasbro to report the chair was defective.[73]

Unlike Baby Trend, Hasbro systematically tested the 1–2–3 on real babies and their caregivers before the product launch. "On Wednesday, March 23, 1994, quantity 24 #731 Playskool 1–2–3 High Chairs were sent out for field test," reads an internal Hasbro memo dated April 1994, one month before the high chair reached store shelves. "23 out of 24 recipients responded."[74] That Hasbro had planned to sell at least 300,000 of these high chairs suggests that a significantly larger sample size was warranted.

Hasbro took some of the field test participants' criticisms of the product seriously. After five testers (twenty–two percent) noted that the high chair's tray was wobbly, the product was sent back to the engineering department for a quick fix. Three testers (thirteen percent) complained that the metal screws holding down the high chair's seat protruded through the cushion. Hasbro switched to a shorter screw without a point. But Hasbro ignored other comments, particularly those regarding the high chair's assembly instructions. In response to the question, "Were the instructions and illustrations clear and easy to understand?" twenty caregivers (eighty–seven percent) responded "No." "I do not believe the average house person would be able to assemble this product without difficulty," wrote one tester. "[The instructions] were somewhat confusing, especially when I tried to adjust the belt length," another complained. "Illustration is different from actual belt on product."[75] Yet the Hasbro memo gave no indication that the instructions would be improved.

While many manufacturers' pre-market testing appears to be inadequate, they do, in a sense, engage in a form of large-scale field testing: the product launch. Every time a parent or caregiver assembles a new, cutting-edge infant product and straps a child into it, a mini-experiment begins. Will the sixteen–year–old daycare center employee put a new infant swing together properly, or will she confuse two nearly identical parts on a diagram? Will the new father listen for the "click" of the portable crib's locking mechanism, or will his baby's cries distract him? Will weak joints cause a high chair to suddenly collapse, throwing a baby to the floor? Unsuspecting consumers in homes and daycare centers submit to such "tests" thousands of times each day. If this "field testing" results in injured or dead babies, the CPSC can recall the product, and coerce the manufacturer to notify a small percentage of the products' users (see Chapter 3). Then the corporate marketing experts return to their focus groups, and the engineers to their drafting tables, eager to fill new vacancies on store shelves with more inadequately tested products.

Voluntary Standards Do Not Address All Known Product Hazards

Early one June morning in 1997, in White Lake, Michigan, Carrie Dorian found her son Brandon dangling lifeless from the side slats of his Cosco metal crib. The eight–month–old baby had squeezed his body through the crib's slats, but his head had gotten stuck, and was pressed against the mattress. The coroner speculated that the infant had struggled for about three minutes to free himself before he lost consciousness and died. Brandon was bruised behind the ears, and he had bled extensively beneath his scalp.[76]

Full-size cribs must comply with mandatory federal safety standards, but these standards do not address all product hazards. Voluntary standards are supposed to fill in the gaps. To prevent children like Brandon from being entrapped, the mandatory crib standard specifies that side slats can be no further apart than two and three–eighths inches—about the width of a can of soda.[77] When Brandon's grandfather assembled the Cosco crib, he had inadvertently mixed up the side and bottom panels. Mandatory regulations do not address the width of bottom-panel slats. Voluntary standards do not address this hazard, either.

Whose fault was it that the crib was misassembled and Brandon was killed? Even after the CPSC received "more than forty–seven reports" of cribs being misassembled in this same manner, and after at least twenty–seven more babies had been entrapped, Cosco continued to deny culpability.[78] Meanwhile, the Dorians' attorney Ven Johnson argued that it was Cosco's responsibility to design defects out of the product. Cosco, he insisted, should have better anticipated what could have gone wrong during the in-home assembly process, and made sure consumers were unable to endanger their children by mixing up the crib's bottom and side panels. The company could have made the bottom and side panels different sizes, so that it would be impossible for parents to mix them up—but it didn't. The company could have stamped a clear label on each panel, warning the assembler not to mix up the two—but it didn't. At the very least, argued Johnson, the crib's instruction sheet should have stated the risks associated with interchanging the side and bottom panels.[79] It didn't.

Eventually, Cosco did change the crib's assembly directions. But the way in which the company undertook this revision led Johnson to conclude that Cosco understood the crib's design could be implicated in Brandon's death. While investigating Brandon's death, the White Lake Township police requested the crib's assembly instructions from Cosco. The company sent instructions that clearly warned against reversing the side and bottom panels: "**Important: Tubing on mattress platform is spaced farther apart than on side rails. Do not use platform as a side rail**" (see Appendix 2–5). But Carrie Dorian had saved the assembly instructions that had come with her son's crib, and in her version, there was no mention of the hazards associated with interchanging the two panels (see Appendix 2–4). "When the two sets of instructions are compared," said attorney Johnson, "you can see that Cosco changed them *after* Brandon's death. They sent the police department the new instructions, not the ones that had been originally included with Brandon's crib."[80] Cosco was never asked to explain the discrepancy between the two sets of directions. A few months after Carrie Dorian filed her lawsuit, Cosco offered her a pre-trial cash settlement (see Chapter 5), and she took it.[81] The CPSC recalled the crib in July 1997, less than a month after Brandon died.[82] (In July 1998, a year after the recall, eleven–month–old Jamie Mosher of Joliet, Illinois was entrapped and died in his Cosco crib. A few days after his death, when a newspaper reporter called Cosco to learn more about the crib, a customer service representative told her the crib had not been recalled and that Cosco had received no reports of accidents associated with the product.)[83]

Why do manufacturers like Cosco fail to design defects out of their products? Why do assembly instructions fail to spell out for consumers, in clear language, the implications of misassembling a product? "Because they can," said Johnson, "and because of money."[84] No one expects companies to anticipate *every* hazard associated with a baby product. Once in a while, no matter how much testing a crib or stroller endures, no matter how thorough and well-intentioned the engineers, a faulty design or defective product will slip through the system. But too often, manufacturers are aware of a hazard, yet refuse to address it.

At the February 2000 infant products standard-setting meeting, CPSC engineer Mark Kumagai presented manufacturers with agency data showing that infants were being injured when their cradles tipped over. Many of the injured children were over six months old. Manufacturers told Kumagai that their product instructions clearly stated that cradles were to be used by infants 0–5 months old.[85]

"I know this is not the *intent* of the product," said Kumagai, recognizing the manufacturers' objections, "but this is what parents are *doing*. Parents are putting ten–month–old kids in these products." And the industry's standard fifty–four–pound test, in Kumagai's opinion, was not addressing the tip-over problem. "I think we should test for a heavier weight if we know that parents are 'misusing' it this way," Kumagai argued.[86]

"Our intent here is to make a standard for five–month–old babies, not ten–month–olds," said committee chair Paul Terronez, a Kolcraft engineer.[87] But Fisher-Price engineer Kitty Pilarz disagreed. "We all have data that shows consumers don't stop using the product when we tell them to," she said, confronting her colleagues head-on. "I would support a higher static load requirement. We know that consumers put older kids in them."[88]

At the meeting's close, the underlying question remained unanswered: Should voluntary standards address how manufacturers would *like* caregivers to use their products, or should they address how people *actually* use them in the real world? The issue was raised multiple times throughout the day and was never resolved. Failing repeatedly to address the issue of "foreseeable" use, the manufacturers demonstrated again and again that their primary goal is to minimize product liability, rather than maximize product safety.

Warning Labels Do Not Reveal Consequences of Behaviors

When six–month–old Jason Shelly had a cold, his mother Rebecca noted, he could breathe more easily sitting up in his Century Products infant swing than he could lying down in his crib. So, as she had done with her first child, Rebecca got into the habit of putting Jason to sleep in his infant swing when he was sick.[89]

At 5:30 a.m. on November 30, 1993, Jason's dad left for work. He didn't check on Jason before he left. A half–hour later Rebecca woke up and fed Jason's two–year–old sister in the kitchen. After a shower, Rebecca went to check on her son. She found Jason hanging from the Century infant swing, his head and neck entangled in its nylon straps. Rebecca called her husband, then her mother-in-law and 911. When an emergency medical team arrived, Rebecca was holding Jason. The baby had no vital signs. According to the police report, Jason was cold and clammy and his skin was gray. Rebecca, the report noted, was "extremely upset."[90]

When the Century 'Lil Napper swing killed Jason in 1993, voluntary standards for infant swings did not exist.[91] Jason's infant swing had come with a usage instruction manual that warned, **"YOUR CHILD SHOULD ALWAYS BE SNUGLY FASTENED WITH THE HARNESS STRAP. THE CONVENIENCE TRAY IS NOT A RESTRAINT SYSTEM. NEVER LEAVE A CHILD UNATTENDED. KEEP CHILD IN FULL VIEW."** The label attached to the swing itself contained none of these warnings. It simply read, "CEN-TURY DEDICATED TO QUALITY. DO NOT USE AS A CAR SEAT. IMPORTANT NOTE: THIS SWING WILL NOT OPERATE PROPERLY UNLESS IT HAS A BAT-TERY. DISCONTINUE USE ONCE CHILD BECOMES TOO ACTIVE OR EXCEEDS 11.4 KGS (25 POUNDS)."[92] Jason weighed 15 pounds.[93]

Between 1990 and 2000, at least sixteen babies were killed by their swings.[94] Although manufacturers and the CPSC were aware of the deaths, a voluntary safety standard for the product was not proposed until 2000. The infant swing com-mittee, headed by Graco engineer Steve Gerhart, drew up a standard that guarded against some causes of infant swing fatalities (i.e., a crotch restraint, to prevent a child from slid-ing down the seat and strangling on the seat belt) but neglect-ed others (i.e., size of leg openings).[95] Human factors psychol-ogist Shelley Waters Deppa, an expert on how infant products are used by babies and caregivers in the "real world," had seri-ous reservations about the proposed infant-swing standard. In a letter to the committee, Deppa pointed out that the stan-dard failed to provide adequate warning statements. "[T]here is no indication whatsoever [in the avoidance warnings] that children can get entangled in the restraints and strangle," Deppa wrote. "The fatal hazard of entanglement and strangu-lation in the safety restraints is not obvious by either the appearance nor function of the seat belt. All of the avoidance warnings could be interpreted by consumers to address the more obvious, common and less severe hazard of falling out of the swing."[96] Deppa's proposed solution: A label that clearly warns parents that their child could die from strangulation if they do not use the waist and crotch restraints in the manner specified by the manufacturers.

There is an important difference between the "avoidance" messages found most frequently on infant product warning

FIGURE 2–1
WARNING

Never leave baby unattended.
Always keep child in view even
while sleeping.
Always use waist straps to retain
baby.
Stay within reach of your child..

IMPORTANT NOTE:
Discontinue use once child
becomes too active or exceeds
25 lbs.

FIGURE 2–2
WARNING

Never leave baby unattended.
Always keep child in view even
while sleeping.
Always use waist straps to retain
baby.
Stay within reach of your child.

Children's abilities develop rapidly
and they can unexpectedly wiggle
out of restraints and strangle in
them or on the tray, causing brain
damage or death within minutes.

IMPORTANT NOTE:
Discontinue use once child
becomes too active or exceeds
25 lbs.

labels and the type of "consequence" warning label Deppa recommended. "Avoidance" messages warn a caregiver NOT to do
something, such as "never leave a baby unattended," but do not
explain why this behavior should be avoided. "Consequence"
warnings, on the other hand, spell out not only which behaviors should be avoided, but describe the consequences of these
behaviors—such as "brain damage or death within minutes."[97]

"Avoidance" warnings, such as the swing warning written
and tested by human factors specialist Jay Martin (Figure 2–1),
do little to compel caregivers to avoid behaviors such as leaving
infants unattended. Clearly stated "consequence" warnings
(Figure 2–2), on the other hand, are better understood by caregivers, result in more accurate perceptions of product risk, and
are more likely to be heeded than the more common "avoidance" warnings, according to Martin's research.[98] Explicitly stat-
ing *why* certain behaviors should be avoided is most important
for products with hidden hazards. The obvious hazard of infant

swings, most parents can tell you, is that a child may fall out if the restraint buckle isn't used. However, very few parents have any idea that infants can be, and have been, strangled by the straps of a swing. A label alerting caregivers to this hidden hazard could be expected to greatly increase compliance with product usage instructions.

Nervous that strongly worded warning statements may scare customers away, most manufacturers do not display adequate consequence warnings on their infant products. But this won't be the case with infant swings anymore. The standards committee voted to accept Deppa's suggestion on consequence warnings (22 for, 4 against). While the message will not be as strong as Martin's proposed warning (Figure 2–2), it will at least mention the hidden hazard of strangulation. For manufacturers to be in compliance with the new standard, they will have to affix the following hazard statement onto their infant swings:

> To prevent serious injury or death from children falling or being strangled in straps, always use seat belt provided.
> Never leave infants unattended in a swing.
> Discontinue use of swing when child becomes too active (approximately 6 months).[99]

By convincing most of the standard-setting voters of the need for consequence warnings on infant swings, Deppa scored a small victory for parents and their babies. However, this important change affects just one product. For consequence warnings to be included on other products, Deppa and other consumer advocates will have to make this case again and again.

Voluntary Standards Exist for Inherently Unsafe Products

In 1994, the American Academy of Pediatrics, the National Safe Kids Campaign, the Consumer Federation of America, and Consumers Union petitioned the CPSC to ban the sale of baby walkers, the product associated with more injuries than any other infant product.[100] In response to the petition, the CPSC issued an Advance Notice of Proposed Rulemaking (ANPR) for baby walkers, initiating the government's *mandatory* standard-setting process. An ANPR notifies industry and all interested parties (i.e., consumer advocates) that the CPSC has reason to suspect a voluntary standard is not stringent enough, and that a product may be dangerous enough to warrant a mandatory safety standard. "Based on currently available information," read the ANPR, "the Commission has reason to believe that unreasonable risk of injury and death may be associated with baby walkers."[101]

A voluntary walker standard had been in place since 1989, but clearly it did not go far enough to prevent walker-related injuries and deaths. Between 1989 and 1994, walker-related emergency room visits rose precipitously, reaching 28,000 visits in 1994.[102] During this time period, eleven children died from incidents involving their walkers (drownings, suffocations, and fatal head injuries). Other children suffered non-fatal skull fractures, concussions, brain hemorrhages, burns, and spine fractures.[103] Most of the injuries (seventy–nine percent) occurred when children under fifteen months tumbled down stairs in their walkers. Other injuries occurred when walkers tipped over, when a walker enabled a child to touch a hot oven, heater, or radiator, or when a child reached up from a walker to overturn a container of hot liquid.[104]

By the time the CPSC issued its ANPR, the agency's walker file was thick with descriptions of hundreds of infant injuries such as these:

> The 9–month old female victim was injured while at home with her mother. The victim's mother stated that the basement door was open and the victim rolled the walker through the door and fell down the stairs. The

victim's mother transported the victim to the emergency room...

The 8–month old victim was injured when she pushed on a gate leading down a set of steps and the victim and her walker went tumbling down the stairs, falling 11–12 carpeted steps. The victim's mother took the victim to the emergency room...

The 7–month old male victim was injured at home while under his mother's care. The victim was sitting in a baby walker and when his mother left the room, the victim rolled the walker to the basement door and rolled down the stairs. The victim and walker fell forward and the victim landed on his head. The victim's mother took the victim to the emergency room...[105]

Walkers are treacherous for one reason: They allow a baby who is not yet able to walk on his own to be mobile. Babies use walkers to travel up to four feet per second, enough time to tumble down stairs, reach the cord of an electric appliance, touch a hot stove, or roll into a swimming pool.[106] Accidents occur quickly, often when a caregiver has turned her attention away from the baby for just a few seconds. Two–thirds of walker accidents occur while children are *in the same room* with their caregiver, demonstrating that the product is so dangerous, it is not even safe for a child to use it while he's *attended*.[107] One pediatric research study showed that walkers account for up to forty–five percent of all head injuries caused by children falling down stairs, pointing out the toll the product takes on public safety. "And, amazingly, even after their babies had been injured by walkers," writes Sandy Jones in the *Consumer Reports Guide to Baby Products*, "one out of three parents put their babies right back in a walker again or used walkers for other children."[108] The evidence is clear: the costs incurred by walker injuries—to individual families and to the public—far outweigh their benefits.

The CPSC often issues an ANPR to warn industry that if they don't develop a more stringent voluntary standard on their own, the agency will promulgate a mandatory standard or ban the product altogether. When the agency deems a specific product dangerous, such as the Graco Converta-Cradle or the Baby Trend portable crib, it can move to have that product recalled (Chapter 3). Although the agency has the authority to recall *all* brands within a product category in one fell swoop—such as *all* brands of walkers or *all* brands of portable cribs—it has not exercised this authority in recent history.[109] Less drastic than a ban, an ANPR gives manufacturers one last chance to make a product safer. This was the case with baby walkers. The ANPR suggested ways manufacturers could create safer walkers: build them too large to fit through standard door openings, or limit their mobility by equipping them with "wheel-stop" mechanisms that act as brakes.[110]

Picking up on the CPSC's hints, baby-walker manufacturers agreed to develop a more stringent voluntary standard. The CPSC backed down, and denied the consumer advocates' petition to ban walkers.[111]

The industry's new voluntary standard, completed in 1997, specifies that walkers must come equipped with at least one feature that will prevent them from tumbling down stairs.[112] But the standard falls short of specifying exactly what that feature must be. Such a standard would be considered "design restrictive"—the type of solution manufacturers invariably reject.[113] Some manufacturers chose to comply with the new walker standard by making the product larger, so that it simply couldn't fit through a standard thirty–six–inch stair door. Others chose a less expensive route: a "friction strip" intended to stop the walker when it hits the edge of a stair and a "parking brake" that is supposed to keep the product and baby in one place.[114]

The CPSC is quick to trot out baby walkers as an example of a product with a voluntary standard that worked. Since the standard has been in effect, the agency claims, walker-related injuries dropped from 28,000 in 1994 to 13,100 in 1998.[115] The CPSC neglects to mention, however, that walker-related injuries have been declining since 1995, two years *before* the new standard was in place.[116] The reason: Walker sales plummeted when sales of a safer replacement product, stationary entertainers, took off. Many—but not all—consumers had gotten the word that baby walkers were dangerous, and were no longer buying the industry's claim that any amount of design modifications could make them safe.

Despite declining sales, walkers continue to injure thousands of babies each year and still account for more emergency room visits than almost any other baby product.[117] As long as walkers continue to be sold, walker-related injuries will persist. "The American Academy of Pediatrics strongly urges parents not to use baby walkers," the doctors' group warns parents in the 1998 book *Caring for Your Baby and Young Child.*[118] In California, walkers are illegal in daycare centers.[119] Yet the CPSC won't ban the product outright, and manufacturers like Baby Trend, Cosco, Graco, Kolcraft, and Safety 1st continue to sell them.[120] While manufacturers' advertising claims of convenience come through loud and clear, the message that walkers are highly dangerous still fails to reach many consumers.

An incident brought to manufacturers' attention by the CPSC at a recent standard-setting meeting highlights the persistent dangers of walkers, despite the new voluntary standard. In the summer of 1998, Bob and Susan Sobel of Comstock Park, Michigan, were thinking of purchasing a baby walker for their ten–month–old son Ian. After seeing an ad on a local television station for the "safest walker on the market," they made their decision. Ian loved his new walker, and Bob and Susan loved it too, because "it kept the child happy and helped him exercise." The walker complied with the new 1997 voluntary standard,

ASTM F–977. The manufacturer had used friction strips and a parking brake to prevent it from tumbling down stairs.[121]

Soon after Bob and Susan bought the walker, they noticed the friction strips had come off and the parking brake had failed. They reattached the strips and kept a closer eye on Ian when he used the product.

While in the kitchen one day with Ian, Susan briefly turned her back to the child. In this split second, Ian followed his older brother to the basement and fell down the stairs in the walker. Luckily, he only cut his head. Bob and Susan calmed their son, then inspected the walker's stopping mechanisms, which obviously had not worked. The parking brake had failed to hold the walker in place and the friction strips had come off again. Over the next two weeks, Bob and Susan estimated that they reattached the five friction strips at least ten times, and Ian fell four more times.

CPSC engineers told this story at the August 1999 standard-setting meeting, hoping to cajole manufacturers to come up with a more stringent walker standard.[122] Friction strips that easily came off were not an adequate solution for walker hazards, they claimed. The manufacturers disagreed, insisting that the Sobels were to blame for Ian's falls, not ineffective friction strips. "The directions said not to use the walker if it is broken," one manufacturer argued, "and these parents apparently knew the product was broken." But most parents didn't know what friction strips were, one consumer advocate countered, much less the importance of making sure they were working. "The problem here is that the parents used the walker even when they knew it wasn't safe," said Jerry Dobrinski, former vice president of product development at Graco, now a recall consultant to infant product manufacturers. "This [CPSC report] says the parents used the walker after it had fallen over four times. These parents should have been picked up for child abuse."[123]

Were the Sobels guilty of child abuse? Or were they simply

guilty of believing a television ad that claimed a walker was safe? "Parents have bought the myth that if you watch your children while they're in the walker, then they'll be fine," said Gary Smith, a pediatrician and director of the Center for Injury Research and Policy at the Children's Hospital in Columbus, Ohio. "That's just not the case."[124] Graco, Century Products, and Safety 1st continue to market the product, despite knowing that walkers send thousands of children to emergency rooms each year. Unlike the manufacturers, the Sobels did not have access to data on walker-related injuries and deaths. Nevertheless, once their child was hurt, they became another industry scapegoat. Parents can't win. Manufacturers maintain it is their right to manufacture and advertise safety claims about products that are inherently dangerous, just as it is their right to conceal product injury data (see Chapter 5). Then, when a child is hurt, they blame the parents.

Theoretically, voluntary standards can improve product safety. But over the last twenty years, mounting evidence has suggested that for many baby products, voluntary standards just aren't stringent enough. A mother who is willing to pay a premium for safety cannot be sure her choice is a good one—even when the product's box flaunts the ASTM compliance seal. What the mother doesn't know can quite literally hurt her child. She will not know that the product may not have been tested on real babies. She will not know the voluntary standard is unlikely to have addressed all the known product hazards. She will not know the "hidden hazards" associated with the product, or the consequences of not using the product exactly as the manufacturer wants her to use it. And she may not know the product is associated with over ten thousand injuries each year, and has been deemed inherently unsafe by pediatricians.

Clearly, the time has come for the CPSC to play a larger role in the standard-setting process for baby products. Kip Viscusi, an economist with a reputation for taking a hard-line *against* government regulation of industry, concedes that children's products warrant stricter regulation. Why? Because, like the Sobels, the buyers and users of these products "cannot always properly assess the risks and undertake the appropriate safety-enhancing actions."[125] Argues trade reporter Warren Shoulberg, "There is only one more voluntary action the kids industry should take: It should volunteer to start working on mandatory safety standards."[126] Paula Markowitz, the president of New Jersey-based infant bedding company PatchKraft, didn't hesitate when asked to sum up the five years she has spent on the ASTM infant voluntary standards committee: "The whole process is a joke."[127]

CHAPTER 3

A Recall Process That Fails to Alert Consumers about Infant Product Dangers

In March 1995, Ann Brown, the newly appointed chair of the Consumer Product Safety Commission (CPSC), welcomed senior industry executives to a conference in Washington to discuss how safety could increase corporate profits.[1] Manufacturers had been nervous when President Clinton appointed Brown, a strong consumer advocate, to head up the CPSC, but from the start the public relations-savvy regulator searched for win-win strategies to carry out the agency's mission. The Safety Sells conference signaled Brown's respect for the corporate bottom line, as did her nascent product safety award. Bestowing the first CPSC Chairman Commendation for Significant Contributions to Product Safety upon the Playskool 1–2–3 high chair in August 1994, Brown announced to the press, "It is a competitive advantage to get this award, and I'm convinced that pretty soon you'll see that competitors won't stand still and let Hasbro have this advantage. They'll start making safer high chairs soon."[2]

Brown sealed her approval of the Playskool high chair by choosing Hasbro C.E.O. Alan Hassenfeld to be a featured speaker at the Safety Sells conference. "Chairman Brown has asked me to talk to you about one specific example of a product that has safety as a key component, where safety really does sell," Hassenfeld told the 175 conference attendees, among them senior executives from Binney & Smith (Crayola), Toys

R' Us, Procter & Gamble, Volvo, Evenflo, Rollerblade, and Whirlpool. "I can think of none better than our award-winning 1–2–3 high chair—award-winning because of the design and the safety elements that are built into it."[3] The chair's rigid crotch restraint, the first of its kind, was intended to prevent the most common high chair accidents, falls and "submarining"— incidents in which babies slide down the seat and strangle on the tray or waist strap.

Hassenfeld had reason to brag. In addition to receiving the CPSC award, the 1–2–3 was named one of the "Ten Best Products" of 1993 by the Juvenile Products Manufacturers Association (JPMA), the industry trade group, prompting retailers such as Toys R' Us, Service Merchandise, Wal-Mart, Baby Superstore, Costco, and Target to place sizable orders.[4] Most important, the high chair struck a chord with parents. Within a year of its 1993 launch, the Playskool 1–2–3 became the best-selling high chair in the nation, despite a retail price well above most of its competitors. Research and development costs for the high chair, which had run in excess of a million dollars, appeared to be paying off.[5]

Soon after the 1–2–3 hit store shelves, however, hints of trouble trickled into Hasbro's customer service lines. As the product worked its way through the distribution system, from retailers' warehouses and stockrooms into consumers' homes, the complaints escalated (Table 3–1). In May 1994, forty–four customers called Hasbro to report that their 1–2–3 high chairs had broken; by the end of the year, customer service representatives were fielding over 150 complaints a month.[6] Yet retail sales remained strong.

By the spring of 1995, hundreds of thousands of Playskool 1–2–3 high chairs were being subjected to the wear and tear of daily use in consumers' homes. In May, more than twelve hundred customers called Hasbro with complaints.[7] There wasn't just one problem, but many. The chair was collapsing after its

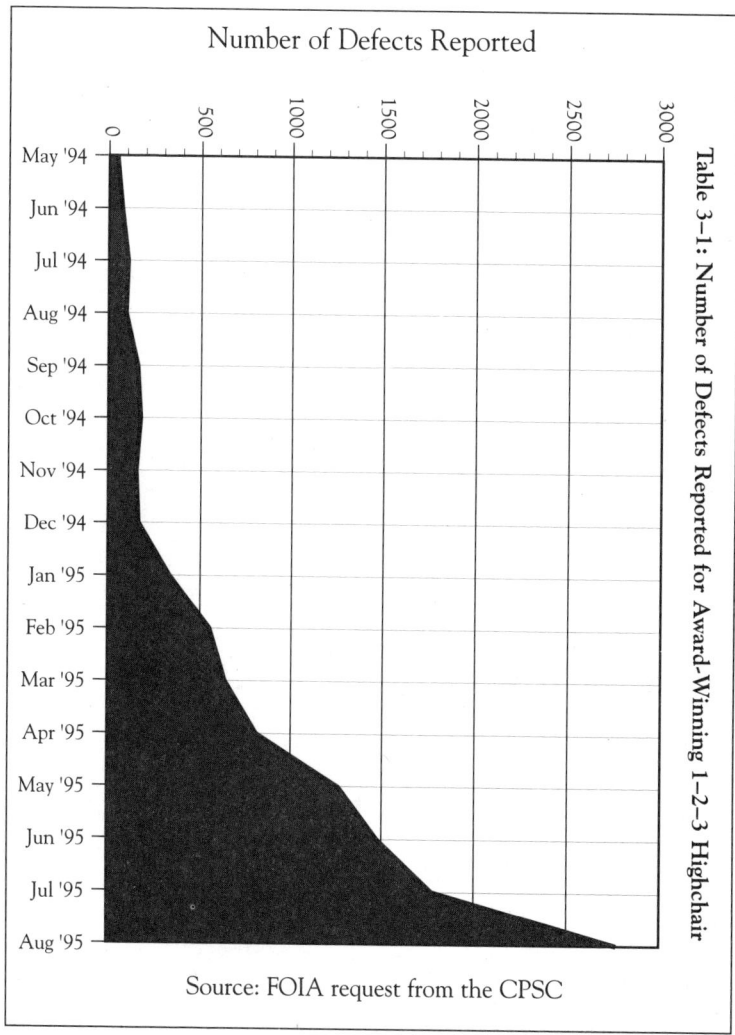

Table 3-1: Number of Defects Reported for Award-Winning 1-2-3 Highchair

Number of Defects Reported

Source: FOIA request from the CPSC

legs broke, the incline levers were defective, the seat pads were ripping, and the height adjusters didn't work properly.[8]

Hasbro executives knew they had a problem. By the end of August 1995, the company had heard from more than 10,500 unhappy customers.[9] Nevertheless, Hasbro continued to manufacture and sell the chair.

Emily Weinberg, of Hartsdale, New York, was not as lucky as the thousands of other toddlers whose 1–2–3 high chair broke. On September 16, 1995, when the fifteen–month–old child's high chair collapsed, Emily fell to the ground and suffered a concussion. "Due to the severity of the fall," the family's pediatrician wrote to Hasbro, "Emily suffered head trauma which resulted in vomiting."[10]

Two weeks later, Hasbro stopped production of the 1–2–3.[11]

"It may have been the Gallo brothers who said they will sell no wine before its time," Hassenfeld boasted at the Safety Sells conference, "but I can assure you, it is the Hassenfeld brothers who will sell no product before it passes our very rigorous safety standards." The C.E.O. continued with safety advice to his competitors: "The most important thing if you have a problem is to nip it in the bud, so that it stays a small problem. Don't be indecisive—move on it right away."[12] Company records indicate that at the time Hassenfeld uttered these words, in March 1995, his company had already recorded 2,483 complaints of defective 1–2–3 high chairs.[13]

Hasbro voluntarily recalled the high chair in October 1995, a year after Chairman Brown bestowed it with her first-ever safety award.[14] The CPSC requests a recall in the face of mounting injuries, manufacturers' consumer complaint lines that won't stop ringing, or hundreds of pages of investigator reports detailing a product's dangers. "The purpose of a recall," says CPSC Chairman Brown, "is to get dangerous products back."[15] But the Consumer Product Safety Act, which gives Brown's agency the power to yank dangerous products off the market, falls short of enabling her staff to get these products out of homes and daycare centers. A recall protects people who haven't yet bought the defective product—but does not go far enough to protect those who already own and use it.

Consolidation of the infant products industry into only a handful of large players, high-speed production lines, widespread distribution by Internet and power retailers like Wal-Mart and Babies R' Us, and the proliferation of targeted media outlets such as *Parent* and *Child* magazines, give manufacturers the ability to deeply and rapidly saturate the marketplace with new products. By the time an infant product is recalled, hundreds of thousands, even millions of units may already be in use. In 1999, the CPSC recalled 95 children's products, adding up to tens of millions of units.[16] Recent recalls include 800,000 Kolcraft car seat/carriers, 355,500 Cosco infant swings, 166,000 Century sport strollers, and 7 million Graco swings.[17]

Agreeing to a recall generally means that a company consents to take two broad actions: to issue a notice to the media and to notify retailers that the product can no longer be sold and must be pulled from store shelves. There is no law or regulation that requires manufacturers to notify parents or daycare centers of a recall directly by telephone or mail. There is no law or regulation that requires manufacturers to advertise a product recall—much like they advertise new products—in magazines or on TV. And there is no law or regulation that requires manufacturers to demonstrate that recalled products are returned or are in some other way taken out of use.[18] High chairs, cribs, strollers, infant swings, and carriers—products parents and caregivers buy specifically to keep a child safe—continue to be used months, even years after they have been recalled. Recycled and resold through garage sales and secondhand stores, passed on to unsuspecting friends, relatives, and younger siblings, products with dangerous and even deadly track records remain in circulation. In a particularly macabre version of Russian Roulette, no one knows who the next victim will be.

It is no accident that manufacturers of infant products cannot account for 70–90 percent of sold infant products after they have been recalled.[19] Manufacturers certainly have the ability to disseminate recall news widely. But the same corporations that spend millions of dollars on market research and advertising each year claim they are incapable of reaching consumers when a product is recalled. The veneer of this claim is scratched easily to arrive at the truth: The last thing manufacturers want is for news of a recall to get *too much* attention. In the short-term, well-publicized recalls are expensive to carry out, and in the long-term, they can invite product liability lawsuits, damage a company's image, and erode shareholder wealth.

How the CPSC Finds Out about Dangerous Infant Products

Manufacturers are legally obligated to notify the CPSC within twenty-four hours of learning that one of their products has a defect that can cause injury or death.[20] Congress enacted this statute as part of the Consumer Product Safety Act, aiming to place the burden of hazard identification on corporations, rather than the financially strapped CPSC. Companies are likely to learn that one of their products is hazardous long before the CPSC is privy to this information, Congress reasoned; therefore, the onus should be on companies to self-report. Congress was right: Problems with infant products typically are discovered through customer feedback. The same consumer who would throw away a malfunctioning toaster rather than make the effort to call the company and demand a new one doesn't hesitate to track down a manufacturer and complain when her two-year-old's high chair or crib falls apart.

Despite the law, the CPSC has never been able to rely on manufacturers to report their own product defects (see Chapter 4). "Industry under-reporting of significant safety hazards continues to be a matter of concern to the Commission," reads the agency's *2000 Budget Request to Congress.*[21] So when it comes to uncovering dangerous products, the CPSC's "compliance" staff must become sleuths. In 1999, the CPSC's division of hazard identification and analysis spent close to $7 million (15 percent of its total budget) uncovering unreported product hazards.[22]

The CPSC jump-starts its hazard identification process with a consumer hotline, a toll-free number the public can call to complain about defective products. This is one place a consumer can be sure her voice is heard: The agency closely monitors the calls for tips that will lead investigators to products that may need to be recalled. However, most people have no idea the hotline exists—in 1998, only 4,300 consumers called it to report hazards associated with all CPSC-regulated consumer products, including infant equipment, toys, yard and garden equipment, tools, construction materials, and home appliances.[23] By comparison, 225,096 infants and children were rushed to emergency rooms that year for toy and infant equipment-related injuries.[24]

Karin Bellholder was one of the few parents who knew to contact the CPSC when her daughter's Playskool 1–2–3 high chair broke.[25] She told the agency that when she put the four–month–old baby in the high chair, the legs separated and the chair collapsed. The infant escaped injury only because Karin was quick enough to break her fall. When Karin called Hasbro's customer service line to report the incident, the company offered to send her a new pair of chair legs. The new legs broke soon after Karin installed them. When she tried to contact Hasbro for the second time, she could not get through. Frustrated, Karin called the CPSC to report the problem. "I have not been able to contact the manufacturer," she told the agency. "The telephone line is constantly busy. Please advise." Karin was one of only twenty–one consumers who called the CPSC to complain about the high chair; more than 10,500 others called Hasbro directly.[26]

The CPSC's main source of information about product-related injuries is its hospital reporting system. At 101 emergency rooms across the U.S., the CPSC has trained hospital staff who collect data on emergency room visitors with product-related injuries.[27] This information is stored in the CPSC's National Electronic Injury Surveillance System (NEISS) database and is available to regulators within seventy–two hours of an accident. But fatal problems with NEISS data limit its usefulness. First, because the system samples only a small fraction of American hospitals, many product-related injuries are never recorded; as a result, CPSC epidemiologists are sometimes unable to make reliable injury projections to the population as a whole. Second, the NEISS database captures only basic demographic information about an injured person (such as age, gender, and body part affected), neglecting information that would allow the CPSC to "assess causality"—to figure out if the accident was caused by a product (for example, a cradle's rocking motion caused an infant to slide into a corner and suffocate), or whether it was purely a fluke. In the absence of such records, motivated corporate lawyers often successfully argue—against a plaintiff in a product liability case or against the CPSC—that their product may have been associated with a child's injury or death, but was not the cause. "Product misuse" is to blame for the incident, the defense argument goes, not the product per se. If the child's mother had been more attentive, or if Grandpa had assembled the crib correctly, or if the babysitter had read all the fine print on the warning label, the child would never have been harmed. In this way, manufacturers routinely blame parents for their child's injury or death.

To augment the emergency room data and the companies' minimal reporting, CPSC staff rely on a patchwork of external data sources, including newspaper stories about product-related injuries and deaths, coroner reports, insurance investigations, reports of lawsuits, and even manufacturers who call the agency to report on competitors' unsafe products. At best, these sources paint an incomplete picture of product-related injuries and deaths.

"Because the CPSC's data sets reveal only a portion of the injury picture," says a 1997 Government Accounting Office report, "the agency underestimates the total numbers of deaths and injuries associated with any given consumer product. The extent of this undercounting is unknown."[28] Undercounting, resulting either from companies failing to self-report hazards or the inadequacy of the CPSC's injury surveillance system, means that it can take months or even years for the CPSC to detect a significant product hazard that manufacturers are well aware exists. Kolcraft received "more than 3,000" complaints about a car seat/carrier that injured forty–two infants before it was recalled, Cosco received "about 3,000" complaints about a tandem stroller that injured two hundred babies before it was recalled, Safety 1st received "more than 700" complaints, including thirty–three reports of injuries, about its bouncing buggy before it was recalled, and Graco received "more than 400" reports of children being injured in its stationary entertainer before it was pulled from the market.[29]

The task of finding dangerous products is daunting. CPSC regulator Marc Schoem refers to his job as "searching for that needle in a haystack."[30] Multiply the fifteen thousand products under the agency's jurisdiction (high chairs, fireworks, garage door openers, roller coasters, etc.) by the countless number of brands within each product category (Cosco high chair, Peg Perego high chair, Fisher-Price high chair, Evenflo high chair, etc.), and it's easy to see why the agency is in a constant state of Sisyphean overexertion.[31]

"The CPSC isn't a typical bureaucracy," says Schoem, who clips a pager onto his belt buckle each night when he leaves the office. "This is not a 9–to–5 job. We have a sensitivity and sense of urgency in what we do. We're available all the time."[32] But no matter how many hours Schoem and his staff work, savvy corporate lawyers and well-funded industry coffers ensure that the agency will never catch up.

How Consumers Are Notified of a Recall

Defective children's products stubbornly resist recalls for one reason: The Consumer Product Safety Act does not hold manufacturers responsible for getting recalled products back to their warehouses. When a product is recalled, manufacturers are required to issue a joint press release with the CPSC, specifying why the product has been recalled and what consumers who own it should do.[33] The notice is sent to the national wire services (AP and UPI), major metropolitan newspapers, and television and radio networks. Each media outlet decides independently whether or not to report the recall.

The language used in a recall press release is negotiated in highly secretive meetings between CPSC compliance staff, lawyers, epidemiologists, and test engineers, and the manufacturer's lawyers, product engineers, and public relations staff.[34] Virtually every word used in a recall notice has been hashed out and debated.[35] While the CPSC requires the press release to state how many children have been injured and killed and to describe the types of injuries sustained, it is in the manufacturer's best interest to play down the product's hazards. As in most negotiations between the CPSC and the industries it regulates, the balance of power tilts heavily toward manufacturers. If a manufacturer refuses to give in on a point, the CPSC can always take the company to court. But the agency must choose its battles very carefully. Suing a manufacturer over the wording of a recall notice is not how an agency with jurisdiction over 15,000 products wants to—or necessarily should—spend its scant resources.[36] The result: The final recall notice is so watered down that it's difficult for anyone to know with any degree of certainty how serious the problem is.

Sometimes, manufacturers even debate the very use of the word "recall." Manufacturers' lawyers carefully consider how the wording of a press release might be used against the company in court, if the parents of an injured baby were to file a lawsuit. Juries are more likely to blame the manufacturer—rather than parental negligence—if they see the word "recall." For this reason, many press releases do not announce a straight "recall," but rather the less alarming "voluntary repair program" or "recall for free repair kit."[37] Since Ann Brown took the CPSC's helm in 1994, the word "recall" has appeared in the majority of recall notices. But prior to 1994, it was possible for manufacturers to carry out a recall without using the word "recall" at all. "The industry doesn't want to use the word 'recall' [in the press releases] because people will think it means they will have to return the product," said one CPSC regulator.[38] His comment suggests that manufacturers would prefer dangerous products to remain in consumers' homes than to be returned to their warehouses.

The case of the Baby Trend portable crib is an especially egregious example of how far a manufacturer will go to dilute public perception of a product's dangers. Baby Trend, a small, California-based manufacturer of strollers, high chairs, and baby walkers, launched its "Home and Roam" portable cribs in 1992.[39] In January 1993, the CPSC learned of an incident involving a toddler who had stood up in his Baby Trend portable crib, causing the crib to fold up and collapse on him.[40] He was knocked down, but not injured, because his babysitter was in the room with him. In February, the same thing happened to another child, except this time, the baby stopped breathing. His grandfather performed CPR and revived him.[41] Regulators met with Baby Trend executives in June to figure out what should be done.[42] In August, before the parties had decided on a plan of action, a crib collapsed on yet another child, and she stopped breathing. The baby's mother revived her, and she subsequently spent three days in the trauma center of a Seattle children's hospital.[43] On September 1, the CPSC sent a letter to Baby Trend notifying general manager Jim Dodds that the agency's staff had made a "preliminary determination" that the Baby Trend Home and Roam portable crib presented a "substantial risk of injury to children."[44] The letter listed the information Baby Trend was now required to hand over to the CPSC, so that the agency could proceed with a thorough investigation. One week later, another Home and Roam crib collapsed, killing a thirteen–month–old boy.[45] One month after this first reported death, on October 8, 1993, the CPSC and Baby Trend issued a press release warning consumers of the hazard.[46] "Urgent Warning On Baby Trend and Baby Express Home and Roam Playpens: Strangulation Risk Cited," read the headline. Nowhere in the press release did it say the product was being recalled. Nowhere in the press release were caregivers urged to return the crib in exchange for a refund—though they were promised an unspecified "corrective action" from Baby Trend and "a free gift valued at $5.00."

In August 1994, almost a year after the "urgent warning" press release was issued, another Baby Trend crib collapsed, this time killing eight–month–old Jared Zalinski.[47] It took the CPSC another five months, until January 1995, to finally issue a press release announcing an official "recall" of the Baby Trend crib. Even then, consumers were not offered a refund or new, safer crib. Rather, they were told to call Baby Trend to arrange "to have their top rail locks replaced free-of-charge." Baby Trend paid the postage.

Recall press releases have gotten clearer in recent years, which is not to say they are clear enough. The award-winning Playskool 1–2–3 high chair's recall press release was ambiguous, at best. In October 1995, the CPSC and Playskool issued their initial release, a "Recall to Repair," which warned consumers that the plastic joints on some of the high chairs had cracked, causing the chair to collapse (see Appendix 3–1).[48] The release reported ten injuries, "including bumps, bruises and one concussion."

Not until the second paragraph do readers learn that "consumers have reported cracks in 1.5 percent of the high chairs sold." One–and–a–half percent may sound like a trivial number—but at that point, Hasbro had sold close to 300,000 chairs. The truly tenacious parent or news director who did the arithmetic would have figured out that 4,500 high chairs were known to be faulty. CPSC records indicate that early drafts of the press release stated clearly that 4,500 high chairs were defective.[49] At some point during the negotiations between CPSC staff and Hasbro attorneys, the figure was changed to 1.5 percent.

Not until the fourth paragraph does the press release instruct consumers what to do if they own this product. First, they should "inspect it carefully for cracks at the pivot joints or elsewhere." If there are no cracks, they are advised to contact Playskool for a repair kit, but they are not instructed to stop using the chair—despite earlier warnings that there is a reasonable chance that cracks will develop, and despite thousands of consumer complaints about problems in addition to faulty joints. If the pivot joints are cracked, owners are told near the end of the press release to "stop using the chair immediately." What parent wouldn't want to know this from the start?

Trouble with the Playskool 1–2–3 high chair didn't end once this initial recall notice was issued. About a year later, the CPSC and Playskool issued a second recall notice for a new problem, this time a "Recall to Repair Restraint Bar" (see Appendix 3–2).[50] The feature that had won the high chair the CPSC's Significant Contributions to Product Safety award was now failing. Hasbro had received hundreds of complaints about broken restraint bars, including at least forty reports of injuries; one child had broken his collarbone. The second recall notice mentions nothing about the injuries described in the previous recall—notably the concussion, or even that the chair had been recalled fourteen months before because its leg joints collapsed. Only the most vigilant, media-savvy parent would have put two and two together to figure out that the Playskool 1–2–3 high chair had defective leg joints *and* a defective restraint bar. The chair was collapsing *and* children were falling out of it. What parent would knowingly buy such a chair? What parent would continue to use the chair if they knew the truth about its safety record?

Frustrated by their inability to get newspapers and TV stations to report recall news, CPSC staff complains that too often, the media ignore their press releases. "The media prints lottery results, but not recalls," griped one agency spokesperson. "The news media should be party in some of these lawsuits that are going after the manufacturers."[51] Consumer advocates counter that the manufacturers who profit from these products should be responsible for disseminating recall news.

Imagine that you are a television news director trying to decide whether or not to devote fifteen seconds of your 6 p.m. broadcast to the Playskool 1–2–3 high chair "recall to repair restraint bar." Is the wording of the press release strong enough for you to consider it urgent news? If so, which part of the release would you report? What action would you advise viewers to take? Would you remember that a press release for the same product crossed your desk fourteen months before? Given the tepid legalese of most recall notices, it's no wonder the press often fails to consider them newsworthy. And it is no accident that when parents do hear about a recall involving a product they own, many of them have no idea what action they should take.

Ambiguous recall notices are a consequence of competing provisions in the Consumer Product Safety Act. On one hand, the Act grants the CPSC the right to approve or disapprove of each piece of communication notifying consumers of a recall.[52] But the Act also prohibits the agency from releasing to the public any company-specific information without the manufacturer's consent (see Chapter 5).[53] Both parties need the approval of the other before a single word goes out to the public.

When the CPSC can't convince a manufacturer to agree to any aspect of a recall—the wording of the press release, the remedy being offered to consumers, or even a concession that the recall is warranted—the agency can sue the company. But a lawsuit of this sort can take years to resolve. Corporate legal coffers can sustain long, drawn-out suits; the CPSC's budget can't. If the agency does take a company to court, the product under dispute can remain on the market while the case is being prepared for, settled, or tried.[54] When faced with a recalcitrant manufacturer, the CPSC must ask itself what is more important: suing Hasbro to label a release a "recall" instead of a "recall to repair restraint bar," for example, or releasing *any* recall notice quickly so that the product can no longer be sold. On a daily basis, the agency must decide whether to allow a manufacturer to take actions that undermine infant safety, or siphon its budget into costly court battles.

"The agency is constantly assessing tradeoffs," says former CPSC lawyer Bob Adler. Softening the press release language is just one example of the "horrible agreements with the devil" the CPSC is constantly forced to make, just to get companies to agree to a recall in the first place.[55]

Why Recall News Too Often Fails to Reach Parents and Caregivers

Imagine yourself in this scenario:

You have had a grueling day at work. As you make your way home through rush hour traffic, you look forward to spending a quiet evening at home with your wife. When you finally walk into the house, your wife—who is seven months pregnant with your first child—asks if you want to order a pizza or Chinese food. She tells you about her day, which sounds even more hectic than yours. You call Maggio's and order a mushroom pizza.

After dinner, the two of you settle in front of the TV with mugs of steaming herbal tea. You feel the day's stress melt away as you sip the tea and watch your favorite sitcom. The main characters are about to have a baby, and it is reassuring to laugh out loud at some of the new-parent fears that have started to keep you up at night.

When a commercial comes on, your wife gets up and you reach for a magazine. But the eerie tone of the announcer's voice pulls both of you back to the TV.

"This important announcement is brought to you by the Evenflo Company, manufacturer of quality infant products. It concerns the safety of your infant—your highest priority, as well as ours." The voice-over reminds you of the emergency broadcast system announcements you sometimes hear on the radio: "This has been a test... this is only a test..." It's a voice that makes you listen.

Perched on the edge of the sofa, the two of you stare unblinking at the screen. A woman about the same age as your wife, dressed in khaki slacks, a flowery blouse, and running shoes, is pulling an infant car seat out of a dark-green family van. When the camera pans to a close-up of the car seat, you realize the passenger is not a real baby, but a stuffed dummy.

"Evenflo is recalling 800,000 On My Way infant car seat/carriers," the announcer says. "The company is urging anyone who owns this product to stop using it as a carrier. You can continue to use the product as a car seat. The car seat is safe—the carrier is not."

An 800-number flashes repeatedly on the top of the screen as the woman unlatches the car seat from its base, turning it into a baby carrier.

"One hundred seventy–six consumers have contacted Evenflo," continues the announcer, "reporting that when the car seat is used as a baby carrier, its handle may unlock unexpectedly, causing your infant to fall or be thrown. So far, eighty–nine babies have suffered injuries, including two skull fractures, three concussions, and dozens

of scrapes and bruises. For this reason, Evenflo is urging all parents, grandparents, babysitters, and daycare centers that own the product to call Evenflo immediately. The call will cost you nothing. Operators are standing by. The Evenflo carrier can seriously injure your infant—please call the 800–number now."

The woman on the screen slides the van door closed and walks up the sidewalk, the baby carrier swinging at her side. Just as she is about to climb her front steps, the carrier's handle breaks. The stuffed dummy falls onto the sidewalk and bounces a couple of times on its head before landing on its back. Evenflo's hotline number continues to flash on the screen.

The entire "commercial" has lasted just a minute. An ad for tortilla chips comes on next. Stunned, you turn to your wife and ask, "What was that?"

"I have no idea," she says, standing up.

"Where are you going?"

"To call my sister," she says. "She's supposed to drop off her car seat and high chair this weekend—for us to use when the baby comes. I've got to find out if she owns this Evenflo On My Way."

❊ ❊ ❊

Part of this scenario is fictitious and part of it is true. Can you tell which is which?

The husband and wife watching the commercial are not real people. Nor is the commercial real—it was never made. The infant skull fractures, concussions, scrapes, and bruises mentioned in the fictitious ad, however, really did occur.

In 1998, Evenflo recalled 800,000 of its popular On My Way infant car seat/carriers, after receiving 176 reports from consumers that the handle unexpectedly unlatched from the carrier, flipping the seat forward and throwing the baby to the ground. By the time the product was pulled from the market, parents had reported 176 incidents of the handle unlatching, and 89 babies had been hurt, many seriously.[56] However,

Evenflo did *not* go on national television to warn parents unfortunate enough to own this defective product that their children's safety was at risk. In fact, Evenflo argued with CPSC regulators that a recall was not even necessary. According to Evenflo, the product was safe—it was the babies' parents who deserved the blame for their children's injuries. The CPSC rarely disparages individual companies publicly, but in this case CPSC chairman Ann Brown didn't hesitate to complain about Evenflo's behavior. "We felt like we've been dragging them every step of the way," she told the press, adding that throughout the process, Evenflo executives "seemed to insist it was the customers' fault."[57]

For years, consumer advocates have urged the infant products industry to better advertise product recalls. Manufacturers respond with a litany of excuses. Cosco, a Canadian-based manufacturer with one of the worst recall records in the industry, has a history of making excuses for its products' failures. Over the past few years, the company has recalled 62,000 crib mattresses (*twelve cases of infant entrapment, including one death*), 75,000 toddler bed guardrails (*sixty–seven cases of entrapment*), 150,000 toddler beds (*fifty entrapments, including one death*), 57,000 strollers (*3,000 reports of locks failing, 250 reports of strollers unexpectedly collapsing and more than two hundred reports of injuries, including a fractured arm, finger, and arm lacerations requiring stitches, etc.*), 580,000 full-size cribs (*227 incidents, including at least twenty–seven entrapments and one death*), 355,500 infant swings (*over three hundred complaints and forty–four injuries*), and 670,000 car seat/carriers (*151 incidents and twenty–nine injuries, including multiple skull fractures*). Of the 151 incidents and 29 injuries caused by its unlatching baby carrier handles, a company spokesperson said, "The incidence of malfunction was .023 percent and Cosco had no reports of serious injuries when the children were restrained according to the instructions and product labels."[58] Regarding the twelve crib mattress entrapments and one death, the company said, "The 12th incident involved a death under confusing and questionable circumstances and was promptly reported to the CPSC."[59]

In a similar vein, the company claims that advertising—at least when it comes to recalls—doesn't work. "Our understanding is that paid advertising has been tried in the past, and has not significantly increased the response rate," says Cosco spokesperson Carol Dingledy. "For one thing, magazine ads typically appear several months after the recall."[60] That children like seventeen–month–old Danny Keysar (killed five years after his Playskool Travel-Lite crib was recalled), ten–month–old William Conahan (killed five years after his Playskool Travel-Lite crib was recalled), and thirteen–month–old Troy Gonzales (killed six months after his Baby Trend crib was recalled) continue to be injured and killed long after a product has been recalled points out the implications of Cosco's self-serving logic.

Contrary to Cosco's public statements, a consumer goods company with 1999 sales of $157 million is surely aware of the power of aggressive marketing—at least when it comes to touting product benefits.[61] In recent issues of infant-oriented consumer magazines such as *American Baby* and *Childbirth*, the company heavily advertised its products.[62] Cosco also relies on tried-and-true advertising tactics such as promotional discounts, recently offering *Baby Talk* magazine readers a ten–dollar coupon toward the purchase of a Cosco tandem stroller at any Baby Depot store.[63]

Cosco is hardly the only infant products manufacturer that relies on targeted advertising to attract consumers' attention. In 1998, Hasbro had sales of $3.3 billion, and the company spent more than $30 million promoting its Playskool brand name.[64] The same year, Hasbro's number-one rival, Mattel, had sales of $5.6 billion and spent $45 million to promote its Fisher-Price products.[65] Yet these same companies resist allocating significant portions of their promotion budgets toward recalls.[66]

No wonder, then, that new parents can quickly rattle off the brand names of the hottest new stroller or high chair, yet are hard-pressed to come up with the brand name of even one product that has been recalled. When it comes to recalls, it's as if the corporate marketing departments suddenly forget everything they know about reaching consumers.

Manufacturers Claim Target Marketing Doesn't Work

The backbone of every successful consumer goods company is a sound marketing plan. The plan identifies which consumers the company will "target" and describes the products the company has created to fulfill these target customers' desires, needs, and demands. Advertising strategy is a key component of the marketing plan, spelling out where, when, and how the products will be promoted.

When manufacturers like Hasbro, Cosco, and Evenflo launch new baby products, they wisely follow the principles of target marketing. Their target customers are easily identified: the parents or soon-to-be parents of infants. Appropriate advertising venues are likewise simple to find. Newsstands, doctors' offices, and mailboxes are flooded with magazines targeted to expecting and new parents, including *American Baby*, *Parents*, *Baby Talk*, *Parents Expecting*, *Child*, *Mothering*, *Healthy Pregnancy*, *Parenting*, *Healthy Kids*, *Fit Pregnancy*, and *New Parent*. Recent issues of these magazines carry slick ads for products manufactured by Cosco, Graco, Playskool, Baby Björn, Baby Trend, Evenflo, Century, and Safety 1st. In the last few years, all of these companies have recalled infant products, yet it is tough to find evidence that any of these companies has paid to prominently advertise a recall in these magazines.

When a company pays to run an advertisement in a magazine, a newspaper, or on TV, the terms of the advertising purchase specify exactly where the ad will be run, and for how many times (for example, two thirty–second spots during the first half–hour of "All My Children"). The company's advertising agency works long and hard to figure out how best to communicate the client's message. But no such arrangements are made when the CPSC asks the media to report recall press releases. Because no money changes hands, television stations can choose to mention a recall only once, or not at all. Unlike paid ads, recall press releases compete with the other news of the day. Newspapers can report a recall on page one, bury it in the left-hand corner of page C25, or omit it completely. Given the tepid wording of most of these notices, it is no surprise that they rarely make headlines.

Infant product companies contend that they *do* use targeted marketing techniques to spread recall news. The most frequently employed tactic: Corporations send recall announcements to pediatricians' offices and to retailers such as Toys R' Us. Companies claim these tactics are more effective than paid ads. "[Magazine advertising] is not as immediate a response as posters placed where parents shop for children's products or take their children for check-ups," argued a Cosco spokesperson.[67] But pediatricians are bombarded with all sorts of requests to post information—and many parents have neither the time nor inclination to peruse a crowded waiting-room bulletin board while holding a sick child. And how many parents have seen recall notices posted prominently in a toy store? Very few, and certainly fewer than those who have seen children's products advertised on Saturday morning TV or in magazines.

Some companies are reluctant to undertake even these minimal efforts to expand awareness of recalls. When Hasbro recalled the Playskool 1–2–3 high chair, CPSC staff asked the company to send a recall notification to pediatricians. Hasbro refused. "Hasbro is not willing to do the pediatrician mailing in conjunction with the CPSC at this time," their lawyer Barbara Finigan wrote to the CPSC. "We believe presently that our press release and coverage has been both timely and adequate."[68] Hasbro's records indicate the when Ms. Finigan wrote this letter, the company had heard back from a mere ten percent of consumers who owned the 1–2–3—coverage somewhat less than "adequate."[69] Ten months later, customer response to the recall was up to 42 percent—which meant that the majority of the defective 1–2–3 high chairs remained in circulation.[70]

A letter of complaint from a Hasbro customer, forwarded to the CPSC, also suggests the company's efforts to notify customers directly of the 1–2–3 recall were insufficient. Four months after the recall, a mother in California wrote to Hasbro Consumer Relations:

> ...I came upon the 10/12/95 CPSC recall notice by mere accident while scanning for general product information on the Internet. I am disconcerted because I completed and returned the warranty card that accompanied the high chair when I received it in September 1995. Why wasn't this information used to inform your customers of the danger associated with your product? It makes me wonder how many of your other customers, with or without access to computers, are unaware of this recall...[71]

CPSC officials report that they are constantly searching for new, creative ways to get recall news to the public.[72] Chairman Ann Brown frequently appears on NBC's "Today Show" to warn consumers about the latest dangerous product. Increasingly, the agency has put a lot of faith in the power of "video news releases" (VNRs)—graphic videos of a recalled product's hazard. The agency sends VNRs via satellite to local and network news stations. But VNRs suffer from the same problem as press releases: Because they are free, the *media* gets to decide if and when they will be aired.

Manufacturers despise VNRs. "They're expensive, and you can't consistently be in the consumer's face saying, 'Sorry, we made a defective product.' It paints with a broad brush when a finer brush could be used," says David Baker, a Washington,

D.C.-based lawyer with Thompson, Flory, and Hine, a firm that has defended numerous manufacturers in product liability cases.[73] Repeated warnings about infant deaths and injuries can drive a company out of business. Kolcraft's resistance to widespread notification methods throughout the Playskool Travel-Lite portable crib recall shows just how far a manufacturer will go to prevent such news from getting "too much" public attention.

Corporate Resistance in Action: Kolcraft and the Playskool Travel-Lite Crib Recall

A $30 million, privately held Chicago corporation, Kolcraft Industries is the seventh largest manufacturer of infant products in the U.S.[74] Although the company is a fraction of the size of the industry's dominant players, Kolcraft has managed to thrive during times of industry consolidation and cutthroat competition. The second best-selling stroller in the U.S. sports the Kolcraft brand name, as do multiple models of top-selling car seats. Kolcraft sales VP Mark Deutchman, in an interview with trade magazine *Small World*, attributed the company's success to value-oriented products and ample advertising in consumer magazines. To address "the safety issue," the trade magazine reported, Kocraft maintains "a legal and product quality assurance department that executes all safety testing and ensures that the company complies with all current safety standards."[75]

In the late 1980s, Hasbro was considering ways to expand its Playskool brand name into the juvenile furniture market.[76] Kolcraft offered a quick solution: The company had recently developed the first portable crib. The crib's light weight, convenient portability, and low price virtually guaranteed its success. Hasbro and Kolcraft struck a deal: Hasbro would license its name to Kolcraft, which would manufacture, distribute, and market the Playskool Travel-Lite portable crib. The crib was launched in January 1990.[77]

When JPMA, the industry trade group, named the Travel-

Lite one of the "Ten Best Products" of 1989, both Kolcraft and Hasbro knew they had a winner.[78] Initial sales to power retailers Wal-Mart, K-Mart, Sears, and J. C. Penney were promising, and it wasn't long before Kolcraft's sales reps had sold more than 11,600 Travel-Lite units.[79]

In July 1991, seven months after the Travel-Lite launch, Roberta Gonzales put her eleven–month–old son Anthony down for a nap in his Playskool Travel-Lite crib. It was 12:30 in the afternoon, a hot summer day in Los Angeles. Roberta waited ten minutes, long enough for Anthony to fall asleep, before checking on him. What Roberta found was this: Anthony's portable crib had collapsed, trapping the infant's neck in the "V" formed by the folded side rails. Roberta pulled her son from the crib, started CPR, and called 911. Anthony was still alive when he reached the hospital, but had gone into cardiac arrest, and soon lapsed into a coma. The infant died two days later, on the Fourth of July. By then, Roberta was under investigation by the Los Angeles County Sheriff's Department for possible child abuse and the homicide of her son.[80]

The L.A. Police Department reported Anthony's death to the CPSC, which then notified Hasbro. "With respect to the above-mentioned [Anthony's death]," Hasbro's lawyer wrote the CPSC, "kindly be advised that this is a product manufactured and distributed by our licensee, Kolcraft Enterprises… [W]e have put them on notice with respect to this product, and you should be hearing from them."[81] Hasbro had washed its hands of the matter. Kolcraft, in turn, denied that the crib was hazardous. "Nothing in the CPSC report or accompanying documents suggest at this point that the Travel-Lite portable crib is defective in any way, or presents a substantial hazard," stated John Staas, Kolcraft's executive vice president of operations.[82]

Four months after Anthony died, on Thanksgiving Day, 1992, Teresa Parkens of Siloam Springs, Arkansas, put her nine–month–old daughter Amanda down for an afternoon nap in a Playskool Travel-Lite crib. Two–and–a–half hours later, the young mother checked on her baby and saw this: The Travel-Lite crib had collapsed, trapping Amanda's neck in the "V" of the folded rails. According to the police report, "it appears the baby awoke from its nap and pulled the soft net-type siding causing the sides to collapse inward which in turn pulled the locking bars down... trapping the baby's neck... cutting off the oxygen supply..." Amanda was pronounced dead on arrival at the hospital.[83]

The next day, an article in the *Northwest Arkansas Morning News* described Amanda's death as a "freak accident." When the reporter had called Hasbro to learn more about the incident, a company employee told her that Hasbro did not manufacture the Playskool crib.[84] Again, Hasbro washed its hands of the matter.

A week after New Year's Day, 1993, Sophie Talling's babysitter put the eleven–month–old child down for a nap in her Playskool Travel-Lite crib. The babysitter took care of eight children in her suburban Los Angeles home. Sophie had a cold, so the babysitter checked on the child often as she slept, every fifteen minutes between one and two o'clock. At 2:15, when the babysitter went in to check on Sophie, she saw this: The Travel-Lite had collapsed, trapping the baby's neck in the "V" of the folded rails. Sophie was pronounced dead at the hospital at 3:12 p.m., becoming the Travel-Lite's third victim.[85]

Sophie's death kicked off a full-fledged CPSC recall investigation. Marc Schoem, CPSC regulator of corrective action and compliance, notified Kolcraft President Bernard Greenberg that the agency had initiated a "preliminary determination of hazard."[86] The CPSC's goal was to determine whether or not the portable crib was dangerous enough to initiate a recall. By law, Kolcraft was required to send the CPSC any information the agency requested on the crib: product-testing data, engineering drawings, records of consumer complaints, pending lawsuits and warranty claims, assembly and use instructions, and two product samples for the CPSC engineers to test. Kolcraft (not Hasbro) had ten days to respond to the request.

On February 12, John Staas responded to Schoem's request with a full "Section 15" report, detailing the history of the Travel-Lite's distribution and marketing. In this letter, Staas noted that Sophie, the Travel-Lite's most recent victim, had been "left unattended" by a "21 year–old baby-sitting assistant who was supervising eight infants."[87] Refusing to admit that the crib was hazardous, Staas nevertheless told the CPSC that Kolcraft had decided to recall it. "Kolcraft does not have sufficient information to conclude that this product contains a defect which creates a substantial risk of injury," Staas wrote. "However, to avoid any possibility of future injuries, Kolcraft will begin an immediate recall of the product."[88]

Next, Staas laid out a "corrective action plan" for the portable crib, detailing the steps Kolcraft would take to notify retailers and consumers that the crib had been recalled. The most effective way to get the crib out of use, the CPSC knew, would be for Kolcraft to notify its customers of the recall directly, by mail. But in this case, such notification methods would be impossible. "Kolcraft does not know how many cribs are in consumer's [sic] hands," Staas wrote to the CPSC. "Kolcraft has no information as to the names and addresses of consumers."[89]

Kolcraft agreed to take the following actions: issue a joint press release with the CPSC, notify the press of the recall, set up a toll-free hotline for consumers, send recall notification letters and posters to retailers, and send a recall "notice" (not paid advertising) to targeted magazines. The company also intended to ask the American Academy of Pediatrics to notify its members about the recall.[90] Crib owners who returned the product to Kolcraft were offered a $60 refund, though the crib's retail price had been between $69–89. When the CPSC suggested the refund should be higher, Kolcraft responded, "most of these cribs [are] three years old."[91]

Issuing a press release was the first step in the Travel-Lite recall notification plan. As happens every time a product is recalled, both the CPSC and Kolcraft had to approve of every piece of communication issued to the public concerning the recall. As a result, the creation of the press release was a painstaking process. Drafts were passed from one party to the next, corrected, reworded, then rewritten again. The final press release, negotiated and agreed upon by both the CPSC and Kolcraft, was issued on February 17, 1993, nineteen months after the first child had been killed. It read, "The Commission has received three reports of infant deaths due to suffocation in these cribs. In each case the infant allegedly was found entrapped in a folded crib."[92]

Next, Kolcraft worked on retailer notification. Again, by law, the CPSC was granted the right to approve all recall-related materials. Nonetheless, Kolcraft chose to send the recall notification letters and posters to retailers *without* the CPSC's blessing.

Bill Moore, the CPSC's lawyer, was angered by the way Kolcraft had been carrying out the Travel-Lite recall. On February 24, Moore wrote to Kolcraft lawyer Judith Oldham:

> We take serious exception with your proposal to print the pediatrician poster in black and white... the pediatrician posters are a centerpiece of your public notice program and should be given every chance to succeed... The staff was very troubled to learn that the retailer letter and accompanying poster you provided to us... had already been sent... The staff had been asking to review the proposed retailer notice for several days... We stood willing and able to give quick guidance for producing effective notice documents... but you never gave us the chance.[93]

Moore detailed other inadequacies in Kolcraft's recall notification measures: The retailer letter included a picture of the crib that did not display the Playskool brand name, it failed to ask retailers to display the poster in a prominent location, and it neglected to ask retailers to attempt to identify crib owners through sales records. "This was a very disappointing effort," wrote Moore, "and it is not likely to be an effective public notice mechanism. The staff wishes to work with Kolcraft to make this an effective Class 'A' (most serious hazard) recall and to prevent further tragedy."[94]

Kolcraft lawyers were alarmed by Moore's letter. Notes taken by CPSC regulator Terri Rogers of a March 1 meeting between herself, CPSC attorney Moore, compliance regulator Marc Schoem, Kolcraft V.P. John Staas, and Kolcraft attorney Kerri Hook, document the company's concern about their vulnerability to lawsuits. Objecting to the "tone and wording" of Moore's letter, Kolcraft attorney Oldham complained about Moore's use of the term "Class 'A' hazard." Griping that Moore's letter had been "prejudicial," Oldham asked the CPSC to purge it from their records.[95] The agency refused her request.

The next point of conflict occurred over video news releases. Kolcraft fulfilled its promise to produce a video demonstrating the crib's hazard—then objected to the CPSC's efforts to disseminate the tape. When the agency requested seventy copies to be sent to its forty–five field offices around the country, Hook took exception. "[S]he said the company does not want 70 tapes out there; does not want the message replayed," read CPSC notes of attorney Moore's conversation with Hook. Reiterating that "the word was already out," Hook claimed Kolcraft was "very happy" with the response rate.[96] At that point, 981 consumers—less than nine percent of Travel-Lite buyers—had returned their cribs to Kolcraft.[97] More than 10,000 cribs were still unaccounted for.

Later that same day, CPSC regulator Marc Schoem also spoke with Kolcraft lawyer Kerri Hook. During this conversation, Hook continued to try to cajole the CPSC into purging Moore's letter, arguing, "it would be 'Exhibit A' in any lawsuit."[98] Schoem refused Hook's request.

Clearly frustrated by her lack of headway with Schoem, Hook played her trump card: She blamed the agency for one of the Travel–Lite deaths. When the CPSC had initiated its formal recall investigation, the agency had told Kolcraft about only two deaths, when in fact there had been three. Why the CPSC either didn't know about one of the deaths, or didn't tell Kolcraft about it, to this day remains unclear. Regulator Marc Schoem recounted his conversation with Hook in CPSC notes:

> Kerri then indicated that she would also point out that the CPSC had information in our files that if we had shared it with Kolcraft, one death could have been possibly prevented. I said I thought that was unfair, that if the firm had done adequate design and testing of the product, they may have found the accident scenario was foreseeable and all the deaths could have been prevented.[99]

For the next three months, Kolcraft continued to keep track of the returned cribs, until the CPSC agreed to close the file in June 1993.[100] At that point, 2,736 cribs had been returned; 76 percent were still unaccounted for.[101]

Sherry Miller, an Indianapolis babysitter, owned one of the Playskool Travel–Lite cribs that remained in circulation. News of the recall never reached Sherry. On October 10, 1996—two–and–a–half years after the recall—Sherry put ten–month–old Christian Hastings down for his morning nap in a Playskool Travel-Lite crib. When she checked on the child, Sherry saw this: the portable crib had collapsed, trapping Christian's neck in the "V" of the folded rails. Christian was dead, the Travel-Lite's fourth victim, the first to be killed *after* the recall.[102]

On May 12, 1998, seventeen–month–old Danny Keysar of Chicago became the Travel-Lite's fifth victim, the second to be killed after the recall.[103] After Danny's death, Kolcraft president Thomas Koltun stated to the press, "Kolcraft is deeply concerned that the recalled Playskool Travel-Lite portable crib continues to be used by parents and caregivers, despite repeated warnings to consumers…"[104]

On August 19, 1998, ten–month–old William Conahan's babysitter put the infant down for his nap in a Playskool Travel-Lite crib at 3:00 p.m. When she checked on him less than two hours later, she found this: the crib had collapsed, trapping William's neck in the "V" of the crib's folded rails. The infant was pronounced dead on arrival at the hospital, becoming the Travel-Lite's sixth victim, the third to be killed after the recall.[105]

After William's death, Danny Kesyar's grieving parents sent a letter to Allan Hassenfeld, C.E.O. of Hasbro, urging him to "help us stop the killing of babies." The couple pleaded with Hassenfeld to step in and assist Kolcraft in retrieving the cribs that still remained in consumers' homes and daycare centers. "Given the success of your multi-billion dollar company," they wrote, "Hasbro clearly knows how to reach American consumers, utilizing its vast financial resources and marketing expertise when selling products. The same methods can and should be used to retrieve products that have been proven deadly."[106]

Two months later, in November, the CPSC issued a press release entitled, "Kolcraft, Playskool Double Reward for Return of Recalled Portable Cribs." The release announced a $120 Safe Child Reward for every Travel-Lite returned and reported that six children had been killed by the hazardous crib.[107] As of January 1999, an additional ninety–one people had called Kolcraft's hotline in response to the doubled reward.[108]

Critics ask why the company waited so many years to offer a bounty, when both Hasbro and Kolcraft knew long ago that the crib was deadly. In fact, it's not clear that any product recalled in recent years has had such a high risk level associated with it: One out of every 2,000 Playskool Travel-Lite cribs sold has killed a child.

The CPSC's Thwarted Attempts to Improve Recall Response Rates

The recall notification method the CPSC most often urges companies to use is direct mail. What could be easier, the agency argues, than sending everyone who bought the product a letter? The problem is that, like Kolcraft, most companies do not capture, store, and update customer name and address information for the purpose of recalls. For a number of reasons, maintaining consumer records is not a task most infant product manufacturers are willing to undertake.

In 1999, fed up with the high number of recalls and low consumer response rates, CPSC officials wondered if it was time for the government to *require* infant product manufacturers to keep track of their customers. The agency convened a one–day "Recall Effectiveness Forum" to discuss the problem.[109] Industry executives, consumer advocates, and federal regulators gave prepared speeches and, in a forum that was at times quite lively, debated the pros and cons of tracking buyers of baby equipment.

CPSC officials championed the idea of Consumer Safety Awareness Cards—customer registration cards that would be packaged with frequently recalled infant products such as portable cribs, high chairs, and strollers. The idea was a simple one: Consumers would fill out their name, address, and phone number on the Safety Awareness Card, then return it to the manufacturer. The manufacturer would store the information and use it to notify consumers if the product was recalled. Registration cards would be a quick, direct way for manufacturers to reach their customers.

As soon as Chairman Brown and her recall compliance staff

finished their opening remarks, objections to a new safety system began to fly. Manufacturers hated the idea. Rick Locker, a defense lawyer who represents the Juvenile Products Manufacturers of America, the Toy Manufacturers of America, and a host of individual manufacturers, argued: "… an old-style registration card, which requires consumers to actually take the card and to fill it out and to mail it back, is not necessarily or particularly going to be effective on a variety of product categories… it's like the old adage, 'you can lead a horse to water but you can't always make it drink.'"[110] Throughout the day, Locker insisted that if manufacturers were to spend time and money on a safety card system, *consumers* would fail to do their part by filling out the cards. Other industry representatives echoed this prediction, until CPSC regulator of compliance Alan Schoem silenced them. "Of course, this is all putting the responsibility on somebody other than the manufacturer of the product, and other than the retailer of the product," said Schoem, "… and what we may want to focus more on is the manufacturers' and retailers' responsibility to get recall notices out to the consumer, their customer who bought their product."[111] Retailers, like manufacturers, are also hesitant to institute product registration. Why? The cost of collecting the information and sending letters to owners during recalls would be "astronomical," explained Mallory Duncan, vice president and general counsel of the National Retail Federation. "This idea is not ready for prime time."[112]

Product registration is not a new idea. In 1993, the National Highway Traffic Safety Administration (NHTSA) passed a law requiring manufacturers to include a registration card with new child car seats.[113] (Car seats are the only durable infant product not regulated by the CPSC.) After consumers return the cards, postage free, the manufacturer maintains their contact information for six years and notifies them in the event of a recall. The cost of this system to manufacturers is estimated to be between thirty cents and one dollar per unit.[114]

The impetus for car seat registration came during the late 1980s, when NHTSA regulators realized that car seats were being recalled at a rate of 10–12 models per year, with consumer response rates as low as 20 percent. By comparison, each year the CPSC recalls about one hundred children's products (not including car seats), with consumer response rates stuck at 10–30 percent. Clearly, a strong case can be made for affixing product registration cards to other baby products.

Car seat registration was a hotly contested topic at the CPSC Recall Forum. The CPSC and consumer advocates argued that industry has an *obligation* to its customers to replicate the car-seat registration program for frequently recalled baby products. Industry representatives claimed consumers would be the weak link in such a program. Consumers, they insisted, would be suspicious of *any* card enclosed in a new product box, believing it to be just another marketing tool. NHTSA officials countered by revealing that 50 percent of new car-seat buyers registered their purchase. Industry representatives objected, claiming *their* numbers were closer to 20 percent. By the close of the Recall Forum, industry leaders had made their position clear: They are unlikely to institute product registration voluntarily, and if CPSC regulators push for mandatory registration, they will ban together and put up a fight. Educating consumers on the importance of infant product registration, the manufacturers implied, is not *their* job.

"I'm having trouble finding what the downside is for manufacturers to gather this kind of information," said Sally Greenberg, a lawyer with Consumers Union, at the end of the day. "I've sat and listened patiently to manufacturers discuss this issue. But I would think, even from a product liability perspective, they would want to be able to say that they have this kind of information for purchasers of their products, they have contacted the consumers in the event of a recall, and they have really done their best to try to get that information out there."[115]

When it comes to notifying the public of a product recall, the CPSC has its hands tied. By law, the agency can require a company to offer consumers a product repair, refund, or replacement—but there is no law stipulating how manufacturers must deliver this news, nor is there a requirement that the company demonstrate consumers actually hear it. As is always the case, if the CPSC thinks a manufacturer should be making a greater effort, and the manufacturer refuses to do so, the agency can sue. But to do so is a long, expensive process that the beleaguered agency can ill afford.[116]

Frustrated with manufacturers' half-hearted efforts to publicize recalls, CPSC officials maintain they are doing the best they can. It's all a matter of tradeoffs, they say. When a manufacturer refuses to advertise a recall, the CPSC is forced to look for the next-best solution. If the company is unwilling to pay for advertising, but agrees to produce a video news release, the CPSC can either accept the plan, or launch an expensive lawsuit to force the company to cooperate. Reflecting on the agency's tough bind, one official said succinctly, "we trade away paid advertising."[117]

"The reason [manufacturers] go into this is to make a profit," says Mary Ellen Fise, general counsel for the Consumer Federation of America. "In exchange, they have the responsibility not to injure or kill someone. Manufacturers have this enormous responsibility, yet the CPSC can't force them to take it. The CPSC doesn't have the resources to litigate every case."[118]

What the CPSC and Manufacturers Know about Recall Effectiveness

There is no subject more likely to elicit excuses, finger-pointing, misleading statistics, and half-truths than the issue of recall effectiveness. The CPSC and manufacturers are equally guilty, and for good reason: Recall effectiveness is the bottom-line measure of how seriously they take infant safety. As CPSC Chairman Ann Brown has said, "The effectiveness of our recalls is really a life and death situation."[119] Each time consumer response to an infant product recall hovers between ten and thirty percent, *everyone* looks bad.

On the surface, figuring out whether a recall has been effective appears to be a simple calculation: Simply divide the number of people responding to a recall (by contacting the company for a product repair kit, refund, or replacement) by the number of units sold. But idiosyncrasies in the way consumers purchase and use infant products makes the calculation, known as a "completion rate" or "consumer response rate," considerably more messy. Parents often throw away or store these products in an attic after infants outgrow them. Therefore, manufacturers argue, the completion rate should be the number of recalled products repaired, replaced, or refunded, divided by the number of products *still in circulation*, rather than the larger universe of products *sold*. The point is a valid one. But "circulation" data doesn't exist. While consumer goods marketers are adept at using sophisticated statistical models to predict product sales, they have yet to develop methods of estimating circulation rates of infant products. Manufacturers certainly have the ability to make these calculations. What's lacking is their motivation to do so.

After the fact emerged that the portable crib that killed Danny Keysar had been recalled five years before his death, a *Chicago Tribune* reporter asked Kolcraft and the four other manufacturers that had recalled cribs with this faulty design for their consumer response rates.[120] Both Kolcraft (11,600 cribs sold) and Century Products (212,000 cribs sold) claimed they didn't know how many consumers they had reached. Evenflo (1.2 million cribs sold) estimated its response rate to be 10 percent. Baby Trend's (100,000 cribs sold) rate was 17 percent. Draco (13,000 cribs sold) had gone out of business. More than one million of these deadly cribs are still unaccounted for.

The CPSC started to worry about low recall response rates in the 1970s, soon after initiating its first recall. In 1979, after CPSC commissioners voted to place the issue on their list of top priorities, Chairman Susan King created a Recall Effectiveness Task Force. Published in 1980, the Task Force's final report remains, to this day, the only comprehensive document on the topic.[121]

The bulk of the Task Force report describes the CPSC's efforts to gauge public awareness of hairdryer recalls. The agency recalled millions of hairdryers when it was revealed that they contained asbestos, a substance shown to be a serious health hazard. CPSC staff conducted telephone surveys of a randomly chosen national sample of adult consumers, as well as a sample of callers to the CPSC hotline. The study revealed the following:

- 85 percent of hairdryer owners were aware that the presence of asbestos in a hairdryer posed a health risk,

- 4.5 percent of consumers who owned the recalled hairdryers took advantage of a repair, refund, or replacement offer in response to a recall (the "completion rate"), and

- 32 percent of consumers stopped using their hairdryer when they found out it had been recalled.

This study quantified what CPSC regulators had suspected—that a sizable group of consumers continued to use recalled products even after news of a recall had reached them. The study then posed the next logical question: *Why?* The agency discovered that "perceived seriousness" of the asbestos hazard played a key role in determining whether or not a consumer stopped using the recalled product. Apparently, the hairdryer recall notices didn't convince many consumers that the product posed a serious health risk. Given the flaccid language of present-day press releases, it is easy to understand why these consumers were unconcerned.

At about the same time Chairman King's Recall Effectiveness report was published, CPSC officials noticed that completion rates varied widely from one recall to the next.[122] Three product categories—televisions, major appliances, and lawn mowers—had completion rates of 70 percent, while the average completion rate for small electrical appliances was closer to 10 percent. The agency scrutinized 242 recalls to find out why. Their findings were unambiguous: Recalls involving *large numbers of relatively inexpensive products with a useful life of only a few years*—a category that includes almost all infant products—require "especially aggressive measures" to produce high completion rates. The most effective "aggressive measure": direct contact with product owners, either by mail, telephone, or personal visit.

Given these findings, it is not surprising that completion rates for infant products remain so low. Not only do manufacturers rarely undertake direct notification measures when a baby product is recalled, but as the Recall Effectiveness Forum demonstrated, they are quick to argue that these methods won't work.

In 1988, eight years after the CPSC's Task Force on Recall Effectiveness released its findings, economists Dennis Murphy and Paul Rubin published "Determinants of Recall Success" in the *Journal of Products Liability*.[123] Using state-of-the-art statistical techniques, Murphy and Rubin identified the factors that determine whether or not a recall is effective. Like the CPSC, the economists found that recalls achieve the highest completion rates when:

- product owners are directly notified of the recall by mail,

- the manufacturer offers an in-home repair (the least burdensome remedy for consumers) and,

- the product is one that appeals to a well-defined group of consumers who tend to read the same specialized magazines and who are particularly anxious about the product's safety.

Like the CPSC's study, the implications of this research for infant product manufacturers couldn't be more clear: Simply tell consumers when a stroller, toddler bed, high chair, or portable crib is recalled—via direct mail and well-targeted ads in magazines such as *Parent*, *Child*, and *American Baby*—and completion rates will rise.

Such common-sense advice is not news to manufacturers, and it is no accident that they choose to ignore it. Manufacturers like Hasbro could blanket the media with paid advertising when a product is recalled, but they don't. Instead, they wait until six babies have been killed by a single product, then issue a press release with the CPSC announcing a "Safe Child Reward." Manufacturers like Evenflo could use strong, clear language in recall press releases, but they don't. Instead, they choose to blame parents for product failures, and, in the case of its defective infant carrier, resist the CPSC's efforts to notify parents of the product's danger.[124] Manufacturers like Baby Trend could offer consumers a full refund when a product is recalled, but they don't. Instead, they wait until a child is killed, then offer parents a $5 "free gift." The manufacturers' trade organization, JPMA, could urge its members to enclose product registration cards with their products, but it doesn't. Instead, their lawyer argues that registration cards are a bad idea because consumers will fail to return them. In sum, the infant product industry could spend as much effort getting recalled products out of circulation as it does getting them onto store shelves and into homes, but it doesn't. Why? Because recalls are bad for business. For the manufacturers, concern for infant safety is a noble goal, but only to the extent that it contributes to the bottom line.

CHAPTER 4

Corporations That Are Fined by the CPSC for Concealing Product Hazards

In 1992, executives at Century Products' crib division, Okla Homer Smith, decided to change the way the company's wooden cribs were assembled. The cribs' side slats would no longer be glued and nailed into place; they would be glued only. The decision was a poor one. The glue wasn't strong enough to keep the slats from coming loose, and in some cases detaching completely from the crib.[1]

The fact that cribs must comply with a mandatory federal safety standard suggests just how dangerous a shoddily constructed crib can be. If a crib's side slats are spaced too far apart, a tiny neck or head can become entrapped, and a child can be asphyxiated. Missing slats on the Century cribs posed this sort of hazard, violating the federal safety standard.

In February 1993, ten months after Century began selling its glue-only cribs, the company learned that a child had been entrapped in one of the cribs, but not killed, when a side slat came loose. A few weeks later, a second child was entrapped. Then it happened again. And again. By June 1993, Century had learned that five children had been entrapped in broken cribs. Despite knowledge of these five incidents, the company continued to sell the glue-only cribs and did nothing to warn its customers of the hazard.

In September 1993, a sixth child was entrapped in a crib that had a missing slat. This time, the child was killed.

The switch to glue-only cribs had become a fatal error. Nevertheless, Century continued to sell the hazardous cribs. Not until January 1994, after 278,000 cribs had been sold, did the company take action: The old manufacturing process was reinstated, and the slats were nailed to the crib as well as glued.

But Century failed to take one more important step—to tell the CPSC what had been going on. Section 15(b) of the Consumer Product Safety Act (CPSA) requires a company to notify the CPSC within twenty–four hours of learning of a product defect that poses "a substantial hazard" or creates "an unreasonable risk" of injury or death.[2] Century didn't say a word to the CPSC about the injuries or death caused by its cribs. In failing to do so, Century allegedly broke the law.

CPSC regulators found out about the death, though they did not yet know about the five non-fatal entrapments. When the agency contacted Century to learn details of the incident, the company's lawyers confirmed that a child had been killed. But that's all they revealed. Claiming the death was a case of "product misuse," Century's lawyers failed to disclose details about the hazardous cribs.

Though Century was not legally obligated to discuss the crib with CPSC staff over the phone, the company could not avoid disclosing what it knew once the CPSC launched an official investigation. The agency demanded that Century file a full "Section 15" report, which was to include details of the crib's design, testing, and manufacturing process and a full account of all injuries and deaths—data the CPSC needed to determine whether or not the product was dangerous enough to recall.

Under pressure from the CPSC, the company finally filed its full Section 15 report on June 30, 1994. For the first time, the agency learned of the five non-fatal entrapments. Sixteen months had passed since Century had learned about the first entrapment—substantially longer than the twenty–four hours required for hazard self-reports. The CPSC and Century jointly recalled the cribs in February 1995, two years after the first entrapment.[3]

This was not the first time Century had failed to report a product hazard. In 1987, the company discovered that the horn on its baby walkers was faulty; children were pulling off the ornament, which posed a choking hazard. Although Century was aware of at least ten choking incidents, the company did not report the problem to the CPSC until 1988.[4] Between 1995 and 1996, the company's popular TraveLite Sport stroller proved to have not just one defect, but two. More than five hundred consumers complained to Century that when the stroller's front wheels hit a curb, the stroller folded unexpectedly—with the child in it. Sixty more consumers reported that the stroller's restraint buckle didn't work, causing children to fall out, and leading to at least forty–nine injuries. Again, the company took substantially longer than twenty–four hours to report the problem to the CPSC—this time, they took a full year.[5] By the time the stroller was recalled in April 1997, the company had sold 166,000 strollers and logged 1,400 consumer complaints, including seventy–eight reports of injuries.[6]

Section 15(b) of the Consumer Product Safety Act granted the CPSC the authority to fine Century $1.25 million for each of the three dangerous products—the baby walkers, strollers, and cribs. But Century, like virtually every manufacturer caught violating the self-reporting statute, paid considerably less. The penalty for failing to report the baby walker defect: $50,000.[7] The penalty for failing to report the defective cribs and strollers: $225,000, combined; the CPSC agreed to settle the two violations simultaneously.[8] To Century Products, a company that was bought by Graco Children's Products for $77.5 million a few months after the crib/stroller case was settled, the fines were little more than a slap on the wrist.[9]

Congress wrote the Section 15(b) self-reporting requirement into the Consumer Product Safety Act to encourage industry candor about potential product hazards. This would be a way for some of the burden of hazard identification to fall on manufacturers, Congress reasoned, in addition to the financially strapped CPSC. What Congress failed to address, however, is that manufacturers have disincentives to self-report. A Section 15(b) self-report often initiates a CPSC investigation, a process welcomed by a company about as readily as a private citizen welcomes an IRS tax audit. The process is burdensome, expensive, time-consuming, and often ends with bad news—a product recall. Sometimes a more appealing strategy is for the manufacturer to quietly fix the defect without notifying anyone—neither its customers nor the CPSC—and then hope regulators don't find out.

Even if the CPSC manages to find out about unreported injuries or deaths, Section 15(b) is written vaguely enough to allow a manufacturer's lawyers to build a strong defense of the company's failure to self-report. The statute does not explicitly state how many consumer complaints, injuries, or deaths constitute a "substantial hazard" or "unreasonable risk" of injury or death. Even if hundreds of children have been injured, company lawyers can always blame caregivers by claiming the injuries were caused by "product misuse." Century received 560 consumer complaints about its TraveLite stroller, including dozens of reports of injuries. Yet company executives claimed they had no duty to report this information, simply because the products "contained no substantial hazard."[10]

When the CPSC has evidence of a Section 15(b) violation, the agency can file suit against the company in civil court. If the parties cannot work out a pre-trial settlement, the suit goes to trial. This has occurred only once in recent history. When asked for examples of cases that have gone to trial, a CPSC spokesperson said he was aware of only one case, against a company that manufactured automatic pitching machines. "I don't know when that was," he added, suggesting the event had not occurred very recently.[11] Why hasn't the CPSC pushed more cases to trial? A trial poses a resource drain the agency can't afford to undertake very often. Manufacturers, on the other hand, have a corral of in-house and outside counsel at their disposal, and are acutely aware of this resource imbalance when they join the CPSC at the bargaining table.

In addition to the dollar amount of a civil penalty, the language that will be used in the final settlement document is at stake. Admissions of guilt can be used against companies down the road, if the parents of an injured or dead child sue. "By entering into the Settlement Agreement and Order," Century's final crib and stroller settlement read, "Century does not admit any liability or wrongdoing."[12] The company paid the fine quietly and moved on.

The CPSC Trades Away Future Civil Penalities

As early as 1983, the CPSC became concerned that companies had little motivation to self-report product hazards. In Senate committee hearings, one CPSC official noted that, as the Reagan administration slashed the agency's resources, the number of Section 15(b) self-reports dropped. In 1989, Robert Adler, a University of North Carolina law professor who served as an attorney-adviser for two CPSC commissioners, did the math:

> It seems inconceivable with agency jurisdiction over 10–15,000 different products distributed by over one million businesses that only 100 to 200 instances arise nationwide that would lead a company to report a possible substantial hazard. In sharp contrast, the Food and Drug Administration receives roughly 18,000 such reports... In addition, consumers file roughly 60–70,000 product liability lawsuits every year. Based on these statistics, one unavoidably must conclude that Section 15(b) is being widely ignored.[13]

Five years later, a *Consumer Reports* article revealed that "few scofflaws are ever punished," largely due to the CPSC's lack of enforcement staff and cumbersome rules.[14]

In recent years, due to Chairman Ann Brown's increased enforcement efforts, the number of self-reports has steadily increased, from 128 in 1984 to 210 in 1999.[15] Since 1996, Brown has increased both the number of civil penalties and their size. Table 4–1 lists all the companies that have paid fines to the CPSC for failing to self-report hazards between 1996 and September 2000.

In 1996, the CPSC won a $725,000 settlement from Cosco, one of the largest civil penalties in the agency's history.[16] On the surface, Cosco was an easy target for Brown's campaign against self-report scofflaws. But when the facts are examined closely, the case becomes less of a clear-cut victory than an illustration of the resource imbalance that continues to exist between manufacturers and the public agencies that regulate them.

In December 1990, Cosco began selling its first toddler beds, described in promotional literature as a "transition bed for children approximately 2 to 4 years old."[17] Retailing for about fifty dollars, the bed used a standard crib mattress and bedding, which made it a low-cost option for parents who could not afford a child's new twin bed. The bed's design was deceivingly simple: the mattress rested on a metal slatted frame, which had tubular, curved metal rails on each end (see Appendix 4–1). Toddler beds were not covered by the mandatory crib standard; nor was there a voluntary standard for the product at this time. (A voluntary standard was not established until 1997).[18]

Two months after the bed hit the market, in February 1991, Ruthann Scarlatella of Cincinnati, Ohio wrote a letter to Cosco, notifying the company that her two–year–old daughter's head had gotten stuck between the headboard's curved rails (see Appendix 4–2). "Please do further testing on this product," Mrs. Scarlatella wrote, "because if a child's (sic) head gets wedged

Table 4–1: Penalties for Failure to Self-Report Product Hazards to CPSC, 1996–2000

Year	Company/Product	Hazard	Fine
1996	JBI playground equipment	protruding hardware	$225,000
	Singer Sewing juicers	flying parts	$120,000
	National Media juicers	flying parts	$150,000
	Taito America arcade games	metal pad	$50,000
	Cosco toddler beds and rails	strangulation	$725,000
1997	Brinkmann smokers and fryers	lacerations, fire	$175,000
	CSA Inc. exercisers	impact injury	$100,000
	Hartman hair dryers	fire	$60,000
	Nutone stereos	fire	$110,000
	Toro riding mowers	impact injury	$250,000
1998	Binky Griptight pacifiers	suffocation	$150,000
	Century Products cribs and strollers	suffocation, impact	$225,000
	COA Inc. cribs	suffocation	$300,000
	Safety 1st bed rails	suffocation	$175,000
1999	Carter Bros. go-karts	death	$125,000
	Shimano bike cranks	fractures, lacerations	$150,000
	Central Sprinkler fire sprinklers	burns	$1,300,000
2000	Black & Decker toasters	fire	$575,000
	Baby's Dream cribs	fingertip amputations	$200,000
	Hasbro infant carriers	skull fracture	$400,000
	Lancaster Candle	fires and burns	$150,000
	L. L. Bean Inc. carrier	falls, strangulation	$750,000

Source: CPSC press release #00–108, May 12, 2000, www.cpsc.gov.

between and they twist themselves out of bed it could be a real deadly situation."[19] Cosco's internal files note that a Cosco customer service representative called Mrs. Scarlatella and told her the toddler bed complied with the crib standard, and "if we change the headboard or footboard I will send a new one."[20]

Over the next ten months, over thirty more consumers called Cosco's customer service hotline and described entrapment incidents similar to the one reported by Mrs. Scarlatella. Two parents called on November 26, 1991. A customer service representative told the first distraught mother "to be sure to use large pillow for child, to set bed up against the wall."[21] The second caller that day reported that she had been woken up by her eighteen–month–old daughter's screams; the toddler's head had gotten stuck in the bed's headboard rails. The child emerged from the incident with only a scrape on her head, but her mother was afraid the next child wouldn't be as lucky. "I am scared to think that maybe some other child can really get caught between these bars," she said.[22] The mother was referred to parent company Dorel Industries' customer service department in Montreal.

A third entrapment occurred this same day, although it was not recorded by the Cosco customer service hotline: When fifteen–month–old Janie Lafayette tried to crawl through the footboard of her toddler bed, her neck was caught between the bed's curved rails, and she was killed.[23]

Two weeks later, on December 13, Cosco engineer Bob Craig called CPSC regulator Theresa Rogers with the news of Janie's death.[24] During this conversation, according to CPSC records, Rogers asked Craig if the company knew of any other toddler bed entrapments. Craig said they knew of two. But an internal Cosco memo, later uncovered by the U. S. Department of Justice, shows that Craig may have known of significantly more than two entrapments. Two days before Craig called Rogers, Cosco engineer Terry Emerson sent Craig (and other Cosco employees) a memo that read, "23 incidents, including death. Craig and Reynolds to come up with warning label."[25] In fact, the memo understated the number of entrapments; Cosco's customer service department had recorded at least three dozen.[26]

Around the time of Janie's death, another new Cosco product began showing signs of trouble. In August 1991, the company launched a new safety device: toddler bed guardrails.[27] The rails, which attached to the side of a bed, were supposed to keep a child from falling out. Consumers could buy the rails separately, to attach to other manufacturers' beds, or they could purchase them as a set with the Cosco toddler bed. The only purpose of the guardrails was to prevent children from falling out of a toddler bed. Neverthless, in November 1991, a mother called Cosco to report that her child had been entrapped not by the toddler bed's head or footboard—but by the guardrails.[28] Two months later, in January 1992, another parent called with a similar complaint. Cosco's internal records of this call and others that followed describe guardrail entrapments in graphic detail, leaving little doubt that the product was hazardous.[29]

One mother called the Cosco hotline to report that she had found her two–year–old son on the floor with his head caught between the mattress and the rail's bottom rung. Under the space allotted on the Cosco complaint sheet for "Description of Consumer's Concerns/Objectives," the customer service representative had written, "Wants it recalled!" The representative "thanked [the mother] for her information, and promised to pass comments along."[30] Another parent called to say that she had been woken up when her son "yelled out in the night."[31] She found his upper body wedged between the guardrail and the mattress, his feet touching the floor and his back pushing against the rail. The distraught mother demanded that "someone up the chain" call her with a solution. The customer service representative thanked the woman for her concern, then offered a $10 refund. The complaint was forwarded to Cosco vice president and general counsel Jonathan Reynolds.

By the time Cosco filed its complete Section 15(b) report for the hazardous toddler beds in March 1992, the company knew of at least four children who had been entrapped in the guardrails, the new "safety device" that was actually causing injuries.[32] Nevertheless, the toddler bed report mentioned nothing about the guardrails. Therefore, when the CPSC moved to recall the toddler beds, the guardrails continued to be sold.

Despite the self-report requirement, Cosco did not notify the CPSC of the alarming guardrail calls. In fact, charged the CPSC in a complaint against the company, "Even though dozens of consumers notified the defendant [Cosco] of guardrail entrapment incidents beginning in November 1991, the defendant waited until February 1993—after the CPSC requested a full report—to come forward with all but the first of the consumer complaints."[33] It took the CPSC yet another year—until June 1994—to recall the product. At this point, Cosco had sold 75,000 guardrail sets, and the company knew of at least sixty–seven entrapments.[34]

Once the guardrail recall was underway, CPSC lawyers turned their attention to a larger issue: suing Cosco for failing to report both the toddler bed and guardrail entrapments in a timely manner. Lacking the staff to put together the suit, the agency enlisted the help of the U. S. Department of Justice. On December 11, 1995, the two agencies jointly filed suit against Indiana-based Cosco in an Indianapolis U.S. District Court, citing the company for failing to report "dozens of consumer complaints of serious safety hazards with the company's toddler beds and guardrails." The agencies sought the maximum fine: $2.5 million in civil penalties.[35]

Despite the ninety–six known toddler bed and guardrail entrapments and one death, Cosco responded to the CPSC's charges by denying that either product was hazardous. "Since August 1991 when sales of the Side Rail [guardrail] commenced," Cosco's lawyers claimed, "it is estimated that the Side Rail has been used over 100 million times with no serious injuries or deaths reported relating to head and/or neck entrapment."[36] In other words, the company defended itself by arguing that most children who had slept in beds with Cosco guardrails had not been entrapped. Those who were injured, the lawyers countered, were "well below the recommended age for the product."[37] But according to Cosco's own records, at least half of the injured children had been two or older, falling within the company's recommended age range.[38] The company also argued that the $2.5 million fine was excessive, because "Cosco is a small company with very thin profit margins."[39] At the time, Cosco's parent company, Dorel Industries, had revenues of $426 million and net earnings of $15.5 million (Canadian dollars).[40]

Justice Department and CPSC lawyers spent the next year in discovery, taking depositions (oral statements given under oath), filing interrogatories (witnesses' answers to questions, written under oath), and exchanging a series of memos—some quite hostile—with Cosco attorneys (see Chapter 5). In August 1996, eight months after the case had been filed, the parties settled out of court. Cosco agreed to pay a $725,000 fine—considerably less than the $2.5 million penalty the government thought the company deserved.[41]

Money was not the CPSC's only concession. As part of the settlement, the agency promised not to seek civil penalties from Cosco for failure to report hazards associated with nine other infant and child products.[42] The CPSC had been monitoring some of these goods for years, as injuries mounted. Among the products now exempt: nine crib models (277 incidents, twenty-seven entrapments, one death), two infant swings (300 complaints, 44 injuries), one toddler bed (lead paint hazard), eight high chair models, eight stroller models, and baby furniture (eleven dresser tipovers, one chifferobe tipover, metal stool leg collapses). Eventually, the cribs, infant swings, and furniture were recalled.[43] But the CPSC could take no action against Cosco for failing to report the injuries in a timely manner.

Cosco, no doubt, was pleased with the settlement. While the fine was one of the largest in the CPSC's history, it had little impact on the company's bottom line. The CPSC had agreed to a liberal installment plan—Cosco paid the fine over five years, in relatively painless $145,000 installments. The company emerged from the ordeal with its reputation and financial health intact. And while the CPSC could offer the Cosco case as an example of Brown's "get tough" stance, neither the agency nor the Department of Justice were compensated for their efforts. Civil penalties of this sort are deposited into a general fund at the Treasury Department, rather than into the agencies' coffers.[44]

Companies Claim Ignorance of Section 15

One defense the CPSC often hears, particularly from small, newer manufacturers, is that they didn't know about the self-reporting requirement. The recent baby boom has spurned a large number of "mom and pop" operations that enter the market with a single product, such as a decorative crib ornament, a soft infant carrier, or an innovative new stroller. There is no check in the system to ensure that these companies are aware of the CPSC, much less the Section 15(b) self-reporting requirement.

To boost awareness, the CPSC took its show on the road in 1999, giving seminars throughout the country on what the agency was and how it operated. In sessions that were both informative and threatening, the agency struck the tone of a stern, albeit caring parent. "Clearly there is serious under-reporting [of product hazards] by industry," CPSC regulator of recalls and compliance Marc Schoem told an audience of manufacturers, lawyers, and consumer advocates in Chicago.[45] Schoem described the agency's "dreaded" special investigations unit, the team of regulators responsible for uncovering dangerous products. The unit pores over the reports of medical examiners, coroners, police, fire, and insurance investigators, searching for "that needle in a haystack"—a dangerous product that warrants a recall. "If everyone reported with Section 15," Schoem said, "then we wouldn't have to do all this." Urging manufacturers to be more forthcoming about suspected hazards, Schoem offered, "we are the type of agency that puts our name and phone numbers on our organizational chart. We want to hear from you. Call us with questions."

After his presentation, Schoem fielded questions from audience members, who displayed more than a trivial dose of skepticism. Manufacturers appreciated Schoem's efforts to demystify his agency's operations, but it was clear the two parties' interests were far from being aligned. What happens when a consumer is seriously injured, asked one audience member, but that injury is rare, and is caused by customer misuse?

"You may call it misuse," replied Schoem, "but we may think it is possible that it will happen again." Schoem then explained that his agency makes this determination by consulting with human factors psychologists, engineers, and other CPSC staff.

"But it may be a remote risk," countered the manufacturer, "yet the CPSC requires us to take some action."

"The question is," said Schoem, "do you wait for the second event to happen? The CPSC tries to err on the side of caution." This is not the proclivity of many manufacturers.

Despite these public relations efforts, it remains too easy for manufacturers to claim ignorance of the reporting requirement. This was the case with Baby Björn, a forty–year–old Swedish company best known for its high-end soft infant carriers. Baby Björn's exclusive U. S. distributor is Regal + Lager, a seven–person business run by husband-and-wife team Bengt Lager and Luanne Whiting-Lager.[46]

In May 1995, Bengt Lager learned from a retailer that a ten–day–old baby had slipped through the leg hole of a Baby Björn carrier and fractured his skull.[47] The child's family lived in Atlanta, where Lager is based, so it was easy for him to visit their home to learn what had occurred. His talk with the victim's family, Lager claimed, made it clear to him that the case was one of product misuse—an isolated incident that wasn't likely to occur again. Still, Lager insisted, his company wanted to do everything it could to make sure the carrier was completely safe. In response to this single incident, Baby Björn began manufacturing a new version of the product with smaller leg openings and altered the product instructions.

A year later, in June 1996, a sixteen–day–old Seattle infant fell out of her Baby Björn carrier and fractured her skull. The baby's mother wrote to Lager two months later, describing "the traumatic and damaging experience that my infant daughter, McLean and I had due to your Baby Björn front-pack [carrier]."[48] About a week later, one–month–old Matthew Gordon fell out of his Baby Björn carrier as his mother Portia Moore reached for a loaf of bread in a San Francisco grocery store. "He immediately let out a high-pitched cry," Moore told a Florida newspaper reporter who was writing a series on dangerous children's products. "I kept saying 'Matthew, I'm so sorry Matthew.'"[49] The infant fractured his skull. Moore, an attorney, reported the incident to the CPSC.[50]

Six months later, in April 1997, a three–week–old New Jersey infant fell out of his Baby Björn carrier and fractured his skull.[51] A few weeks later, a CPSC investigator paid an unannounced visit to Regal + Lager's Atlanta office. The investigator asked the Lagers many questions that day, most of them focused on the infant injuries. The couple admitted they were aware of Matthew's incident, but claimed they knew nothing about the three other skull fractures. Matthew Gordon's injury was "the first complaint of this type they have ever received involving the baby carrier," wrote the CPSC investigator in his notes.[52]

Ten weeks later, in August 1997, CPSC Central Region Office director Eric Ault wrote to Bengt Lager, informing him that the agency had made a "preliminary determination of hazard." The letter requested that Regal + Lager "voluntarily" recall its Baby Björn carrier.[53] The Lagers hired Rick Locker, the New York-based defense attorney for the Juvenile Product

Manufacturers Association (JPMA), to represent them. In a September 1997 response to the CPSC's request, Locker denied that the carrier was hazardous: "[I]t is the company's position that such incidents were purely the result of unreasonable misuse of the product and not a defect in the product itself... it is the company's position that the Baby Carrier does not contain a defect which could *reasonably* create a serious risk of injury and should not be recalled."[54] Locker had made it clear that Regal + Lager was not going to recall the product without a fight. Meanwhile, stores continued to sell the Baby Björn carrier.

Four months later, in January 1998, a fifth infant fell out of his Baby Björn carrier. The three–week–old Rhode Island baby suffered a concussion.[55] In February, an eleven–day–old California infant fell out of his carrier as his father bent down to retrieve something from a kitchen cabinet. Luckily, his father caught him before he hit the ground, and the baby was not hurt.[56] In March, the Lager's attorney, Rick Locker—who was intimately acquainted with the CPSC's self-report requirement—informed the CPSC that Portia Moore's (the mother of victim Matthew Gordon) lawyer had notified Regal + Lager that he knew of additional Baby Björn carrier incidents. Locker hesitated to take the opposing lawyer's claim seriously. "This may just be chest pounding on behalf of the plaintiff's attorney," he wrote to the CPSC, "in order to obtain a settlement of his claim."[57]

Six weeks later, in May, a thirteen–day–old Seattle infant fell out of his Baby Björn carrier and fractured his skull. A nurse in Seattle called the CPSC to report the incident.[58] Three weeks later, Regal + Lager submitted to the CPSC articles from twenty magazines around the world that gave the Baby Björn carrier rave reviews, describing it as a "safe, desirable and highly recommended" carrier.[59]

In July 1998, the Lagers flew to Washington, D.C. to meet with CPSC staff. Continuing to insist that the falls were occurring because parents were not properly securing their children in the carriers, the Lagers informed the CPSC that they could not carry out a recall without the approval of Baby Björn executives in Sweden. The Lagers then told the regulators that the carrier was once again being redesigned by the Swedish manufacturer. CPSC staff pointed out that a new carrier design would not address a fundamental problem: Consumers were still using the existing Baby Björn carriers with no knowledge of the potential for injury, and the product continued to be sold in stores.[60]

Two weeks after this meeting, in August, an eighth baby fell out of his Baby Björn carrier in Winchester, Massachusetts and fractured his skull.[61] In September, a one–month–old Pittsburgh child fell out of her Baby Björn carrier and fractured her skull.[62] Two weeks later, Portia Moore wrote to CPSC Chairman Ann Brown, asking why the carrier had not yet been recalled. Moore had seen a recall notice for an Evenflo soft carrier, a product that was similar to the Baby Björn carrier, but had injured far fewer babies. Why was the Baby Björn still on the market? "As a mother, I am very concerned about this because babies are continuing to fall though the leg holes of the carrier," Moore wrote, "and suffer serious injuries including bruised brains, skull fractures and subdural hematomas."[63]

Clearly, by the fall of 1998, the CPSC had ample evidence that the Baby Björn carrier was hazardous enough to recall. Facing another meeting with CPSC staff in early October, the Lagers were growing nervous. The JPMA trade show was coming up at the end of the month; this is where they and the rest of the industry clinched most of their sales. If Regal + Lager was unable to sell the carrier at the show, the small company could go bankrupt. The Lagers persuaded Baby Björn president Björn Jakobson to fly in from Sweden to D.C. for the meeting with the CPSC. On the night of October 21, following their meeting with the CPSC, the Lagers and Jakobson agreed to recall the carrier—after successfully resisting the agency's recall efforts for more than a year.[64] Soon after, Lager and his associates set up a Regal + Lager booth at the JPMA show in Dallas. Optimistic that his engineers would create a "product fix" shortly, Lager told no one about the upcoming recall. Conducting business as usual, Lager took orders for the carrier, despite having no idea when the merchandise would be shipped.[65]

Five days after the JPMA show, Baby Björn engineers in Sweden sent "retrofit" drawings to the CPSC for their approval. Because all the babies who had slipped through the leg holes had been small, between seven and eight pounds, the engineers proposed adding an extra band to the carrier, another check to keep these tiniest of children in place.

While waiting for the CPSC's approval, Lager sent letters to all of his retail customers, requesting that they ship back their Baby Björn carrier inventories. Within a few days, Regal + Lager's Atlanta office was flooded with returned products, but Lager still had no replacements to offer his customers. "We were frustrated with the amount of time it took CPSC to approve our drawings and retrofit," said Lager. "It took them about four weeks."[66] In the meantime, on November 5, a Sonoma, California baby fell out of her carrier and suffered internal bleeding.[67] On November 17, CPSC compliance officer George Gayman wrote to notify the Lager's attorney Rick Locker that, "[I]t is time for us to proceed with the development of a corrective action plan."[68] It was time to write the recall press release.

Negotiations over the press release wording got underway between Lager and the CPSC. By the time the notice was ready and the CPSC had approved the carrier "retro-fit" it was Christmas. Afraid the recall would get lost in the holiday shuffle, the CPSC held it until January 21, 1999, three–and–a–half years after the first child had fractured his skull.[69]

To this day, Bengt Lager views himself as an innocent victim of the CPSC's "confrontational" approach to recalls. Insisting he wanted "to do the right thing" from the start, Lager claims he has a hard time understanding the agency's need to treat him as an adversary. As a distributor for a European-based manufacturer, he alleges he was ignorant of the CPSC's self-report requirement. He became defensive with the CPSC, he claims, simply because he was scared. "You get the feeling that the CPSC looks at manufacturers as evil people. People that make products that hurt kids on purpose," Lager said. "No one does this. This is the basic misunderstanding that sets the terms of the recall negotiation process—that manufacturers are evil people."[70]

Portia Moore does not describe Lager as "evil," but she has called him a liar. In a lawsuit filed six weeks before the carrier was recalled, she charged that Regal + Lager knew of at least eight newborn babies who were seriously injured after falling through the leg holes of their Baby Björn carriers. Instead of notifying the CPSC and the public of the hazard and recalling the carrier, Moore charges in her suit, "Regal + Lager has lied to the parents of the injured babies, lied to the Consumer Product Safety Commission, lied to the plaintiffs in this case, and lied to this Court, in an attempt to cover up the dangerous effect."[71]

Did Lager, in fact, lie to the CPSC when he claimed he only knew about one of the early carrier-related injuries? This is the type of difficult question CPSC lawyers face when deciding whether or not to sue a company for failing to report a product hazard. If, as Lager claims, he was not aware of the infants' falls, he has broken no laws. Which highlights a fundamental flaw in the recall system: Manufacturers are not legally responsible for tracking injuries and deaths caused by their products. Regal + Lager maintained no customer complaint files.[72] When asked by the CPSC investigator, in 1997, if she knew of any injuries, Bengt Lager's wife and business partner, Luanne, recalled "one or two complaints" about babies falling out of their carriers. But when she contacted the babies' parents, she remembered, they told her everything was okay.[73]

Some companies, like Mattel (owner of the Fisher-Price brand name), do maintain extensive consumer affairs departments that collect the sort of information the Lagers claim they did not have. Mattel employs a support staff of 150–250 people whose job it is to answer the 2.5 million calls the company receives each year through its customer hotline.[74] James Walter, Mattel's vice president of product integrity, concedes that most of the information the consumer affairs department gathers from customers is related to marketing—consumers' perceptions of Mattel's toys and infant products, feedback about how the products are being used, and suggestions for product improvements. "But along with that comes a lot of safety information," Walter remarked in his speech at the CPSC's 1999 Recall Effectiveness Forum (see Chapter 3). He then suggested why some companies might resist building departments like Mattel's: The CPSC's self-reporting requirement may put companies that capture consumer feedback—in particular, details about product hazards and injuries—at a regulatory disadvantage. Why? "Because when you're asked [by the CPSC] to provide information concerning consumer contacts and problems that you've had with the products," Walter said, "if you have a very, very good system for capturing that information, then you have a lot of information to offer. If you don't have a very good system you may be able to say, 'We've had very few calls, we've had very little interest; we've had very few incidences.'"[75] In other words, the way the CPSC's self-reporting requirement currently stands, ignorance is not only a viable excuse, but a savvy business strategy.

Portia Moore settled her case with Baby Björn out of court, but she was prohibited from disclosing details of the settlement terms to the public (see Chapter 5).[76] In the meantime, Bengt Lager has joined the JPMA board of directors with the goal of educating the trade group's members about CPSC policy and recall procedures. "If you go to the JPMA show," says Lager, "at least half of the manufacturers there have no idea of the self-report requirement."[77] In his opinion, the industry trade group should keep its members updated on regulatory information, so that all manufacturers will be aware of their obligation to self-report hazards. "[Recalls are] the kind of thing manufacturers don't want to think about," Lager says. "You know you should do these things, but you don't prepare. Your priorities are different. You want to increase sales and market share. Every company should have a recall plan, but they don't."

Regal + Lager now has a recall plan in place. But will the CPSC charge Lager's company with failing to self-report the carrier's hazards? More than a year after the recall, Lager was still waiting to find out.

Regulatory and Legal Systems That Allow Companies to Keep Consumers in the Dark about Dangerous Children's Products

Brand-name baby products injure tens of thousands of American children each year. Portable cribs and the Graco Converta-Cradle alone are responsible for more than two dozen infant deaths; bath seats are responsible for sixty–six more. And yet most parents remain ignorant about these product dangers. Why, after so many infant deaths and injuries, do these hazards remain largely unknown to even the most safety-vigilant parents? Because manufacturers have fought hard for, and won, the right to keep these very public matters private. Statutes in the Consumer Product Safety Act, in conjunction with a legal system that permits the infant products industry to conduct its business shrouded in a thick veil of secrecy, keep news of hazardous products and corporate wrongdoing from ever reaching the public.

Section 6(b): The CPSC'S Reverse-FOIA—The CPSC Pays for the FTC's Mistake

Oddly enough, the story of the infant product industry's concealment of safety data begins thirty years ago, with a Federal Trade Commission (FTC) secret investigation of a new brand of automobile antifreeze. In 1970, the DuPont Corporation introduced its revolutionary new antifreeze, Zerex. A notch above its competitors, Zerex was "self-sealing," a property that prevented the antifreeze from leaking out of car radiators. DuPont hired top-flight advertising agency BBD&O to create television commercials for Zerex—in 1970, an extravagant marketing strategy for a product as mundane as antifreeze. Focusing on Zerex's competitive advantage, BBDO's work culminated in a graphic "show me" ad. Television viewers across the country watched raptly as an ice pick bashed through a can of Zerex. Rather than leaking through the punctured can, the antifreeze sealed. Consumers were convinced of the company's claim, and sales of Zerex began an upward trajectory.[1]

The FTC, however, didn't buy it. Shortly after the first ads were aired, the commission set out to prove that DuPont's self-sealing claim was a sham. The FTC's ultimate goal: to get Zerex off the market. Regulators went about their investigation quietly, never letting DuPont know what they were up to. In fact, DuPont executives learned of the government's charges the same way the public found out—from a FTC press conference held Thanksgiving week, 1970. With great bravado, the agency accused DuPont of trying to bilk consumers into buying a product that fell far short of its advertising claims. Zerex was *not* self-sealing, the FTC announced to the press, and in fact, the product was likely to *damage* a car's cooling system. Advertising agency BBD&O was named as a co-respondent in the case.[2] Zerex sales plummeted.

As it turned out, the FTC had made a mistake. Tests conducted throughout the months following the press conference revealed that Zerex did exactly what its advertising had claimed it would. A year later, the FTC dropped its charges, but by then, DuPont's profits had taken a beating.[3] The FTC's original warning got considerably more press than the retraction, and sales of Zerex never recovered. The federal agency had annihilated a brand.

The legacy of the FTC's Zerex blunder has been long-lasting and pervasive. For at the same time this story was playing out, Congress was in the midst of hashing out the details of the Consumer Product Safety Act, delegating responsibilities to the Consumer Product Safety Commission. Like the FTC, the CPSC was to be the federal overseer of consumer goods manufacturers that preferred not to be regulated. At the heart of the Consumer Product Safety Act was the question of how much power the CPSC would be given vis-à-vis industry. The Zerex debacle still fresh in their minds, the CPSC's congressional architects vowed to make sure the new agency would not have the authority to do to *any* corporation what the FTC had done to DuPont. Section 6(b) of the Consumer Product Safety Act was Congress's backlash against the FTC.

Manufacturers Control What the CPSC Can Divulge

The Freedom of Information Act (FOIA), enacted by Congress in 1966 under the belief that "an informed electorate is vital to the proper operation of a democracy," provides the public with direct access to documents held by federal agencies.[4] The Act has some exemptions (primarily to protect the confidentiality of trade secrets and the names of victims), but it has become an invaluable tool for lawyers, consumer advocates, and journalists. FOIA law stipulates that federal agencies such as the CPSC must respond to requests for information within ten days.

Despite the ten–day law, the CPSC can take months to answer a FOIA request. Section 6(b) of the Consumer Product Safety Act—the legacy of the FTC's DuPont blunder—is to blame. Called a "reverse-FOIA," 6(b) grants manufacturers the right to review all product-specific information that the CPSC releases to the public. In other words, before the agency sends anyone—consumer advocates, journalists, or parents seeking safety advice—information on any specific product, the CPSC must notify the company of the request, then send them the file to review. The company has thirty days to evaluate the FOIA request. If the company disputes the accuracy or fairness of the information in the file, the CPSC must determine whether or not these concerns are legitimate. When the parties don't agree, the CPSC's Office of General Counsel gets involved, and suddenly the request for information has become a federal case.[5] Ultimately, the dispute can go to court, but the CPSC has little incentive to take these matters this far. Financially strapped, with never enough resources to do its work, the agency is unlikely to make a 6(b) legal battle one of its top priorities. Manufacturers know this. "Any manufacturer willing to contest a pending release of information about its product," says former CPSC lawyer Bob Adler, "can delay, and occasionally prevent, its release simply by threatening to litigate whether the agency followed 6(b) procedures."[6]

The CPSC is the only federal health and safety agency with information disclosure restrictions as stringent as 6(b).[7] Understandably, CPSC staff resent the time and resources they devote to this obligation. In 1999, the CPSC spent $1.4 million to process FOIA requests, about $400,000 of this amount on 6(b).[8] Clearly, safeguards should have been in place to prevent the FTC from disparaging Zerex so publicly, without first giving DuPont the chance to defend itself. But critics claim 6(b) is overkill. Says CPSC Chairman Ann Brown, "You have to understand that 6(b) is imposed upon us, and it is the bane of our existence. They tell us in our statutes to get information out to consumers. Then they tell us that we can't do it unless we give industry that information. That really gives industry the control of the information flow process, and the consumer should be in control of that."[9]

Consumer groups have appealed to Congress to rescind 6(b) several times—one case even made it to the Supreme Court—without success.[10] Today, when consumer advocates and regulators are asked what most undermines the CPSC's ability to disseminate product safety information to the public, most respond with a resounding, "6(b)."

Why Buying a Safe Car is Easier than Buying a Safe Infant Swing

Imagine that a couple, expecting their first child within the next month, is in the market for both a new car and a slew of infant products. The mother-to-be wants to learn as much as she can about the safety track record of individual cars before visiting a dealer's showroom. While enticed by the roominess of sports utility vehicles (SUVs), she is concerned that some brands may not be as safe as their large, chunky exteriors portray them to be. Where should she begin her search? Guessing that the government will be the source of the most credible, objective information, she turns to the National Highway Traffic Safety Administration (NHTSA), the federal agency responsible for overseeing the safety of motor vehicles. Scanning the agency's website (www.nhtsa.gov), she quickly zeroes in on the data she is after: the federal government's safety ratings for most brands of SUVs. Each brand is rated on a variety of measures—driver's and passenger's frontal crash tests, driver's and passenger's side crash tests, and airbag protection. Through the NHTSA site, she can link to other car safety-related sites, like www.hwysafety.org and www.crashtest.org.

Examining the ratings, the mother-to-be learns that the 1999 Dodge Durango scores only two stars out of a possible five on the driver's side frontal crash test, four stars on the passenger side test, and provides no side airbag impact protection. According to NHTSA, a safer choice would be the Nissan Pathfinder or the Mercury Mountaineer, both rating four and five stars on all crash tests. Linking to the www.hwysafety.org site, she comes to understand the importance of the various crash tests. Ending her search, she sends away for the booklet

"Shopping for a Safer Car," confident that she has found the information she needs to make a wise purchase decision.

Next, the mother-to-be turns her attention to baby equipment. She and her husband have already bought a crib, and she's had a baby shower, but there are a few items her friends have told her she shouldn't live without. One of them is an infant swing. Nothing can lull a baby to sleep more quickly, her best friend has told her, and the swinging motion calms even the most colicky infant. The woman begins her search with the two books she received at her shower: *Baby Bargains* and *Consumer Reports Guide to Baby Products*. Immediately, a sentence in *Baby Bargains* jumps off the page, heightening her concern: "Remember to observe safety warnings about swings, which are close to the top ten most dangerous products as far as injuries go."[11] The book doesn't explain what these dangers are, nor does it say anything about their prevalence. But it does recommend a "best brand": Graco. She wonders what *Consumer Reports* has to say about Graco.

Consumer Reports names swing manufacturers—Graco, Evenflo, and Fisher-Price—but falls short of recommending a specific brand. Beneath the manufacturer listings, the expectant mother finds a half-page warning titled, "Swings Require Vigilance."[12] It is here that she learns why infant swings are dangerous: Babies can fall forward in a swing and suffocate, and older babies can pull on a swing leg and topple out. Wondering how to reconcile this new information with the endorsement of her friends, she decides—as she did when searching for safety data on cars—that the government would be the best source for unbiased, objective recommendations on infant products.

Logging into the CPSC website (www.cpsc.gov), the first thing the woman learns is that, unlike NHTSA, the CPSC doesn't test or rate any of the products it regulates. The site lists infant swings that have been recalled, but there is no information about swings that are currently on the market. Checking the recall list, she tries to figure out if certain manufacturers have better or worse track records than others. This is when she learns that Graco, the brand *Baby Bargains* recommended, recalled seven million infant swings in the spring of 2000, after 181 babies had been injured, nine babies had fractured bones or were knocked unconscious, twenty–two infants had been caught by the swing at the neck or chest, and six babies had died.[13] The recall occurred after *Baby Bargains* had been published.

Graco wasn't the only manufacturer that had sold dangerous infant swings. Adding up the numbers, the mother-to-be discovers that over the last few years, an additional two million swings were recalled by Century Products (*multiple deaths by strangulation*), Little Tikes (*cuts, bruises, and a broken elbow*), Carlson Children's Products (*suffocation*), Newco (*cuts and bruises*), Playskool (*bumps, bruises, and a broken nose*), and Cosco (*bumps, bruises, and a concussion*).[14] There must be a safer brand of swings, she thinks. Why else would all of her friends swear by them? Intent on finding a safe swing, she calls the CPSC for advice. This is when she collides with Section 6(b).

The Consumer Product Safety Act imbues the CPSC with one non-regulatory responsibility—to investigate, analyze, and disseminate to the public information on injuries and deaths associated with consumer products. However, 6(b) largely prohibits the agency from carrying out the "dissemination" component of this mandate. CPSC regulators know which infant swings are associated with the greatest number of injuries and deaths, but 6(b) prevents them from releasing this information on their website or over the phone. Once a product is recalled, the injury and death count becomes public knowledge, but before a recall notice is issued (by which time hundreds of children may already have been hurt), 6(b) forces anyone who wants this information to jump through hoops to get it.

A parent seeking safety data on infant swings—or any product regulated by the CPSC—can secure it in one of two ways.

Both require her to file a Freedom of Information Act Request (see Appendix 5–1 for instructions). The quickest option is to file a FOIA request that asks for "all incidents of injury and death, brand names not necessary" associated with infant swings. Within a few weeks, the CPSC will send a computer printout describing each infant swing incident that occurred in the time period specified. Incident descriptions will be brief and brand names will be blacked out. The following reports were included in a FOIA request for infant swing incidents occurring between 1990 and 1999:

> A 13–month old child died from asphyxiation caused when the child's head/neck became entangled inside a seat belt loop that was protruding from the back of a baby automatic swing seat.

> A 1.5 year old female fell from her seat in an indoor infant swing. The child sustained a bump to her forehead and a bruised left eye. She was treated at home and has fully recovered from the incident.

> The victim, an 8–month old female, was found by her mother entangled around the neck in the harness strap of a battery operated infant swing. The victim was pronounced DOA at a local hospital. The official cause of death was hanging.[15]

The full report described ninety–four infant swing incidents, including twenty–five deaths. While information of this sort may help a parent assess dangers posed by the swings in general, it will do little to help her identify the safest brand.

The mother's second option is to file a FOIA request for "all incidents of injury and death" associated with infant swings "with brands identified." This request will yield hundreds of pages of data, but by the time it arrives, the woman's baby may have outgrown the product. And of course, because 6(b) forces the agency to get the final go-ahead from every company before they can fulfill the FOIA request, the process can take many months, sometimes up to a year. Then, when the data arrives, the effect of 6(b) will be obvious: pages deleted, sentences blacked out, and entire documents withheld.

Had the mother-to-be filed a FOIA request for "all incidents associated with the Century 'Lil Napper infant swing," she would have received hundreds of pages of information, including: a photograph of a dead nine–month–old baby who was strangled by his swing; a police department report classifying a baby's swing strangulation as "death—suspicious circumstances"; a picture of a doll hanging face-down in a swing with restraint straps around her neck, positioned by the mother of a victim to illustrate for investigators how she had found her dead son; descriptions of babies' autopsies; a grandmother's desperate letter requesting financial assistance from Century Products for her uninsured grandson's emergency tracheotomy (he was a "near-miss"); and the heartbreaking letter of a mother who found her son dead, early one morning, strangled by the swing's restraint system.[16] A two–page letter from the CPSC's FOIA officer would have told the mother-to-be that the agency had withheld certain documents "where the manufacturer has requested confidentiality."[17] What should she make of this chilling data? Is Century a worse brand than others? Does any other manufacturer make a safe swing? Should she scratch infant swings from her shopping list altogether? The CPSC is not permitted to tell her.

It takes little more than a few clicks on the NHTSA website for a consumer to find out which cars are safe and which are not. In contrast, for a parent to learn which infant products are safe, she must master the art of FOIA requests, then wade through hundreds of pages of documents that describe the minutiae of childhood injury and death. In the end, she must draw her own conclusions about the product's safety. Why doesn't the CPSC summarize its data into a format that would help parents make wiser purchase decisions? Because Section 6(b) forbids the agency from doing so. Thanks to 6(b), the manufacturers of hazardous infant products never have to worry that the CPSC will one day tell an expectant mother, "Don't buy that brand, it's dangerous."

Court-Sanctioned Secrecy: How Manufacturers Usurp the Legal System to Keep News of Dangerous Products from Reaching the Public

The U. S. legal system plays a valuable role in government regulation, particularly in largely unregulated industries like infant products.[18] When a family sues a manufacturer for the wrongful injury or death of their child, or the CPSC sues a manufacturer for failing to self-report product hazards, the courts provide a forum for the truth to be told about the company's pre-market testing and sales practices. In addition to compensating the family or the U. S. government monetarily, a judgment against the manufacturer can contribute to public safety. News of a verdict against a manufacturer—particularly a company that sells baby products—will travel quickly, alerting other consumers not only of the product's danger, but also of the company's actions. Infant product manufacturers have strong incentives to make sure news of this sort is kept out of the limelight.

An injury or wrongful death lawsuit brought by a family against a manufacturer is filed in the family's local state or federal trial court. Often, in addition to the manufacturer, the suit names the product's retailer as a defendant. Some suits, like the one filed by the Zalinskis after their son was killed by a Baby Trend portable crib, also name the industry trade group, the Juvenile Products Manufacturers Association, as a defendant.[19] To win a verdict under the current doctrine of strict liability, a plaintiff in a product liability suit must demonstrate that a defective product caused a child's injury or death.[20] During the discovery process, attorneys for both sides gather testimony relevant to the case, through depositions of key witnesses and interrogatories. The discovery process entitles the plaintiff's lawyers to scrutinize the defendant's internal documents; for manufacturers, this includes notes taken during product-safety review meetings, executives' memos, consumer complaints logged by the company's customer service department, reports of product testing labs, and so on. The content of these documents can determine the outcome of a case.[21]

From the start, the discovery process is stacked to favor the defendant. While the plaintiff desperately needs the manufacturer's documents, the manufacturer has the most to lose by surrendering them. The discovery process becomes a battle for information, as plaintiffs' lawyers demand a company's internal documents, and the company strives to keep the documents to themselves. Ralph Nader and Wesley J. Smith, authors of *No Contest: Corporate Lawyers and the Perversion of Justice in America*, describe the process like this:

> In the 1950's and 1960's there was a popular television game show called I've Got a Secret. On the program, four celebrity panelists tried to discover a contestant's "secret" by asking a series of questions that could be answered yes or no. If the celebrities failed to guess the secret, the contestant won a cash prize. It was all great fun.
>
> Today, big law firms and their corporate clients play their own version of the game. Only, the action isn't televised, there are rarely celebrities, and the game isn't fun at all. The corporate lawyer version of I've Got a Secret allows evidence of corporate wrongdoing, evidence relevant to public policy debates and consumer interests, to remain hidden, frequently from the public and sometimes even from victims of the wrongdoing. It is a dangerous strategy, with grave consequences for the public welfare.[22]

Over the years, manufacturers have invented an arsenal of

stonewalling tactics to prevent plaintiffs from gaining possession of incriminating documents and to keep evidence of corporate wrongdoing from reaching the public. Their tactics are shockingly successful. Corporate lawyers, generally paid by the hour and equipped with abundant resources, are strongly motivated to resist plaintiffs' attorneys' requests for information. Plaintiffs' attorneys, who usually are compensated only if they win a case, and then take a percentage of the monetary award, view the discovery process as "overhead." It is in their best interest for discovery to move quickly. This rarely occurs. "The plaintiff's efforts to obtain information exclusively in the defendant's possession will frequently be met by a wall of unyielding opposition," write product liability attorneys Francis Hare, James Gilbert, and Stuart Ollanik in *Full Disclosure: Combating Stonewalling and Other Discovery Abuses*. "Although the practice of stonewalling has been with us for as long as discovery has been allowed, in recent years corporate defendants in complex litigation have raised the practice to a new art form."[23]

United States v. Cosco, Inc.: A Lesson in Stonewalling

In 1996, the CPSC teamed up with the U.S. Department of Justice to bring suit against Cosco for failing to report hazards associated with its toddler beds and guardrails (see Chapter 4). Having recalled the toddler beds in 1992 and the guardrails in 1994, the agency already had plenty of well-documented evidence that the products were hazardous. To win the case, the plaintiffs—the CPSC and the Department of Justice—would have to demonstrate that Cosco had known of the products' dangers, and had failed to notify the CPSC when dozens of parents called to complain that their children had been entrapped in the guardrails and beds. Cosco's lawyers stonewalled throughout the discovery process, relying on a number of efficacious tactics—excessive delays, boilerplate objections, and evasive responses.

Department of Justice attorneys William Zoffer and Joseph Gergits sent their first set of interrogatory questions and document requests to Cosco's lawyers on February 7, 1996.[24] Twenty–five pages long, the questions covered a lot of ground. How did Cosco evaluate the products' safety before they were sold? What kind of internal system did Cosco have in place to relay consumer complaints of entrapment to the company's executives? What did Cosco do with the recalled toddler beds that had been returned or that had never left the warehouse? To try the case fairly, the Department of Justice needed answers to these questions, as well as the company's records of product tests, analyses, marketing, consumer complaints, and entrapments.

A month after receiving the plaintiffs' interrogatory and document requests, Cosco lawyers Peter Winik and Minh Vu asked for a thirty–day extension—the first of many delays.[25] When they finally responded in April, their incomplete answers suggested there was much the company wanted to keep secret. Listing fifteen boilerplate general objections, including the Department of Justice's definitions of "Cosco" and "the original toddler bed," Cosco's lawyers quibbled with any question they considered vague, ambiguous, overly broad, or that "would subject Cosco to oppression, harassment, and undue burden and expense."[26] In response to the plaintiffs' request for information about the fate of the recalled toddler beds, Cosco's lawyers complained that the answer would expose the company to "undue burden and expense."[27] Furthermore, they claimed the question was irrelevant to the suit and would not lead to the discovery of admissible evidence.[28] Winik and Vu offered only that some of the headboards and footboards of the recalled beds had been destroyed, others had been "reworked," and the mattress platforms had been "salvaged."[29]

A week later, government lawyer William Zoffer voiced his annoyance with Cosco's evasive responses. In a letter to Winik and Vu, Zoffer argued that the company's handling of the recalled toddler beds *was* relevant to the case, as it bore heavily on Cosco's credibility, a point central to the suit.[30] Cosco's lawyers had also put off Zoffer's request for the names of the customer service employees who had fielded toddler bed and guardrail complaints, saying only that they would provide the names, "upon request and with reasonable notice." "For the record," Zoffer responded, "you are requested *again* to furnish this responsive information." Zoffer also took issue with the company's failure to provide the names of those involved in Cosco's product safety committees. Zoffer needed the names, Cosco's lawyers knew, to draw up a list of Cosco employees who would be asked to give depositions. By withholding this information, Cosco was unnecessarily delaying the discovery process.

Over the next month, Department of Justice and Cosco lawyers met to try to resolve these discovery disputes. Cosco attorney Winik agreed to supplement some of the company's original answers. But by the first week of June, Cosco had provided no new information. "These matters have been dragging for some time," Zoffer wrote to Winik, requesting his supplemental answers by the close of business the next day.[31]

Cosco responded immediately, but once again produced only a fraction of the information Zoffer had requested. According to Winik's response, the recalled toddler beds had been "processed through the Returned Goods Department," but no one at Cosco could remember who, exactly, had handled them.[32] Nor, apparently, could any executives recall what they had done upon learning of the bed and guardrail hazards: "Cosco cannot identify with specificity the timing of any actions it took or communications it made upon learning of the various reports of entrapment incidents."[33] The company did, however, furnish a list of executives on its Product Review Committee and Product Safety Task Force—though no one could tell Zoffer what was discussed in these meetings. Why? According to Cosco, no minutes were kept.[34]

In the Department of Justice's next letter to Cosco's attorneys, lawyer Joseph Gergits expressed his extreme displeasure with "continuing shortcomings in Cosco's responses to our interrogatories and document requests."[35] Among the most egregious omissions was Cosco's obstinate refusal to disclose what had happened to the recalled toddler beds. For the first time, Zoffer revealed the source of his continued interest in the issue: He had documents that suggested the company had diverted the beds to Mexico, where they had been sold. "Furthermore, other documents that we possess," wrote Gergits, "establish that the principals at Cosco were arranging for (or at a minimum were fully aware of) this diversion to Mexico while they were reporting to the CPSC that all non-conforming beds were being destroyed."[36] Gergits gave Cosco a week to come up with a satisfactory answer. Otherwise, he would ask the judge to order Cosco to respond.

Cosco lawyer Minh Vu responded ten days later—and again failed to answer the question. "[W]e have investigated your allegations and have determined that there is no basis to change the response at this time," Vu wrote.[37]

As it turned out, Cosco executives never had to tell anyone what they had done with the recalled toddler beds. Soon after the Department of Justice took its first deposition—of former Cosco CEO David Zike—the case was settled out of court.[38] Cosco's stonewalling had paid off: For $725,000, the company was able to put an end to all of the government's questions.[39] By settling the case, Cosco avoided the repercussions that were sure to ensue when the company's executives answered pointed questions under oath, in depositions and in court. Cosco vice president of manufacturing Robert Schwartzkopf never had to explain the memos that were sent to him by employee Don Dillman, which informed Schwartzkopf that thousands of recalled toddler beds had been "reworked" for Mexico.[40] Quality control/product standards manager Bob Craig never had to reveal why he had told CPSC compliance officer Terri Rogers that he was aware of only two toddler bed entrapments, shortly after being copied on a memo that put the count at twenty–three.[41] Nor did Craig, who was identified as Cosco's "CPSC representative," have to explain why he had decided to "fix" the toddler bed entrapment problem by adding a warning label to new units sold, rather than taking the product off the market and notifying customers of the beds' hazards.[42] Lacking the resources to fight Cosco indefinitely, the Department of Justice and the CPSC were all too willing to take the money and move on to the next case. The result: Consumers continued to remain in the dark about Cosco's dismal track record on infant safety and the highly suspect actions of its executives.

Confidential Settlements: Manufacturers Make Sure Parents Don't Talk

One cold March day in 1989, sixteen–month–old Michael Bancroft's mother's Toyota was struck head-on by another car. The impact of the crash killed the oncoming car's driver. Michael broke his neck, was permanently paralyzed from the waist down, and retained only partial use of his arms and hands. He had been strapped into a Kolcraft booster-style car seat.[43]

Michael's family sued Kolcraft. During discovery, the family's lawyers learned that other manufacturers of booster car seats recommended the product for children *over thirty pounds*. The National Highway Traffic Safety Administration (NHTSA) had a more stringent weight limit: *over forty pounds*. Kolcraft, however, claimed its seat was safe for children between twenty and forty pounds. Michael weighed twenty–two pounds—within Kolcraft's generous weight recommendation, but not within NHTSA's or those of most other manufacturers. The Bancrofts' attorneys had multiple experts reconstruct the accident, and filmed "sled tests" of the car seat ejecting a test dummy the same size as Michael. "Our engineering team quickly came to the conclusion that 20 pounds was inappropriate," said Stephen Kiely, who led the plaintiffs' legal team.[44]

Three months after Michael's accident, Kolcraft raised the recommended minimum weight for its booster car seats to thirty pounds, up from twenty. The company claimed the change had nothing to do with safety. Rather, it was purely a marketing decision, made "to bring them into conformity with other manufacturers."[45] Why did Kolcraft originally choose a car-seat weight restriction that was far more lax than that of its competitors? The answer to this question remains a mystery. The Bancroft case never went to trial, and Kolcraft's defense lawyers went to great lengths to ensure no one would ever learn what happened to Michael Bancroft. In exchange for a settlement payment, Michael's family and lawyers signed a confidentiality agreement that stipulated they would never reveal Kolcraft's name to the public. Kolcraft was identified as the manufacturer of the boy's car seat only after relentless journalists tracked down the case through public court records. The records revealed that Kolcraft had offered the Bancrofts $4.25 million, plus scheduled payments for Michael's ongoing care that could have brought the final settlement to more than $10 million.[46]

The Bancroft family's dilemma is played out in lawyers' offices everyday. Should a family push their case to trial, or settle quietly and move on with their lives? A trial can bring public attention to an unsafe product and spotlight corporate wrongdoing. For this reason, many product liability lawyers view the dissemination of product safety information as an important part of their job. "A lawyer who discovers evidence that a product is designed defectively or is inherently hazardous or who discovers repeated evidence of neglect causing injury, has an overriding responsibility to see that the information is disseminated as a means of avoiding further injuries," wrote the Bancroft's lawyer Stephen Kiely, in *Massachusetts Lawyers Weekly*, a year before he settled the Kolcraft car seat case.[47]

But sometimes when a lawyer wants to take a case to trial, his clients feel otherwise. Parents who take the witness stand in a court trial face the likelihood of being blamed by the manufacturer's lawyers and their expert witnesses, repeatedly and aggressively, for the injury or death of their child. When the Zalinski family sued Baby Trend for the wrongful death of their son, Baby Trend's lawyer asked Jared's mother questions intended to demonstrate she was a bad parent. Her crimes? She had set up Jared's portable crib near window blind cords that could have injured Jared, and she had failed to install plug protectors on all of the electric sockets in the house.[48] All but the most resilient parents will seek to avoid such an ordeal and settle their cases out of court, even if this means signing a confidentiality clause.

Despite the Bancrofts' attorney's strong statements about the importance of disseminating public safety information, when Kolcraft offered his clients millions of dollars to settle, he allowed his clients to take the money and sign the gag order. Why? "In the end, I agreed," said Kiely, "because my job is to secure proper care for my client. And I deemed it inappropriate for the confidentiality agreement to stand between my client and the settlement."[49] When a child is not killed by a product, but severely injured like Michael Bancroft, the rewards of settling out-of-court are ratcheted up another notch: The staggering costs of medical care are often overwhelming. An offer of ongoing payments over the rest of the child's life becomes too important to pass up. Overburdened by the cost of Michael's medical care, concern for "a larger public interest" was a luxury the Bancroft family simply couldn't afford.

Confidential settlements have become the norm in industries like juvenile products, where a company's financial health rests heavily on its ability to project a nurturing, caring, safety-conscious image to the public.[50] This trend toward secrecy has spawned an intense debate between plaintiffs' and defense lawyers.[51] Plaintiffs' lawyers, resentful of being forced to choose between a client's immediate needs and the safety and welfare of the public, have been pushing for the past ten years for legislative solutions. Since 1990, a handful of states have passed "sunshine" laws that prohibit the courts from keeping secrets from the public. Florida's 1990 Sunshine in Litigation Act, one of the most stringent, prohibits any confidential settlement that conceals information about "public hazards."[52] In 1993, Washington State passed the Public Right to Know bill, prevailing against the strong opposition of Boeing Aircraft and other local manufacturers. Louisiana passed a similar bill in 1995. But in many states, including California, industry has used its clout to persuade legislators to vote down sunshine laws. Senator Herbert Kohl of Wisconsin has introduced right-to-know legislation at the federal level, with no luck.[53]

Professor Arthur Miller of Harvard Law School, among the more vocal advocates of settlement secrecy, argues that courts should remain a place where "private parties bring a private dispute"; therefore, plaintiffs have no right to force a defendant to disclose information the company considers to be confidential.[54] But is it a company's right to determine what information should remain confidential? Miller's critics argue that when a company markets a product that endangers public safety, that company loses the right to keep product information a secret. Miller claims further that prohibiting confidential settlements will decrease the incentive for corporations to settle out of court and further burden the already overloaded U.S. court system. In fact, there is no empirical evidence that this occurs; settlement rates have *not* decreased in states with strong sunshine laws. Why? Companies remain strongly motivated to settle before the very public scrutiny of a full-blown trial.[55]

It is time, consumer advocates insist, for the corporate game of "I've Got a Secret" to end. Secret settlements conceal safety information that can, quite literally, kill a child. "The time has come to enact a federal anti-secrecy law," argues attorney

Andrew Miller. Access to public court records like settlement agreements should be limited only when a judge has determined that the records do not conceal information about public hazards. "Overall, anti-secrecy legislation will provide the public with access to information that can be used to foster change and work to safeguard the world in which we live."[56]

Standing in front of the juvenile products aisle at Wal-Mart, a parent sizing up a Cosco baby swing or stroller may be able to draw a few conclusions about the product's manufacturer. The sheer amount of Cosco goods on the shelves could lead her to the correct conclusion that the company sells more car seats, strollers, cribs, and play yards than just about anyone else.[57] Maybe she's seen her friends' babies enjoying Cosco products, or she may have been enticed to the store by a Cosco ad while flipping through *Childbirth* or *American Baby* magazines in her obstetrician's office. It is quite likely, however, that she will know next to nothing about Cosco's safety track record. She will have no idea that since 1990, the company has recalled over 2.5 million product units, accounting for over four hundred injuries and at least three deaths (see Table 5–1). She will have no idea that the U. S. Department of Justice fined the company for allegedly withholding safety information from the CPSC. She will have no idea that multiple Cosco employees who were implicated in the safety-information cover-up today play a significant role in the voluntary standard-setting process for infant products. Why? Because the U. S. regulatory and judiciary systems allow Cosco—and all other juvenile product manufacturers—to dupe trusting parents and caregivers into believing that their baby products are infallibly safe.

Table 5-1: COSCO Juvenile Product Recalls: 1990–2000

Product	Date	Units	Incidents	Injuries	Deaths
Toddler beds	4/92	155,000	50+	50+	1
Toddler bed rails	6/94	75,000	67	67	0
Crib	12/95	190,000	230	N/A	0
Youth furniture	1/96	585,000	11	3	0
Infant swings	4/97	355,500	300+	44	0
Cribs	7/97	390,000	47+	27	1
Car seat/stroller	12/97	6,000	0	0	0
Tandem strollers	2/99	57,000	3,000	200+	0
Crib mattress	2/99	62,000	12	12	1
Car seat/carrier	7/99	670,000	151	29	0
TOTAL		2,545,500	3,868+	432+	3

Safety Information about Cosco products that most parents don't know exists. [58]

CHAPTER 6

What Parents Can Do to Keep Their Infants Safe

The hot new product at a recent Juvenile Products Manufacturers Association (JPMA) trade show in Dallas was a round mahogany crib adorned with a leopard-print canopy, leopard-print crib draperies, leopard-print diaper bag, leopard-print crib sheets, and tiny leopard-print infant pillows. Retail price: $2,000, accessories not included. For the mother less concerned with lavishly decorating her infant's bedroom than with keeping the baby entertained while she scratches together dinner, there were stationary "activity centers"— updated versions of old-fashioned baby walkers. And for parents sold on the notion that it's never too early to prepare their child for admission to the Ivy League, manufacturers with auspicious names like Em-bry-on-ics and Brilliant Beginnings hawked recordings of classical music for the developing brains of embryos and infants.[1]

The JPMA trade show is a once-a-year opportunity for retailers to comparison shop (the show attracts 400–500 manufacturers each year) and tactually scrutinize an orgy of high chairs, cribs, strollers, cradles, playpens, car seats, baby swings, bouncers, diaper bags, crib mobiles, bassinets, carriers, and whatever else the marketing people have dreamt up to fulfill the needs, wants, and desires of their target market: guilty, indulgent, starved-for-time new parents. The show's atmosphere is festive; a local high school marching band greets attendees at the door. The noise level increases throughout the day, as buyers and sellers gab about market research, hash out prices, and toast their deals with celebratory cocktails. It's a feel-good affair, all four days of it. And why shouldn't it be? These people are in the business of making babies and their parents happy. It would be tough to find a more worthwhile, cheery profit motive. The fact that the industry is enjoying a boom like it's never seen before is simply well-deserved icing on the cake.

In 1985, American consumers spent $1.5 billion on infant equipment, or $400 per live birth. By 2000, industry sales had more than tripled, to $4.9 billion, or $1,256 per live birth.[2] The days are long gone when parents prepared for a child's birth with just four pieces of equipment: a car seat, high chair, full-size crib, and stroller. Now, by the time a toddler learns to walk, odds are she already has been lulled to sleep in a cradle or bassinet, toted through shopping malls in a hard-handled carrier, bounced in a baby bouncer, bathed in a bath seat, pushed in an infant swing, put down for a nap in a portable crib, and strapped into a baby walker or stationary entertainer.

What has fueled this buying frenzy? Demographers offer a couple of explanations. Beginning in the mid–1970s and continuing through the mid–1990s, the original baby boomers reached childbearing age and created a baby "boomlet" of their own. At the same time, American women have delayed childbirth until they are older and more financially secure. While the birth rate of women 20–29 years old has remained relatively constant since 1985, the rate has increased markedly among women over thirty. For women in their thirties, the birth rate has increased without interruption since 1978, by ninety percent. The birth rate of women in their forties increased eighty–seven percent between 1981 and 1997.[3] These trends have not gone unnoticed by baby product manufacturers. Older, relatively more affluent parents prepare for the birth of a first child differently than they would have in their twenties. "There are a lot of women over 35 having children," said Kim

Whittaker, founder of Baby Faire, a multi-city marketing extravaganza attended by tens of thousands of parents willing to pay $7 apiece to view the latest children's products. "They're really ready now and they want to do it right and get all the right things."[4]

Grandparents, who are healthier and living longer than ever before, are indulging their grandchildren too, frequently helping out with big-ticket items like cribs and nursery furniture. They've also spawned a trend of "double purchases": a second portable crib, car seat, and/or infant swing for the baby to use when she visits grandma and grandpa.[5]

Demographics go a long way toward explaining the industry's explosive growth, but the consumer psychology behind these purchases should not be overlooked. Excited, overwhelmed, and often laden with anxiety about the enormous turn their lives are about to take, first-time parents are a marketer's dream. "What's in store for us?" they ask. "How will we know what to do?" And included in every expectant parent's question repertoire: "What should we buy?" Plunged suddenly into a product category with which they have little or no experience, parents-to-be engage in a relentless search for product quality and safety information. Manufacturers are quick to jump in and help educate them. Some companies, like Safety 1st, address the fears of these new parent-consumers head-on. Reads a recent ad in *Childbirth* magazine:

> If you think that getting a good night sleep is a thing of the past, think again. Safety 1st understands the anxiety that new parents face each night, hoping that their child sleeps safely and soundly throughout the night. Now, we can help with the new Safety 1st Angelcare Sound Monitor & Movement Reassurance System. Offering innovative advancements in nursery monitor technology, this system provides a continuous sound and motion detection link to your sleeping baby.[6]

Others seek to reassure novice buyers with product features they'll recognize from their more carefree, pre-baby lifestyle. This ad in *American Baby* magazine makes a stroller sound like a kid-sized mountain bike:

> Cosco's Explorer All-Terrain Stroller can handle the tough stuff—rutted forest trails, gravel lanes, muddy parking lots—as well as those everyday annoyances like uneven walkways and bumpy paths. With all-around suspension, sturdy steel frame, removable molded tray, and zip-off vented canopy/windshield, this stroller is right on track with the features you need and the quality you expect.[7]

Savvy, well-educated consumers routinely claim they don't pay attention to advertising and are smart enough to recognize marketers' exaggerated promises. But expectant parent-consumers are quick to suspend their skepticism as they thumb through magazines like *Parenting*, *American Baby* and *Fit Pregnancy*—publications notorious for the thin line they draw between advertising and editorial content. In 1998, *American Baby* asked its readers, "Which products can't you live without?"[8] More than five–thousand parents mailed, faxed, and emailed their responses. The winners: a Fisher-Price bouncer seat, a Graco open-top infant swing, Mondial Industries' Diaper Genie, the Evenflo Exersaucer, Playtex's spill-proof cup, Huggies overnight diapers, Pampers Premium Diapers, a Graco portable crib, Medela's breast pump, a Fisher-Price musical infant gym, the Evenflo On My Way car seat/carrier, Baby Björn infant carrier, a Camp Kazoo pillow, Braun's ear thermometer, and Desitin diaper rash ointment. The losers: the parents who bought the three products on this list that were recalled shortly after the *American Baby* article was published. Two hundred and seventy–nine babies were injured and six were killed by the recalled products: the Graco swing (one–hundred and eighty–one falls and six deaths), the Baby Björn carrier (nine falls, including six skull fractures), and the Evenflo car seat/carrier (eighty–nine injuries, including skull fractures and concussions).[9] Contrary to *American Baby's* claim, these infants' parents would have been able to "live without" these award-winning products.

"Of course, no one would contend that humans are Pavlovian dogs that run immediately to the store or telephone to buy advertised products," say Michael Jacobson and Laurie Ann Mazur in their anti-advertising polemic, *Marketing Madness: A Survival Guide for a Consumer Society.* "And not all advertising is a sinister instrument of thought control—some actually provides useful information... But, like air pollution and acid rain, commercialization has crossed the threshold into the danger zone, and it is time to consider remedial action."[10]

When it comes to buying baby equipment, there is one clear remedy to advertising overkill: education. Parents must learn to seek information that reveals the flip side of infant product manufacturers' claims. Cosco portrays its Explorer stroller to be as tough as a mountain bike—but has Cosco made reliable, injury-free strollers in the past? Do the research and find out. Baby Björn claims to provide your baby with "the best," but is their carrier really safe? Do the research and find out. Ultimately, parents can rely on no one—certainly not the manufacturers—to tell them the truth about these products' safety records. Yet the truth can be discovered. It may take a bit of work, but in the end, it could be the most important work a parent ever does.

Keeping Your Infant Safe: What to Do Before Your Baby is Born

Read the Right Books

The expectant parent is likely to face her first dose of "buyer's confusion" when simply trying to figure out which books to read. Bookstore and library shelves bulge with parenting books, all of them written by experts promising the most important, up-to-date information on keeping your baby healthy and safe. Best-selling staples like *What to Expect* and the Sears' *Baby Book* dispense invaluable advice on infant care, but fall short of addressing the specific hazards of nursery products.[11] Although Dr. Spock's *Baby and Child Care* has an excellent chapter on injury prevention (e.g., "Why do we all have so much trouble taking the necessary actions regularly? I think it's because of a natural human tendency to go through life with an attitude of 'It can't happen to me.' So the first step is to stop denying the possibility of an injury."), it does not address product-specific dangers.[12]

Unlike most baby-care books, the American Academy of Pediatrics' *Caring for Your Baby and Young Child* does not mince words. If a product is dangerous, the pediatricians say so: "[T]he American Academy of Pediatrics strongly urges parents not to use baby walkers."[13] The book doesn't recommend specific brands, but it does identify the hazards of most products and suggests product features that reduce these hazards. For example, after identifying falls as the most serious danger associated with high chairs, the books instructs parents to "select a chair with a wide base, so it can't be tipped over if someone accidentally bumps into it."[14] *Consumer Reports Guide to Baby Products*, also issues strong warnings (e.g., "Don't use a pressure-mounted gate to block steps and stairs. *Consumer Reports'* tests have shown that pressure-mounted gates can dislodge under child-level forces").[15] Going one step further than the other books, the *Consumer Reports* guide recommends specific brands. A full chapter is devoted to recalls, and the chapter "Keeping Your Child Safe" does a good job of explaining what parents can do to prevent childhood injury. Keep in mind, though, that it is not enough to rely solely on this book: A product recommended one day by *Consumer Reports* may be recalled the next.

Access the Right Websites

Do not rely on manufacturers' websites to provide unbiased safety information. A web address ending in ".com" signals that the company's first priority is to make a profit. For unbiased safety information, turn to the government or a non-profit organization. Web addresses ending in ".org" or ".gov" signal that the organization's top priority is more likely to be child safety. (Exceptions include trade groups like the Juvenile Products Manufacturers Association, which have non-profit status and are entitled to an ".org" address.)

The CPSC is working to get all infant product manufacturers to post recall information on their websites. Many companies already post recalls, but their lists are often incomplete and the language is watered down. For example, Evenflo softens the seriousness of its product recalls on its website, first by renaming them "safety notifications."[16] Next, the company frames product hazards not in terms of corporate wrongdoing, but parental incompetence: "Companies have safety notifications to prevent customers from possible injury or harm. Product misuse, such as using a product incorrectly or for a purpose not intended has also led companies to have safety notifications." For some recalled products, Evenflo does not post the CPSC's official press release, but rather rewrites it with the company's own public relations spin. In 1998, Evenflo recalled 800,000 On My Way car seat/carriers. The CPSC press release noted, "(T)here have been 176 reports in which the carrying handle latch unexpectedly released, resulting in 89 injuries to children, including bruises, concussions and skull fractures." Failing to mention the type and number of injuries, Evenflo's website merely supplies the vague warning that, "Injuries can occur."

The following websites are a good place to start your search for reliable child-safety information:

General Child Health and Safety Organizations

- American Academy of Pediatrics: (847)228–5005; www.aap.org

- National Safe Kids Campaign: (202)662–0600; www.safekids.org

- U.S. Consumer Product Safety Commission: (800) 638–2772; www.cpsc.gov

- The Consumer Federation of America: (202)387–6121; www.safechild.net

Special-Interest Health and Safety Organizations

- The Danny Foundation, a nonprofit devoted to crib safety: (800) 83–DANNY; www.dannyfoundation.org

- Kids In Danger, a nonprofit devoted to notifying parents of dangerous recalled children's products: www.kidsindanger.org

- Back to Sleep Campaign, a government program dedicated to teaching sleep safety: (800) 505–CRIB; www.nih.gov/nichd

- Sudden Infant Death Syndrome Alliance: (800) 221–SIDS; www.sidsalliance.org

Car Seat Recommendations and Installation

National Highway Traffic Safety Administration (888) 327–4236; www.nhtsa.dot.gov. This site provides a list of nationwide locations where parents can have their car seats installed for free by specially trained car seat technicians: www.nhtsa.gov/people/injury/childps.

A 1999 study by the Safe Kids Campaign found eighty–five percent of parents did not install or use their car seats correctly. The most common errors: the car seat safety belt did not hold the seat in tightly enough, and the harness straps were not snug enough.[17]

Also keep in mind that car seats are stamped with a manufacture date. Car seat recalls can affect only those seats manufactured within certain dates. For example, the Fisher-Price Safe Embrace 79700 is rated very highly overall, yet seats manufactured between May 19, 1997 and March 29, 1998 were recalled.[18]

Sign Up for the CPSC's Automatic Recall Notification Program

Call 1–800–638–CPSC and ask to be put on the agency's mailing list, or sign up via their website (www.cpsc.gov). Whenever a product is recalled, you will be notified automatically. The service is free.

Be Wary of Hand-Me-Down Products

Before accepting a used infant product from a friend or relative, or buying one at a rummage sale or second-hand store, first check with the CPSC to make sure it hasn't been recalled (www.cpsc.gov). In 1999, the CPSC conducted a national study of consignment and resale (thrift) stores to determine the prevalence of recalled products in these retail outlets. National organizations like the Salvation Army and Goodwill stores were included in the study. The results: The CPSC found recalled products in sixty–nine percent of second-hand stores. Hazardous cribs were among the most prevalent recalled product for sale.[19]

Be Very Suspicious of Hand–Me–Down Car Seats

When someone offers you a used car seat, be sure to ask them whether it has ever been involved in an accident. On impact, a car seat can crack internally, though you may not notice any external damage. Cracked car seats may not protect your child if you are in a car crash. Before you install any used car seat, check the NHTSA (www.nhtsa.dot.gov) website to make sure it has not been recalled. (Car seats are regulated by NHTSA, not the CPSC.)

Resist Uninformed Impulse Buys

Research products before making trips to baby stores or surfing the Web. Not only can impulse purchases lead you to spend beyond your budget, they can endanger the safety of your child. You may need to visit the store a few times before you make your purchase decision. The first time you go, jot down the names and model numbers of products that catch your eye. Then go home and do the research to make sure they are safe, before you return to the store to buy.

File a Freedom of Information Act (FOIA) Request with the CPSC

In some cases, your safety research will lead you to more questions than answers. To find out more about the safety of a product category (e.g., infant swings) or a brand (e.g., Graco infant swings), file a FOIA request with the CPSC, following the instructions in Appendix 5–1. This requires good planning, as the information may take a few months to reach you. Yet a FOIA request is the only way to get reliable safety information for products that have not been recalled.

Do Not Buy Products That Have Dangerous Track Records

Baby walkers, bath seats/rings, hard-handled infant carriers, infant swings, and toddler beds are all popular products that have proven to be dangerous, even deadly. Consider why you want such a product, and whether it is truly necessary. Never use a walker or baby bathseat/ring; there is no situation where using one is safe (see Chapter 2).

Keeping Your Infant Safe: An Ongoing Process

Read and Pay Attention to CPSC Recall Press Releases

Although CPSC press releases sometimes trivialize a product's dangers, with practice, you can figure out what has occurred. All releases indicate how many children have been injured or killed while using the product. Death and injury data offers the most important clue about the magnitude of the danger.

Do a Product Recall Audit of Your Daycare Center and/or Baby-Sitter's Home

Parents often donate used baby equipment to their daycare centers or baby-sitters. Do not automatically assume that this equipment is safe; many daycare centers fail to keep up with recall news. Don't be shy about educating your daycare provider about the dangers of recalled products. Also, don't overlook daycare sites like those that have recently popped up at gyms, shopping malls, and supermarkets.

Sign Up Others with the CPSC's Recall Notification Service

As soon as a product is recalled that your friend, relative, baby-sitter, or daycare center owns (which is almost certain to happen!), you will become their hero.

Tell Your Friends When You Learn About a Recalled Product

Do not keep recall news to yourself. When you find out about a product's dangers via a recall notice or a FOIA request, become part of the education process by spreading the word to your family and friends who have small children.

Check a Product's Safety Record Before Giving it Away

If you are planning to give a used baby product to a friend, first look it up on the CPSC website to make sure it has not been recalled. Do the same before donating the product to a daycare center, church sale, or a thrift shop.

Check a Product's Safety Record After Bringing it Out of Storage

Just because a product was safe for one of your children does not mean it will be safe for the next. Keeping in mind that it can take years to launch a product recall, be sure to double-check a product's safety record on the CPSC website.

Read Product Warning Labels and Take Them Seriously

Warning labels are the closest a manufacturer will come to divulging a product's true dangers. If a label says, "Never leave a child unattended," this means you must not leave a child alone, for even a minute, while you answer a doorbell or attend to another child. Keep in mind that it is in a manufacturer's best interest to soften product warnings so that customers will not be scared away. Deciding not to buy a product is sometimes the best decision.

Read and Make Sure You Fully Understand All Product Instructions

If you do not understand a product's assembly or usage instructions, call the manufacturer and ask for clarification. Remember, instructions do not have to be tested with "real" consumers, and are often written by product engineers, not parents. If the instructions confuse you, chances are, other parents don't understand them either. If enough parents call, the manufacturer may decide to write the instructions more clearly the next time around.

Do Not Use a Secondhand Product if it Doesn't Come with Instructions

Many injuries occur when parents are given a used product without a box or the original instruction sheet. Call the manufacturer to request instructions and do not use the product until you have read and understand them.

Become an Activist

Contact your representatives in Congress and share your concerns about dangerous children's products. In 1999, Illinois passed the Children's Product Safety Act, making it illegal to sell or lease a recalled or unsafe children's product. Linda Ginzel and Boaz Keysar (www.kidsindanger.org), the parents of Danny Keysar, the toddler killed by a recalled portable crib in 1998, worked tirelessly to get this law enacted in Illinois, their home state. In July 2000, Michigan passed a similar law. In November 1999, The Daniel Keysar Memorial and Children's Consumer Product Safety Act was introduced to Congress on the federal level. The bill requires manufacturers of children's products to do a better job of notifying consumers when one of their products is recalled. You can do your part by urging your senators and representatives in Congress to support this bill. And you can lobby politicians in your state legislature and senate to pass bills similar to those enacted in Michigan and Illinois.

What to Do If Your Child is Injured

If your child is injured by a product, do not automatically assume—as many parents do—that the incident was a fluke, or that it was your fault.

Call the CPSC to Report the Injury (1–800–638–CPSC)

The agency relies on consumers to notify them of product-related injuries, and is anxious to hear from you. If your child was hurt, others may have been hurt as well. Calls such as yours can determine whether or not a dangerous product remains in stores or is recalled. Your complaint will be heard and acted upon.

Call the Manufacturer to Report the Injury

A frequent manufacturer defense is that they "didn't know" a product was hazardous because no one called to complain. Manufacturers are obligated, by law, to notify the CPSC when consumers have called them to report product defects or hazards. Your call may help the CPSC get a dangerous product off the market. Be sure to let the manufacturer know that you will also be in touch with the CPSC.

If Your Child was Injured Seriously, Get in Touch with a Product Liability Lawyer

A lawsuit can compensate you for medical bills, bring publicity to a dangerous product, and force a manufacturer to clean up its act. The trial lawyer's trade association, the Association of Trial Lawyers of America, can put you in touch with lawyers who have experience in juvenile products litigation: 1–800–424–2725, or www.atlanet.org.

CHAPTER 7

What the U.S. Government Must Do to Improve the Safety of Baby Products, and How Parents Can Help

On an October morning in 1982, twelve–year–old Mary Kellerman of Elk Grove Village, Illinois woke up at dawn with a sore throat and a runny nose. Her parents gave her an Extra-Strength Tylenol and sent her back to bed. At seven a.m. they found Mary crumpled up on the bathroom floor. A few hours later, she was dead. That same day, twenty–seven–year–old Adam Janus of Arlington Heights, Illinois collapsed in his home. The paramedics who found him tried to jump-start his heart, but Adam died in the hospital that night. His grieving brother, twenty–five–year–old Stanley, died a few hours after learning of Adam's death. Stanley's wife of three months, nineteen–year–old Theresa, died two days later. Within a few days, medical examiners and public health officials, working around the clock, zeroed in on what the seemingly inexplicable deaths had in common: All four victims had taken Extra-Strength Tylenol capsules that had been laced with cyanide. Before the week was out, the contaminated capsules killed three more Chicago-area residents, bringing the death toll to seven.[1]

Tylenol manufacturer Johnson & Johnson (J & J) wasted no time recalling twenty–two million bottles of the best-selling pain reliever. Heading an emergency strategy group at J & J's New Jersey headquarters, CEO James Burke and President David Clare devoted every waking hour to the crisis. Recognizing they needed all the help they could get to alert the public of the danger, J & J executives opened the company's doors to the media. Fifty employees were assigned to handle the consumer and press calls flooding J & J's phone lines; meanwhile, Burke flew to Washington on a company helicopter to enlist the help of the FBI and the Food and Drug Administration (FDA). J & J ran a series of sixty–second television ads on the major TV networks, urging consumers to throw out their bottles of Tylenol and promising to replace them soon with new, "tamper-resistant" containers.[2] The company's medical director, Dr. Thomas Gates, told the viewing public, "We want you to continue to trust Tylenol."[3] J & J offered a $100 million reward for information leading to the conviction of the person who poisoned the Tylenol capsules.[4]

Meanwhile, in Chicago and its suburbs, where all of the poisonings had occurred, police cruised the streets, warning residents of the Tylenol danger with bullhorns. Boy scouts knocked on doors with the news, and church groups organized telephone drives to reach people who might have missed the TV and radio alerts. Police distributed cyanide antidote kits to all Chicago-area paramedic units. School administrators sent notices home with children. Bus and subway workers helped to spread the news via public transportation.[5]

Within ten days of the first Tylenol death, the *Washington Post* ran a feature story titled: "Tylenol's Maker Shows How to Respond to Crisis." Lauding J & J for demonstrating "how a major business ought to handle a disaster," the *Post* noted that J & J responded quickly and communicated to the public that it was "candid, contrite and compassionate."[6] Seizing responsibility for the recall, the company worked hand-in-hand with the press and government agencies to enforce it. J & J readily destroyed millions of returned Tylenol bottles that were likely to have been completely safe. By the time the numbers were tallied, J & J had spent over $100 million on the recall. "From the day the deaths were linked to the poisoned Tylenol until the recall… Johnson & Johnson has succeeded in portraying itself to the public as a company willing to do what's right, regardless of cost," reported the *Post*.[7] *Newsweek* and *Fortune* magazines ran similar stories, praising J & J for acting quickly and containing the number of deaths.[8] Demonstrating an astonishing level of corporate candor, J & J president Clare told a Kansas City reporter that after learning of the first poisoning, he had reached for a bottle of Extra-Strength Tylenol and paused. "I looked at that bottle, I looked at that capsule, and I said to myself, 'I know there's nothing wrong with that.' But I hesitated."[9]

Three years after the crisis, authorities still hadn't found the person who had filled the Tylenol capsules with poison. But Tylenol had completely regained its pre-crisis market share, and J & J had survived what had been called "one of the biggest disasters in the history of the drug industry."[10]

Poisoned Extra-Strength Tylenol killed seven people.[11] The Graco Converta-Cradle killed more than a dozen.[12] The Playskool Travel-Lite portable crib killed six children, and cribs with a similar faulty design killed seven more.[13] Bath seats have killed about six dozen babies.[14] In each of these cases, the result was the same: Innocent people were killed by products that were supposed to be safe. Yet corporate response to these tragedies could not have been more different.

The Tylenol poisonings were not caused by J & J, yet the company took full responsibility for them. It is no accident that J & J was able to contain the Tylenol deaths within a few days. Infant products have caused many injuries and deaths, yet when these hazards emerge, manufacturers typically demonstrate greater concern for their corporate image than for consumer safety. Confronted with more than a dozen Converta-Cradle deaths, a Graco lawyer told "Dateline NBC": "Common sense tells you a company with Graco's reputation and social consciousness would not put a product on the market that presented a health risk to the very children that are going to use it."[15] Given such a blanket assertion of Graco's infallibility, it is no accident that infants continued to die in Graco cradles for more than two years after the product recall. After the first infant was killed by a Century Lil' Napper infant swing, a Century Products lawyer wrote to the CPSC, "Century does not believe that a safety-related defect exists with respect to the swings. Century does not believe that there exists any possible injury associated with the products when the swing occupants are properly supervised."[16] Given the company's knee-jerk "the-child-was-left-unattended" defense, it's not an accident that a fourth child was killed by the Century infant swing two years after the product was recalled.[17] When ten–month–old Tyler Anderson became the Happy Camper portable crib's first fatality, Evenflo spokesman Robert Potter said, "This play yard (portable crib) comes with a full set of instructions. The parents didn't provide those to the baby-sitter nor instruct the baby-sitter how to use it. She knew it was set up improperly and used it anyway. That is gross negligence."[18] Given this prevalent, "blame-the-baby-sitter" defense, it is no accident that at least two more children died and over one hundred were injured in Evenflo Happy Camper cribs.[19]

For decades, the infant products industry has operated with minimal government regulation. The industry has proven itself to be incapable of handling this responsibility. In an interview with the trade magazine *Home Textiles Today*, Juvenile Products Manufacturers Association (JPMA) executive vice president Bob Waller made his organization's priorities clear. One of the trade group's important roles, challenged Waller, was to stop the CPSC from zeroing in on individual manufacturers and to "shield" the industry from the agency's regulatory efforts.[20] Clearly, when this kind of anti-consumer, anti-safety attitude pervades an industry's highest echelons, it is time for the federal government to step in.

The system that has given manufacturers the green light to manufacture products that injure tens of thousands of babies each year is in dire need of an overhaul. Changes must be made at every point in this broken system. But it would be wrong for parents to assume that manufacturers will make these changes on their own, or that the government will somehow spontaneously legislate and enforce stricter safety regulations. It is time for consumers to send a clear message to manufacturers: We are watching, we are concerned, and we will act.

How Industry and the CPSC Can Improve the Safety of Baby Equipment

1. Improve the Voluntary Standard-Setting Process

In 1968, four years before the CPSC was created, President Lyndon Johnson appointed the National Commission of Product Safety (NCPS) to assess the country's need for a federal product safety agency. The commission's final report, issued in 1970, made many recommendations, none stronger than a pointed argument *against* voluntary standards, which already existed for some products. "Industry self-regulation, in particular consensus voluntary standards," summarized the NCPS report, "[is] legally unenforceable and patently inadequate."[21] In case after case, the report noted, manufacturers chose not to comply with the standards, or industry neglected to write standards for specific products; voluntary standards that did exist were simply too weak.

From the start, the CPSC intended to follow the NCPS's advice. Aiming to regulate aggressively, the agency focused on promulgating mandatory safety standards for consumer products. But with jurisdiction over 15,000 products, regulators soon discovered that this plan was neither feasible nor sufficiently pragmatic. The Consumer Product Safety Act is "heavily weighted with procedural requirements," explains former CPSC lawyer Bob Adler, "that made it virtually impossible to set standards at other than a snail's pace."[22] As a result, the CPSC has sought out less resource-intensive alternatives to mandatory standards—typically, voluntary standards written by industry.

Despite their many flaws, voluntary standards surpass mandatory standards in one crucial respect: speed. In most cases, manufacturers can write and agree upon a standard more quickly and with fewer resources than the federal government can.

In theory, voluntary standards, in conjunction with a strong recall system, are a viable alternative to mandatory standards. A voluntary standard should operate as a first check in the system. If the standard isn't stringent enough, or if a manufacturer chooses not to comply with it and subsequently markets a dangerous product, the CPSC can step in to get the hazardous product off the market and out of homes. But in the last ten years, as the industry has enjoyed explosive growth, the pace of the manufacturers' marketing departments has far exceeded that of their voluntary standard-setting committees (Chapter 2). Infant carriers, cradles, swings, and bath seats were all on the market for years before the industry even began to work on a voluntary standard for these product categories.

Instead of focusing on mandatory standards, the CPSC's resources would be better spent on improvements to the voluntary standard-setting process. "If we go to all the trouble to develop a standard at an ASTM meeting," says infant bedding manufacturer Paula Markowitz, "then we have to be proud of that standard, and we should feel confident that it is a good standard…"[23] Yet Markowitz is not proud of the crib bumper-pad standard she helped to write, complaining that it is "incomplete and doesn't make sense."

The government faces a clear goal: It must take the necessary actions to ensure that voluntary standards are a meaningful indicator of a product's safety. Given industry's history of resistance to regulation, the CPSC must be prepared to push the limits of its authority. The first step: The agency must reduce the pro-industry bias of voluntary standards by encouraging ASTM to significantly increase the participation of consumers in the standard-setting process. If the CPSC has evidence that a voluntary standard is too lax, the agency should not hesitate (as it has done in the past) to replace it with a mandatory standard. Finally, if a product hazard cannot be adequately addressed with a mandatory standard, the CPSC must act to ban the product altogether.

A. Increase Consumer Participation in Standards Meetings

The industry trade group, JPMA, oversees the (ASTM) standard-setting meetings for infant products, deciding which products will be discussed, when committees will meet, and for how long. Excluded from the planning process, consumer advocates object that the JPMA's unilateral decisions reinforce their outsider status. A few weeks before the February 2000 meetings, the JPMA sent a letter informing all attendees that the crib committee's meeting had been canceled. Why? No reason was given. In August 2000, the JPMA distributed the schedule for the October ASTM standards meetings: The crib committee meeting was again called off, as were meetings to develop voluntary standards for walkers and hook-on chairs.[24] Why? The letter didn't say.

As described in Chapter 2, the power imbalance between the manufacturers and consumers who make up ASTM voluntary standard-setting committees is glaringly obvious. ASTM insists its committees are balanced and impartial—and yet manufacturers, their testing labs, and consultants typically outnumber consumer advocates by a margin of at least four-to-one (see Appendix 2-2).[25] The two sides tend to vote as blocs, with manufacturers generally favoring the status quo or less stringent standards, and advocates fighting against the odds for new, tougher safety requirements. The result? A few hard-working individuals have taken on the full burden of protecting babies from dangerous products.

Mary Ellen Fise, general counsel for the Consumer Federation of America, is one such person. A tireless advocate for children and their parents, Fise is the last line of defense against manufacturers pushing through inadequate voluntary standards. Over the past decade, Fise has been instrumental in creating new safeguards for most infant products currently on the market. A savvy participant in the standards meetings, Fise knows how to prioritize issues, how to work behind the scenes to further her causes, when to fight and when to back down.

For years, Fise has argued that manufacturers need to do a better job of providing consumers with contact information, so that they will know whom to call with questions or complaints about a product. At a February 2000 ASTM meeting on a new voluntary standard for toddler bed rails, Safety 1st vice president Paul Ware objected to a provision requiring manufacturers to print their mailing address directly onto the product. After debating the issue with engineers for a long while, Fise suddenly broke off and focused her gaze directly across the room, on Ware. "Why do you *not* want your company's mailing address on the product?" she asked him, pushing the stoic Ware to reveal his true motives.[26] He refused to answer. Engineer Kitty Pilarz of Fisher-Price jumped in, suggesting that manufacturers be given the choice of printing either a mailing address or a toll-free telephone number on the bed rails. Fise moved quickly, turning Pilarz's comments into a formal motion that forced a vote on the issue. Fise won: Ware cast the single dissenting vote.[27]

What would have happened if Fise had missed the bed rail meeting? What if she had decided not to pursue the mailing address issue? In all likelihood, the meeting would have had a different outcome. ASTM committees are in desperate need of more advocates like Fise. Not until ASTM alleviates its pro-industry bias by encouraging more consumer input will voluntary standards be a reliable indicator of a product's safety.

ASTM is just one of hundreds of safety standard-setting organizations worldwide. ASTM's Canadian counterpart, CSA International, has developed a process that pays more than just lip service to the crucial goal of involving consumers in the development of safety standards. Parents, grandparents, and caregivers sit side-by-side with engineers at the standard-writing table, providing manufacturers with the crucial perspective of product users. As the manager of CSA's Consumer Services Program, Jeanne Bank recruits and trains ordinary citizens to become members of standard-setting committees for consumer products. Bank searches out qualified candidates by encouraging members of consumer groups to get involved and by advertising on CSA's website (www.csa-international.org). Though Bank refers to her consumer participants as "volunteers," CSA pays their out-of-pocket travel expenses, including airfare, hotels, and meals. During an orientation program, the consumer representatives become acquainted with the organization's policies and procedures, and with substantive information about their specific committee. This training gives them the confidence and knowledge they need to contribute to the standard-setting process.

Following CSA's lead, ASTM needs to take action to reduce the pro-manufacturer bias of its standards-setting process. The first step: Create a consumer program to actively recruit qualified consumer representatives and train them to be productive committee members.[28] The CPSC could be a valuable partner in such a program. Because CPSC regulators interact closely with consumer groups, they could recommend potential representatives to ASTM and assist in recruiting them. In addition, CPSC engineers, human factors psychologists, and compliance (recall) staff could lead training sessions, educating recruits on technical issues. The CPSC has a strong motive to push this initiative forward: An increase in the numbers of competent consumer negotiators at the standard-setting table can be expected to bring about better standards and safer products.

Industry Action: The voluntary standard-setting process for infant products needs to alleviate its pro-industry bias by encouraging increased consumer input. The industry, through ASTM, must develop a program that actively recruits and trains consumers to participate in standard development.

CPSC Action: The CPSC must encourage ASTM to eliminate its pro-industry bias by increasing consumer input into the standard-setting process. The agency must partner with the infant products industry to actively recruit and train consumers to take part in the process.

Consumer Action: Join consumer organizations that are working to increase consumer participation in voluntary standard-setting and share your concerns. The following groups are involved in standard-setting for baby equipment, and are a good place to start: Consumer Federation of America, Consumers Union, The Danny Foundation, and Kids in Danger (see Appendix 7–1 for contact information).

B. Encourage Industry to Hire Impartial Engineers To Test Products

Not only are consumer advocates outnumbered and overworked at ASTM voluntary standards meetings, but their questions are often dismissed by the engineers as technically naïve or ill-informed. Because the safety tests that make up the ASTM standards are created and conducted by the manufacturers themselves, they can hardly be termed unbiased. And yet, typically lacking engineering degrees, and the resources to obtain data from impartial testing labs, consumer advocates are powerless to dispute the results presented by industry engineers.[29] At the February 2000 cradle committee meeting, Mary Ellen Fise pointed out that many cradle injuries occurred when the product tipped over.[30] She questioned engineers about a potential oversight in the existing cradle standard: "What happens when you test a rolling [wheeled] cradle on different floor surfaces? Does the cradle tip over on carpeting?"[31] The engineers told her that cradle stability was unaffected by floor surface. Fise was skeptical. How could a cradle *not* tip over more easily on a carpeted surface than on linoleum? To her, it just didn't make sense. But because the engineers claimed to have conducted the necessary tests, she had no choice but to accept their answer.

Underwriter's Laboratory (UL), a suburban Chicago-based standards organization, provides an alternative model of product testing and standard-setting. Founded in 1894, UL is the largest safety testing laboratory in the world, with a reputation so strong that today, no major American retailer will sell a TV that lacks the UL seal.[32] What is the secret of UL's success? In a word, impartiality. Unlike ASTM, UL maintains its own staff of *independent* product engineers, who play an active role in standards development. Sitting side-by-side with manufacturers' engineers, government regulators, and industry consultants at the standard-writing table, UL's engineers drive the process, eliciting manufacturers' technical expertise, practical experience, and concerns before they institute a safety standard. UL engineers make the final standards decision, *not* the manufacturers. UL manager of global consumer affairs John Drengenberg, an electrical engineer employed by the organization for thirty-four years, bristles at what ASTM calls "industry standards." "UL does not develop 'industry standards,'" he says, "because industry does not have the final say."[33]

ASTM and UL differ in another important respect: the way products are tested once a standard is written. Manufacturers can hire UL engineers to test their products for compliance to a UL standard. ASTM does not employ engineers to test products, so manufacturers hire outside testing companies like ACTS Testing Labs and Intertek Testing Services to do this work (see Appendix 2–2). But these testing companies are hardly independent; their engineers show up at ASTM meetings, rarely make substantive contributions to the standard, then vote as a bloc with the manufacturers. In other words, they defer to the manufacturers to set the standard, then test the manufacturers' products for compliance to this same standard. Playing the role of "yes men," they do little to ensure the standard is a good one to begin with.

The Draco All Our Kids portable crib is one of too many baby products that was certified through the ASTM process, yet was ultimately recalled. In 1993, Draco hired Detroit Testing Laboratory to test the crib for compliance to the ASTM portable crib standard, F406–89. The testing lab's conclusion: "The sample met all the requirements of the specification."[34] Yet a few years later the crib was recalled, after it killed a child and its design was deemed faulty by CPSC engineers' tests.

Historically, UL has stayed out of the business of developing standards for infant products, allowing ASTM to capture virtually all of this market. Why? According to UL manager John Drengenberg, this industry has been particularly resistant to UL's method of independent, third-party testing. UL's recent experience with full-size cribs is a case in point. In 1993, the Danny Foundation asked UL to develop a new full-size crib standard. Executive director Jack Walsh judged the voluntary standard for cribs to be dangerously inadequate.[35] After studying the cribs CPSC had recalled, Walsh concluded that the most frequent crib hazard was posed by side slats that too easily came off, creating a strangulation hazard not addressed by either the mandatory or voluntary crib standard (see Chapter 4 for discussion of Century cribs).

Walsh convinced UL to develop a new, more stringent crib standard. "We got involved because each year fifty kids are killed in cribs," Drengenberg explains, "and it wasn't much different than the other [products] we test."[36] The final UL standard added a requirement that side slats be tested for joint strength, bending, and impact—but there were no takers. "Usually when we write a standard, people [manufacturers] come flocking," says Drengenberg. "With this [the crib standard], now, nobody wants it." Crib manufacturers apparently felt the death rate under the current voluntary standard was a figure they could live with.

In 1999, Mary Ellen Fise joined UL's Board of Directors. While she respected many aspects of UL's procedures, she saw room for improvement. Her first goal for the organization: To increase the presence of consumers in their standard-setting process. Fise designed a pilot program for UL, launched in 2000, to recruit and train consumer representatives. The UL reps will be trained in three areas: procedures (e.g., how UL committees operate, and how safety standards are written), subject matter (e.g., how do toasters work?) and how to best represent consumer interests (e.g., when to push a point in a meeting and when to give up).

The CPSC does not have the authority to dictate to industry which organization (e.g., ASTM, UL) it employs to oversee the voluntary standards-setting process. However, the agency can certainly encourage manufacturers to improve the safety of their products by hiring truly independent engineers to participate in standard-setting and product compliance testing.

CPSC Action: Encourage manufacturers to hire truly independent engineers to contribute to the standard-setting process and to test products for standards compliance.

Industry Action: Hire truly independent engineers to play an active, "devil's advocate" role in the standards-setting process, and to test products for standards compliance.

C. Increase the Involvement of Pediatricians and Human-Factors Psychologists in the Voluntary Standard-Setting Process

Parents rely on manufacturers' product boxes and instruction sheets to specify a product's age of intended use—how old a child must be to use the product, and the age at which she will outgrow it. Yet few parents have any idea of the debates and guesswork that typically surround a simple warning such as, "Intended for use by children ages 1–3 years old." At the August 1999 voluntary standard meeting for cradles and bassinets, manufacturers struggled with the seemingly straightforward issue of setting a

safe age range for these products. While most meeting participants agreed that cradles and bassinets should be used by infants
only until they are able to roll over on their own, there was little agreement on the age at which this occurs.[37] Some babies can
roll over at two months, while others don't develop the skill
until they are three or four months old. The manufacturers could
not agree on how to communicate this developmental difference
to parents as simply and directly as possible on the products' safety warning. An age-based warning such as "Intended for use by
infants 0–4 months old" could endanger the developmentally
mature infant who can roll over at two months. Fisher-Price
engineer Kitty Pilarz proposed an alternative warning statement
based on behaviors rather than age, such as: "Discontinue use
when infant is able to roll over and/or push up on her own."
Because such a warning accounts for developmental differences,
it could give parents a more accurate means of judging when a
product is appropriate for their child than a traditional age-based
warning. But behavior-based warnings could confuse the parent
who is accustomed to looking for age-based intended use instructions. The manufacturers struggled with the issue for close to an
hour, failing to reach an agreement—and delaying the safety
standard for cradles and bassinets for at least another six months,
until the next meeting.

Product engineers may be unsure about when it is no longer
safe for a baby to be put in a bassinet or cradle, but pediatricians
resolved this issue years ago. "[R]emember that infants grow
very fast," warns the American Academy of Pediatrics in the
book *Caring For Your Baby and Young Child*, "so the cradle that
is sturdy enough one month may be outgrown the next... Your
baby should graduate [from a bassinet or cradle] to a crib *around
the end of the first month or by the time he weighs ten pounds*
[emphasis added]."[38] Why were values such as "two to four
months" discussed at the cradle standards meeting, when pediatricians warn that infants should graduate from the product by

the time they are one month old? Perhaps because many parents would hesitate before spending $50—$150 for a product with a useful life of only one month.

Dr. Robert Tanz, the medical director of the Violent Injury Prevention Center at Children's Hospital in Chicago, and an associate professor for Education in the Department of Pediatrics at Northwestern University Medical School, is deeply disturbed by the baby product industry's track record, and the CPSC's history of dragging its feet on recalls. "A doctor doesn't care if a product injures children because it was 'misused' or it was defective," says Tanz, "if so many kids are hurt, there is something wrong with that product.[39]" In 1990, the American Academy of Pediatrics created a committee on Childhood Injury and Poison Prevention.[40] This group of pediatricians meets annually to share their research on infant injury. As practitioners and researchers at the forefront of this public health topic, pediatricians certainly have much to contribute to the voluntary standard-setting process.

CPSC and Industry Action: Encourage the American Academy of Pediatrics to become a member of ASTM, and to send at least one pediatrician to voluntary standard-setting meetings for children's products.

Consumer Action: Share your concern about product-related children's injuries and deaths with your pediatrician. If she is uninformed about the industry's poor track record on safety, tell her what you have learned from this book and encourage her to contact the American Academy of Pediatrics and the CPSC to learn more.

As experts on how children and their parents use products in the "real world," human factors psychologists also have much to contribute to the standard-setting process. Too often, the CPSC and manufacturers solicit these experts' advice only after children have been injured by a product, rather than beforehand, as a preventative measure. While a couple of human factors experts are members of ASTM infant products committees, they rarely attend the meetings. No outside party pays for their travel expenses, and as private-practice consultants, few of them can afford to leave their businesses for four days, twice a year. Typically, they send written comments and objections to proposed standards, which are discussed by the group. Because the psychologists aren't present to explain or defend their positions, it is easy for the manufacturers to dismiss them. In January 2000, Shelley Waters Deppa, president of Safety Behavior Analysis, Inc., a Maryland-based human factors consulting firm, sent a three–page letter to the ASTM infant swing committee, objecting to several aspects of the proposed new infant swing standard: the restraint system, the size of leg openings, and the warning statement. After discussing each of Deppa's points, the group accepted a modified version of her warning-statement proposal (see Chapter 2).[41] However, the product engineers dismissed her concerns about the restraint system and leg opening as "not persuasive," as recorded on the official meeting notes.[42] If Deppa had attended the meeting, she might have been able to convince the engineers of the importance of more stringent safety design precautions for infant swings.

The CPSC had been tracking infant-swing injury and death statistics for years before manufacturers began to work on a voluntary safety standard. After the Century Lil' Napper swing's restraint harness strangled a child in 1993, then nearly strangled another in 1996 (the baby had to be airlifted to a children's hospital, where he underwent a tracheotomy and spent eleven days in intensive care), the agency launched an investigation of the product to determine whether it should be recalled.[43] CPSC human factors specialist Catherine Sedney assessed the strangulation risk posed by the swing's restraint system. Her conclusion: The risk of strangulation increased the longer the swing was used.[44] As swings got older, parents and caregivers were more likely to have misplaced the product instructions, causing them to improperly replace the restraint harness after cleaning. When installed incorrectly, the harness could strangle a child. The CPSC didn't convince Century to recall the swing "voluntarily" until another child was killed, in 1997.[45]

Sedney's analysis has strong implications for ASTM's voluntary infant swing standard. If she (or one of her colleagues in the private sector) had attended the standards meetings in 1999 or 2000, she may have been able to convince the group to incorporate what she had learned about infant swings from the Century investigation into the industry-wide standard. Perhaps she could have convinced manufacturers to adopt an extra set of warnings to guard against misassembly, or she could have reinforced Deppa's views on leg openings. Clearly, the involvement of human-factors experts would go a long way toward improving the safety of infant products.

Industry Action: Each time a new or substantially revised ASTM voluntary standard is developed, it should include an analysis by at least one independent, private-practice human factors specialist (who specializes in infant products and is unaffiliated with any manufacturer). JPMA should commission this report, and pay the travel expenses for the expert to present his/her analysis at the meetings.

CPSC Action: Each time a new or substantially revised ASTM voluntary standard is developed, it should include an analysis by a CPSC human factors specialist (with expertise in infant products). The agency should require this person to participate in the standard-setting meetings.

D. Establish Clear Time Frames and Benchmarks for Voluntary Standards

While industry may write its voluntary standards in less time than the CPSC writes its mandatory ones, this does not mean the process is a swift one. Most voluntary standards are under development for two to five years. "[T]hat the private sector takes a long time to develop standards is simply [because] it is not a full-time job for the people involved," explained Richard Goodemote, Sears' testing and development director, in 1975 Senate hearings. Goodemote's words hold true today. Manufacturer stonewalling further slows the process. "Whoever comes to the meeting," says manufacturer Paula Markowitz of her experience on the crib bumper-pad standard committee, "we have to discuss their extraneous points forever. You can be a professional saboteur at these meetings to keep anything from ever getting done."[46]

Certain conflicts surface time and again, such as the repeated wrangling over warning statements (Chapter 2) and the question of whether manufacturers should be required to stamp their contact information on products. Each time the issue arises, manufacturers and consumer advocates engage in a lengthy debate. While Mary Ellen Fise was able to resolve the issue of manufacturer contact information within the bed-rail committee, she has to fight this battle for every product, and has been doing so for years. Often, these discussions end with the industry engineer who is chairing the committee relegating the issue to the "memory sheet," to be dealt with at the next meeting. In November 1997, the CPSC asked the bath seat committee to add a suction-cup performance requirement to the slowly developing bath seat standard.[47] "No decision was made on whether there should be a performance requirement for suction cups," read the CPSC's meeting notes, "The issue was put on the memory sheet."[48] At the next meeting, in April 1998, CPSC engineer John Preston recommended that the bath seat standard require two suction cup-related components: A statement warning parents not to use the product if a suction cup comes off, and a performance test to address how strongly the cups attach to the product. Again, manufacturers' engineers relegated the suction-cup issue to the memory sheet. It languished there until February 1999, when the bath seat committee finally agreed to discuss Preston's proposal. At this point, the bath seat committee had been working on a standard for five years. During this time, forty–five children drowned while using bath seats. The descriptions of these bath seat deaths, found in the CPSC files, suggest the consequences of the manufacturers' decision to stall correction of a known product hazard:

> Toppled over, floating face down; 4 suction cups but only 3 present.

> Still in seat, face in water, seat upright; 4 suction cups but may have been missing.

> Tipped over, submerged; 4 suction cups but only 2 present.[49]

In July 2000, fed up with the bath seat committee's inaction, consumer advocates took matters into their own hands. Led by Mary Ellen Fise, representing the Consumer Federation of America, nine consumer groups (including The Drowning Prevention Foundation, Kids In Danger, California Coalition for Children's Safety, and The Danny Foundation) filed a formal petition with the CPSC, asking the agency to ban the product altogether. Motivated by the increasing bath seat death toll, the petition voiced strong concerns about the adequacy of the new bath seat standard, including "the efficacy of draft requirements for suction cups."[50]

While some product engineers have a sincere desire to move voluntary standards forward, others have been allowed to abuse the process for their own means, putting babies at unnecessary risk. No one understands this more clearly than the dozens of parents whose infants have drowned while using bath seats. The CPSC needs to put an end to this dangerous and disruptive behavior by ensuring that voluntary standards are completed in a reasonable amount of time.

CPSC Action: The CPSC should set a time limit on the voluntary standard-setting process for infant products. By analyzing its product-related injury and death data, the agency will be able to set urgency-based deadlines for each product. In no circumstance, however, should a standard be in development for more than two years. If industry exceeds the CPSC's deadline, the agency should begin the mandatory standard-setting process.

Consumer Action: Consumers can speed up the process by refusing to buy baby products that do not comply with an ASTM voluntary standard. Manufacturers have been "working on" voluntary standards for the following products for years: bassinets, cradles, portable bed rails, soft-frame infant carriers, infant swings, and baby bouncers. Write to JPMA, the industry trade group, to express your disapproval of manufacturer stonewalling and your decision to boycott these products until meaningful industry-wide safety standards are in place (see Appendix 7–1 for contact information).

Each year, tens of thousands of children are rushed to hospital emergency rooms for product-related injuries. Some juvenile products are associated with more injuries than others. In 1998, strollers topped the list, followed by walkers and baby carriers (see Table 7–1). At the August 1999 voluntary standards meeting for strollers, CPSC engineer John Preston revealed that between January 1999 and July 1999, the agency's "emerging hazards" staff had identified a substantial increase in the number of consumer complaints about problems and hazards associated with baby strollers.[51] In just one year, according to CPSC records, stroller complaints had almost doubled.

That strollers injure more than fifteen thousand children each year, and walkers injure thirteen thousand, should be unacceptable. The CPSC must do a better job of heading off such injury epidemics by encouraging the industry to write more stringent voluntary standards and by promulgating mandatory standards for products the manufacturers have failed to make safe.

CPSC Action: The CPSC should set a benchmark limit (e.g., one thousand injuries per year) on the number of injuries that can occur before the agency formally asks the industry to improve a voluntary standard, initiates the mandatory standard-setting process, or moves to ban a product altogether.

2. Improve the Product Recall System

"The best insurance against a recall is a quality product," state marketing professors Craig Smith of Georgetown University and John Quelch of the Harvard Business School.[52] Too many infant products manufacturers ignore this sound advice. Lax voluntary standards, coupled with the difficulty of promulgating mandatory standards, heighten the need for a strong, effective recall system. But by any measure, CPSC's current system simply doesn't work. Recall news too often fails to reach consumers, leaving hazardous products in circulation, sometimes for years. Manufacturers water down press release language, often trivializing serious product dangers. Rarely paying to advertise recalls, manufacturers routinely foist responsibility for disseminating the news onto the press. And manufacturers dismiss as impractical the CPSC's efforts to register frequently recalled children's products.

"[E]vidence suggests that recalls frequently are not taken seriously [by manufacturers]," report professors Craig and Quelch. "Many companies seem satisfied with low recall

Table 7–1: Hospital Emergency Room Visits Related to Baby Products, 1998	
Product	# of emergency room visits
Strollers	15,032
Walkers	13,146
Cribs	10,735
Baby carriers	8,205
High chairs	8,111
Crib extensions/Bed rails	2,207
Infant swings	1,254

response rates...which, while meeting the letter of the law, may leave many consumers dissatisfied if not endangered."[53] Clearly, it is time for the CPSC to flex its regulatory muscle and take control.

The CPSC estimates the average recall costs an infant products manufacturer, at most, about a couple of hundred thousand dollars.[54] Cosco estimated that its toddler bed recall, which included replacement kits, administrative costs, and "net loss in customer returns," was $550,000.[55] Johnson & Johnson, by comparison, spent over $100 million on the Tylenol recall.[56] In 1990, when Perrier discovered high levels of benzene in its bottled water, the company recalled 160 million bottles, at a direct expense of over $30 million.[57] It's no accident that the Tylenol and Perrier recalls were effective, while most infant product recalls are dismal failures. A company should view a recall as a catastrophic event, not as a trivial, tax-deductible cost of doing business. Only when recalls become *prohibitively* expensive will manufacturers become willing to commit more resources to product testing.

A. Write Stronger, Clearer Press Releases

In recent years, current CPSC Chairman Ann Brown has recalled over two hundred consumer products a year.[58] But any crackdown on dangerous products will fail to have an impact if the media doesn't report the news. CPSC public affairs officer Russ Rader claims that journalists too often fail to give prominent play to recalls.[59] But news directors' desks overflow with unsolicited "news"—press releases and reports from corporations, non-profits, and government agencies alike, all angling for a precious column inch or a brief mention on local TV. Lacking a clear indication of the product's hazard and written in muddled language (the result of negotiations with manufacturers' lawyers), the CPSC's press releases are too easily lost in the shuffle.

An examination of the press releases churned out by the CPSC in a single month, June 1998, clarifies the agency's own contribution to this information overload. Responding to Danny Keysar's death, the CPSC issued a press release urging parents to stop using the Playskool Travel-Lite crib, which had been recalled five years earlier. As shown in Appendix 7–2, the agency issued eighteen other press releases that same month.

Clearly, some of these press releases were more newsworthy than others. And the fact that another child was killed by a Playskool Travel-Lite a few weeks after this latest release was issued offers indisputable evidence that the news didn't reach everyone who needed to hear it. Internally, the CPSC does categorize recalls by their urgency, sorting them according to the following system:

Class A Hazard: when a risk of death or grievous injury or illness is likely or very likely, or when serious injury or illness is very likely.

Class B Hazard: when a risk of death or grievous injury or illness is not likely to occur, but is possible, or when serious injury or illness is likely, or moderate injury or illness is very likely.

Class C Hazard: when a risk or serious injury or illness is not likely, but is possible, or when moderate injury or illness is not necessarily likely, but is possible.[60]

The CPSC's hazard rating system is an internal guide "for selecting the level and intensity of corrective action."[61] Class A recalls warrant the "highest level of attention," and call for a manufacturer to take the most aggressive actions to notify consumers. The Playskool Travel-Lite crib, which killed three children before the recall (and three after), was designated a "Class A" recall; the Baby Björn carrier, which was associated with at least a half–dozen head injuries before it was recalled, was categorized as "Class B."[62]

Why doesn't the CPSC publicize these hazard levels in its recall notices? The agency's fear, say current and former CPSC employees, is that the media would not consider B– and C–level hazards newsworthy.[63] Given the agency's complaints that the press rarely gives prominent play to *any* recall, this logic makes little sense.[64] What does the agency have to lose? The more significant impediment, and one that regulators are loath to articulate, is that *manufacturers* do not want the public to know when a recall has been rated Class A, the most serious hazard. "What would eventually happen is that industry would start fighting recalls and the CPSC would get fewer voluntary agreements to recall," says former CPSC lawyer Bob Adler.[65] And the agency is hesitant to take any action that would *decrease* the number of recalls. In other words, recalls are not publicly rated according to hazard level because manufacturers want to keep this information a secret. The CPSC could respond to this bullying by suing to get a recall, or even by suing to include the hazard level on a recall press release. The agency has a strong incentive to avoid litigation, an activity that consumes vast resources.

Consumer advocates have proposed remedies to this dilemma, but the CPSC has hesitated to heed their advice. "The solution is to have strong language in the press release that cannot be negotiated away," said Adler, "[language] that will be strong and will tell people very clearly that the product is dangerous. There must be some 'magic words' in the press release, so the public will know what's going on."[66] Mary Ellen Fise of the Consumer Federation of America suggests, point blank: "Press releases should tell people the consequences if they continue to use the [recalled] product, and they should very clearly say, 'using this product may result in death.'"[67]

CPSC Action: The CPSC must develop a boilerplate recall notification press release. When a product is recalled, a manufacturer will be unable to negotiate away language conveying the seriousness of a product's hazards. In addition, all recall notification press releases must include the CPSC's hazard-level rating.

Consumer Action: If you read a recall press release and think the language is watered down, or you don't completely understand the hazard, call the manufacturer and the CPSC to complain about it.

B. Disseminate Recall News through Product Registration and Paid Advertising

Manufacturers routinely argue that there is little they can do to increase consumer response to infant product recalls from current levels of 10–30 percent. These corporations certainly don't lack the resources to increase response rates—what they lack is the motivation to do so. Response rates are low for many reasons, none as troublesome as manufacturers' deep-trenched refusal to take two crucial actions: to maintain adequate customer databases so that product owners can be notified quickly and directly when a product is recalled, and to pay to place recall notifications in the same media they use to advertise their products.

For decades, the CPSC has been exploring the idea of requiring manufacturers to enclose registration cards in frequently recalled children's products such as high chairs, portable cribs, and infant swings.[68] "[T]o be most effective, based on our historical data, we must get into homes directly, right to the owner of the recalled product," regulator of recalls and compliance Marc Schoem told a roomful of manufacturers and consumer advocates at the agency's 1999 Recall Effectiveness Forum. "We must directly notify the consumers of the problem and offer them a remedy... that is quick and not burdensome."[69] Product registration cards are a simple and inexpensive solution to this problem.

In March 1993, the National Highway Traffic Safety Administration (NHTSA) passed a rule that requires manufacturers to attach a product registration card to every new car seat.[70] The NHTSA rule mandates the size of the card, the language used, and the information requested from consumers. It is time for the CPSC to follow NHTSA's actions and make registration cards mandatory, not optional.[71]

CPSC Action: If manufacturers refuse to institute a mandatory product registration system on their own, the CPSC should use its regulatory authority to force them to do so. Manufacturers must be required to enclose, with all durable baby equipment (e.g., portable cribs, infant swings, high chairs), a postage-paid safety registration card imprinted with the product's model number.

Industry Action: To ensure consumer compliance with the product registration program, the industry trade group, JPMA, should voluntarily undertake a consumer education program that explains the importance of filling out and returning registration cards.

Consumer Action: When you buy a car seat, be sure to fill out and return the safety registration card that comes with

it. For all other infant products, fill out and mail the warranty card (leave the marketing information blank if you
want to)—this is the best chance you have to be notified
directly if the product is recalled. If you buy a product that
does not come with a safety registration or warranty card,
make one yourself (see sample form in Appendix 7–3).
Add a warning to the card: Tell the manufacturer that if
you are not notified of a product recall, you will take legal
action against the company if your child is injured (see
Appendix 7–4 for manufacturer contact information).

"The Commission encourages companies to be creative in
developing ways to reach owners of recalled products and motivate them to respond," advises the CPSC's *Recall Compliance
Handbook*.[72] Among the suggested notification techniques: paid
television and/or radio notices, paid notices in national newspapers and/or magazines targeted toward users of the product,
and paid notices in the local or regional media. Yet CPSC staff,
when pressed to generate examples of manufacturers that followed any of the agency's paid notification recommendations,
grope for recent examples. One regulator came up with only
two: Lane Furniture advertised a 1996 recall of its cedar chests,
and Fisher-Price advertised its 1998 Power Wheels recall.[73]
"The manufacturers come back to us and say they never advertised the product originally, so they shouldn't have to advertise
a recall," the regulator explained. "We don't want to have to use
our time and resources to sue to get them to advertise the recall,
if we can get them to do other things [such as producing video
news releases]."[74]

Historically, the CPSC has not always caved in when manufacturers balk at spending real money on recall notification
tactics. In 1978, when consumer response to a Bassett Furniture
crib recall was not what the CPSC thought it should be, the
agency cajoled the company into undertaking more aggressive
measures. Bassett took out paid ads in magazines targeted to the

parents of newborns, mailed notices to every U.S. household known to have a child under twenty–one months old, and sent warning posters to every U.S. pediatric clinic and maternity ward. The result: Consumer response rose from twenty–five percent to forty–five percent for one crib model, and from seventy–seven percent to eighty–six percent for the other.[75]

The time has come for the CPSC to prevail upon manufacturers to undertake *effective* recall notification techniques. It is unconscionable that the agency should be forced to decide whether or not to sue a company for failing to disseminate news of a product that has killed multiple children and can be expected to strike again.

CPSC Action: For Class A Hazard recalls, the CPSC must require manufacturers to undertake the following effective recall notification techniques: direct notification of consumers and paid recall notifications in targeted outlets such as parenting magazines.

CPSC Action: The CPSC should publicize recall effectiveness rates on its website, so that consumers will be able to find out which companies make a concerted effort to get recalled products out of circulation and which companies are satisfied with low consumer response rates.

C. *Improve the Recall Remedies Offered to Consumers*

When the Playskool Travel-Lite portable crib was recalled after killing three children, manufacturer Kolcraft offered consumers a $60 refund, though the product's retail price had been $69–89.[76] After three more children were killed, Kolcraft finally doubled the refund to $120.[77] Given the high level of risk posed by this product, why didn't the company offer the "bounty" from the start? Why did the manufacturers of cribs with the same faulty design—Baby Trend, Century, and Evenflo—offer "free repair kits" in lieu of a product replacement or refund?[78]

Because to do so would have been expensive, and because they knew the CPSC would not force them to.

Graco's remedy for its recall of seven million infant swings in April 2000 is a textbook case of corporate penny-pinching. Revealing that six children had died in the swings and nine others had suffered bone fractures and concussions, the recall press release instructed swing owners to call a toll-free number to request not a refund or a safer replacement swing, but a "free safety restraint."[79] If a parent heard the recall reported on the nightly news, and subsequently called the number, she would have been met with a pre-recorded message that instructed her to leave her name and address and told her that a "free upgrade kit" would arrive at her house within two to four weeks. What was the parent supposed to do with her swing while waiting for the repair kit? Could she be sure the repair kit would eliminate the swing's fatal hazard? The pre-recorded message didn't answer these questions, and the parent was given no opportunity to ask them of a Graco customer-service representative. The recording did state clearly that Graco would send only one kit to an address—so daycare centers and babysitters who owned more than one Graco swing had to jump through an extra hoop: The message instructed them to call a different number to obtain their "free swing upgrades." The babysitter who called the second number would have been instructed by yet another pre-recorded message to leave her name and telephone number, and would have been assured that someone would return her call "as soon as possible."[80] "As soon as possible" turned out to be about three weeks.

Receiving a small package from Graco about a month after her initial call, the typical parent was likely to have been both disappointed and confused by its contents. The repair kit—intended to keep a child from being *killed* by the swing—was nothing more than a flimsy strap and six small pieces of plastic. The accompanying instruction sheet was certain to test the reading skills, technical comprehension, and patience of even the most diligent parent. Cluttered with a series of busy diagrams, it was divided into sections titled: "To Remove Your Old Waist Belt," "To Attach the New 3-Point Restraint," "To Attach the Buckle," and "To Modify the Seat Pad."[81] Struggling to repair the hazardous swing, more than one parent is likely to have resented paying $70–120 for a product that had killed children and had been deemed unsafe by the federal government.

A partial refund or a repair kit such as Graco's is an insufficient remedy for a product categorized as a Class A hazard. When a product poses a great threat to public safety, the first priority of the manufacturer and the CPSC should be to get it out of homes and daycare centers. An effective means of signaling the seriousness of a recall to consumers is to offer a refund significantly higher than the original retail price.

CPSC Action: The remedy for a Class A recall should be a "bounty"—a cash refund at least double the product's retail price.

Consumer Action: If you think a recall remedy has been slow to arrive, is confusing, or insufficient, call the manufacturer and the CPSC to complain. Be clear about what problems you are having (e.g., can't get through to a manufacturer's hotline, don't understand repair kit instructions, etc). Tell the CPSC how much you paid for the product and explain why you don't think what is being offered is good enough.

The CPSC can sue a manufacturer for failing to cooperate with any aspect of the recall process: the remedy offered consumers, the press release wording, or consumer notification techniques. However, the agency rarely exercises this authority.[82] Once the agency deems a product hazardous, the CPSC's foremost priority is to act quickly. The faster a recall is in place, the faster dangerous products will be removed from store shelves. Suing a manufacturer over recall terms slows down this process. Sitting at the bargaining table, manufacturers are well aware of the CPSC's desire to get the recall in motion, and they use this knowledge to their advantage.

In 1980, an internal CPSC recall task force criticized the agency for its hesitancy to litigate when recall negotiations break down. While the task force was addressing the larger issue of whether or not a company was willing to recall a product at all, the task force's lessons apply to all forms of manufacturer resistance to recall effectiveness. "The Task Force identifies several long-term costs associated with the historic infrequency of [such] litigation," reads the final report. "[W]e conclude that if the Commission wants to utilize its recall authority routinely as a formal regulatory response to product hazards... and to make clear that it will seek formal remedies if negotiations break down, it would appear that some amount of litigation... is necessary."[83] Despite short-term costs, it would be in the CPSC's long-term best interest to occasionally sue a manufacturer whose actions—or, more typically, inaction—suggest a blatant disregard for the safety of its customers.

Twenty years later, the same issues are at stake. As long as the CPSC continues to back down from its threats to sue, manufacturers will continue to scoff at the agency's bargaining table demands. To achieve credibility and clout, the agency must exercise its authority to sue to improve recall response rates.

CPSC Action: To increase its clout during recall negotiations, the CPSC, as suggested by its own task force in 1980, must push recall authority to its limits and increase its litigation of recalcitrant manufacturers.

What Congress Must Do to Increase the Safety of Juvenile Products

While there is much the CPSC can achieve by pushing its authority to its limits, some needed changes extend beyond the boundaries imposed by the Consumer Product Safety Act. For this reason, Congress must intervene to expand the CPSC's regulatory authority. Specifically, Congress must help the CPSC boost the number of manufacturers' hazardous products self-reports, give the agency the right to release manufacturer-specific safety information to the public, put an end to secret settlements that jeopardize public safety, and increase the agency's budget to a level that allows it to stand up to deep-pocketed corporations. Consumers can help the CPSC fight for these important changes by telling their congressional representatives: We are counting on you to reign in corporations whose products injure our children.

1. Congress Must Act to Increase Industry's Self-Reporting of Product Hazards

Disseminating recall news to consumers is a tough challenge for the CPSC. Even more problematic, however, is finding hazardous products in the first place. Section 15 of the Consumer Product Safety Act requires companies to self-report product hazards, and yet many children's products companies completely ignore the statute. Since 1996, *seventy–five percent* of the hazardous children's products recalled by the CPSC were not reported to the agency by their manufacturers; the CPSC found out about the incidents from consumers or through their own surveillance methods.[84] This is true, despite the fact that consumers are significantly more likely to report faulty products to the manufacturer than to the CPSC. With more than two million companies manufacturing or selling consumer products in the United States, it has been estimated that the CPSC should receive at least two thousand hazard self-reports each year.[85] In 1999, the agency received a mere 210 self-reports.[86]

The case of the Century Products Travel-Lite stroller is a graphic illustration of the CPSC's manufacturer scofflaw dilemma (see Chapter 4). In 1997, the CPSC sued Century for failing to report 560 consumer complaints about the stroller, including forty–nine reported injuries. The company quietly paid a fine, but refused to admit wrongdoing; Century claimed it had no duty to report the 560 incidents to the CPSC.[87] How could Century Products have so grossly "misinterpreted" the CPSC's self-reporting requirement? Michael Lemov, an attorney specializing in product-safety and trade regulation law, argues that the wording of Section 15 of the Consumer Product Safety Act is to blame. In short, the section requires manufacturers, distributors, and retailers to report to the CPSC any "substantial product hazard," which is defined obliquely as "a product defect which (because of the pattern of defect, the number of defective products distributed in commerce, the severity of the risk, or otherwise) creates a substantial risk of injury to the public."[88]

"While some legal scholars may have a grasp of what these words mean," complains Lemov, "it's not clear what 'substantial risk of injury' means to a busy executive attempting to both market a product and comply with safety laws."[89] It is difficult to fathom how any "busy executive" at Century Products concluded that 560 reports of defective strollers—which included failing locks and seat belts—did *not* create a substantial risk of injury to the public. Such decisions add fuel to the argument that the typical infant products executive is busier with marketing than with protecting consumer safety.

The CPSC routinely confronts another drawback of Section 15 self-reports: Most of the hazards reported by manufacturers are "B–" or "C–level" hazards, rather than the most serious level "A's."[90] The CPSC must track down these most dangerous products on its own. Seeking to reel in the most serious product defects, consumer groups pushed for an amendment to the CPSA—and scored a partial victory. The new reporting requirement, added as Section 37 to the CPSA in 1994, stipulates that companies must report hazards if:

A product is the subject of at least three lawsuits filed in federal or state court,

Each lawsuit alleges that the product was involved in a death or grievous bodily injury (i.e., mutilation or disfigurement, dismemberment or amputation, the loss of important bodily functions, injuries that require extended hospitalization),

Within a two–year period, each of the three lawsuits ends with an out-of-court settlement or in a court judgment that favors the plaintiff (victim).[91]

The intent of Section 37 was to provide an additional, yet objective, definition of when a manufacturer has a duty to report a product hazard to the CPSC. However, consumer advocates claim that Congress watered down the proposed amendment to such a degree that its usefulness was undermined from the start. Limited by the narrow criteria that must be met before a manufacturer's reporting obligation is triggered, Section 37 has done little to increase company self-reports. Why? First, the amendment overlooks the fact that manufacturers sometimes settle with victims' families without any court intervention; such cases would not apply to the lawsuit or settlement "count." Similarly, Section 37 ignores those lawsuits that are not settled or disposed of by a court judgment within the relatively short two–year time frame.

Perhaps the Section 37 loophole that most undermines child safety is the stipulation that a product be implicated in death or grievous injury. Many infant products are hazardous to children, but do not meet Section 37's stringent definition of "grievous injury." The Century Travel-Lite stroller was clearly hazardous—it folded unexpectedly with the child in it, and its restraint buckles unlatched at least fourteen–hundred times by the time the CPSC issued the recall press release—yet the seventy–eight reported injuries were "merely" bumps and bruises.[92]

Seeking to strengthen Section 37, the Consumer Federation of America supports a proposal that would amend the CPSA's

Section 15 self-reporting requirement. The proposed change would require a manufacturer to report a product to the CPSC when, within a two–year period, it is the subject of *any combination* of three civil actions filed, settlements in civil actions, settlements of claims where a civil action was not filed, or court judgments that involve an allegation *of death or injury*. Under this change, manufacturers would not have to determine whether or not the injury was a "grievous" one, the reports to CPSC would be required within twenty days instead of thirty, and companies would not have to wait for a final settlement or court judgment to be rendered.[93] The changes would both broaden and clarify the situations in which a company has an obligation to report a product hazard, and would produce reports in a more timely manner.

Congressional Action: Congress must strengthen Section 15 of the Consumer Product Safety Act with an amendment that eliminates the subjectivity surrounding whether or not a manufacturer has an obligation to report a product hazard to the CPSC.

Another way to increase the number of Section 15 self-reports is to increase the penalties levied on companies that are caught not reporting. Currently, when the CPSC files suit against a company for violating Section 15, its enforcement tools are severely limited. As of 2000, the maximum fine the agency was able to impose on a non-reporting company was $1.65 million.[94] In May 2000, First Lady Hillary Clinton and CPSC Chairman Ann Brown held a joint White House press conference to announce legislation aimed at cracking down on recalcitrant companies. "CPSC has to do its own detective work to find out about the problem products and seek recalls," read the press release announcing the legislation. "Increasing CPSC's authority and expanding its product injury reporting network will mean that dangerous products are recalled faster."[95] The most significant aspect of this legislation: eliminating the current $1.65 million cap on the maximum fine the CPSC can impose on a company. Such a provision could make it prohibitively expensive for companies to break the self-report law.

Congressional Action: Congress must approve the proposed legislation that eliminates the $1.65 million civil penalty cap on companies that violate Section 15 of the CPSA by failing to self-report hazardous products.

Consumer Action: Contact your representatives in Congress and tell them you support legislation that eliminates the $1.65 million civil penalty cap for violation of Section 15 of the Consumer Product Safety Act.

Eliminating the civil penalty cap is just one step needed to motivate companies to report product hazards. Of the twenty–two fines imposed by the CPSC for failing to self-report between January 1996 and August 2000, only one penalty exceeded $1 million; Central Sprinkler was levied $1.3 million for failing to report seventeen fires that resulted in four injuries.[96] Seventeen of the twenty–two fines (seventy–seven percent) were for $300,000 or less—hardly a punitive damage for companies like Dorel Industries, Cosco's $425 million parent company, or $3 billion Hasbro. Why are the fines so light? Lacking the resources to endure long, drawn-out litigation, the CPSC's incentive is to settle each case quickly. Manufacturers know this as they sit across from the CPSC's lawyers at the settlement bargaining table.

As the Cosco toddler bed and guardrail case demonstrated (Chapter 4), the CPSC not only trades away fines, but future civil penalties as well. The CPSC and Department of Justice had a strong case against Cosco's failure to report dozens of toddler bed and guardrail entrapments. Yet, even in this most egregious of cases, the CPSC was unable to bring the full force of its regulations down on the company and levy its maximum fine. The company agreed to pay $725,000 over a period of five years, and in return the CPSC promised not to pursue future penalties for nine other Cosco products, including some that were later recalled.[97] The agency struck an even more benign deal with Century Products, which agreed to pay $225,000 for withholding information on its hazardous strollers and cribs.[98]

Congress must step in to level the playing field between the CPSC and the companies it regulates. One simple solution would be to increase the agency's annual legal budget to *meaningful* levels, giving it the resources it needs to see these suits through to trial. In addition, Congress should add an amendment to the CPSA that prohibits the agency from trading away future penalties in its settlements. Likewise, to strengthen the prohibitive effect of settlement payments, damages should be paid up front, in one lump sum.

Congressional Action: Congress should significantly increase the CPSC's legal budget, so that the agency will have the resources it needs to follow through on its threats to sue manufacturers.

Congressional Action: The CPSC should be prohibited from trading away future penalties in Section 15 settlements.

Congressional Action: The CPSC should be prohibited from allowing settlements to be paid over time. Payments should be made in one lump sum, to signal to stockholders and financial analysts that the company has been fined for allegedly breaking the law.

2. Congress Must Allow the CPSC to Release Product-Specific Safety Information

Even the harshest critics of government regulation of business acknowledge that perfectly functioning markets work only when consumers are fully aware of the risks their choices entail.[99] Simply stated, the safest portable crib on the market should cost more than a shoddily constructed one, and this choice should be clear to consumers. But today, the market for infant equipment is anything but "perfectly functioning." Why? Because Section 6(b) of the Consumer Product Safety Act requires the federal government, at the insistence of industry, to withhold safety information from the public. When it comes to buying baby equipment, parents have no way of knowing the risks their purchase decisions entail.

A 1980 *University of Pennsylvania Law Review* article articulated industry's rationale for 6(b) censorship:

> The CPSA requires manufacturers to submit large quantities of commercial data to the CPSC. The interest of these manufacturers in preventing FOIA disclosure is representative of the concerns of many American businessmen. These suppliers of data fear the consequences of release of this information to the public, particularly when the persons seeking such information under the FOIA are competitors, potential litigants, the press, labor organizations, or consumer groups.[100]

The article draws the battle lines: Nosy, litigious consumers and their advocates are the enemies of industry. This distrustful attitude is evident to anyone who has received, in response to a CPSC FOIA request, files purged of "confidential" documents by manufacturers' lawyers.

"At the heart of the controversy over [company-specific information] disclosures is the potential for unwarranted adverse publicity," argued the 1980 *University of Pennsylvania Law Review* article.[101] But what corporate actions *do* warrant "adverse publicity"? Suppose that in one year, the CPSC discovers that four infants had died while sleeping in their Graco swinging cradles. In all four cases, the medical examiners listed the cause of death as SIDS, not suffocation caused by the crib.

Should a parent who calls the CPSC for information on cradles be privy to the medical examiners' information? Should a journalist working on a cradle story for *Childbirth* magazine have access to this data? Suppose that a year later, the CPSC learns that eight more infants have died of unexplained causes in their Graco cradles. How many infants must die before Graco *deserves* the negative publicity that may surround the company when news of this safety hazard reaches the public?

Adverse publicity is unwarranted only when those who release it do not take the steps to ensure that it is accurate. In 1972, when the FTC publicly disparaged Zerex, the agency had not ensured its information was accurate. DuPont had every right to argue it had been the target of unwarranted adverse publicity. But thirty years later, because of the FTC's single capricious act, infants and children are being injured and killed because manufacturers argue they are *entitled* to keep safety information from the public. When the government is required to be an accomplice in corporate censorship that results in injured and dead children, the system has gone terribly awry.

CPSC regulators take great measures to ensure the fairness and accuracy of their data. They systematically gather injury information from a national sample of hospital emergency rooms. Their hotline logs consumer complaints. Their field staff conduct in-depth investigations of reported incidents. Medical examiners, coroners, and police departments throughout the country notify the agency of product-related deaths. When the agency is determining whether or not a product is hazardous enough to recall, the staff takes months, sometimes years, to scrupulously build its case. Of course, at times a specific piece of this information, such as a consumer complaint, will turn out to have been capricious or unwarranted. Collectively, however, the agency's investigations have proven to be quite capable of uncovering accurate patterns of injury and death.

The debate over Section 6(b) boils down to a fundamental

choice: Do manufacturers have the right to censor product safety information, or do consumers have the right to know the risks involved in the products they buy? It is time for Congress to opt for the latter, and do away with 6(b).

Congressional Action: Congress must repeal Section 6(b) of the Consumer Product Safety Act.

Consumer Action: Contact your representatives in Congress and tell them you are concerned that manufacturers require the CPSC to censor product safety information from parents. Tell them you want Section 6(b) of the Consumer Product Safety Act repealed.

3. Congress Must Outlaw Secret Settlements That Undermine Child Safety

Secret settlements, signed routinely by the parents of children who have been injured or killed by a faulty product, are little more than hush money: A wealthy corporation offers a large sum of money in return for vows of silence about its wrongdoing and the product's hazard. When another child is injured or killed by the same product, his parents are unaware that their child is the second, third—or in the case of the portable cribs, the thirteenth—victim. "The public policy issues raised by court secrecy are national in scope," stated the Association of Trial Lawyers of America and the Society of Professional Journalists in a 1990 report. "[C]ourt-approved secrecy agreements and protective orders can keep the facts about hazardous products and practices from the public. They can shield secrets that can be deadly," the report concluded.[102]

In 1990, the Supreme Court of Texas amended the Texas Rules of Civil Procedure to set clear standards that a company must meet before requiring a settlement agreement to be kept secret. The most important aspect of the new law is its presumption of openness. "It is up to the person who desires to seal those records and foreclose public consideration of them to shoulder the burden of proof at every instance," said Texas Justice Lloyd Doggett, who was instrumental in passing the "sunshine law."[103] In other words, a company cannot secure a confidential settlement unless a judge decides that the corporation's privacy interests weigh more heavily than any adverse effect the secrecy may have on public safety.

Under the Texas sunshine rule, Kolcraft would not have been permitted to impose secrecy as a condition of its settlement with the family of Michael Bancroft, the boy permanently crippled when his car seat failed to protect him (see Chapter 5). But because Michael's accident occurred in Massachusetts, not Texas, his family had little choice but to sign the secret settlement.[104] When Kolcraft settled another car seat case in 1995, however, news of the settlement did reach the press. In 1992, Connie Roland was driving on a Florida highway when a car struck the rear of her Ford Explorer. The Explorer rolled over three times, killing Roland's thirteen– and eight–year–old nephews. Roland's three–year–old son Kasey, who had been strapped into his Kolcraft car seat, was thrown from the car. Kasey survived the crash, but suffered long-term brain damage. The Roland family sued Kolcraft, and attacked the design of the car seat. In 1995, while denying liability, Kolcraft settled the lawsuit by paying the Rolands $2 million.[105] Details of the case and final settlement were available to the press—and therefore to consumers who may have owned the same car seat.[106] Why couldn't Kolcraft persuade the Rolands to sign a gag order? Because the accident occurred in Florida, a state that in 1990 passed the "Sunshine in Litigation Act," which prohibits settlement agreements that conceal public hazards.[107]

By restricting the flow of information, secret settlements undermine the safety of America's most vulnerable citizens: our children. As of 2000, about two dozen states had adopted "sunshine laws" that seek to diminish courtroom secrecy.[108] It is time for legislators to pass a federal Sunshine in Litigation Act that specifically addresses cases in which the public safety of children is at stake.

Congressional Action: Legislation must be passed on the federal level that makes confidential settlements illegal when a child has been injured or killed by a consumer product.

Consumer Action: Contact your representatives in Congress and tell them you want to put an end to secret "gag" settlements that keep news of dangerous products from reaching parents.

4. Congress Must Restore the CPSC's Budget to Its 1974 Level

In 1997, the Government Accounting Office (GAO) conducted an in-depth investigation of how the CPSC allocated its resources. At the time, the agency carried out its mission with a budget of $42.5 million and a full-time-equivalent staff of 480 employees. "[A]fter adjusting for inflation," the GAO calculated, "the agency's budget has decreased by about 60 percent since 1974. Similarly, CPSC's current staffing level represents 43 percent fewer positions as compared with the agency's 1974 staff."[109]

By 2000, the CPCS's budget had increased slightly, to $50 million, while its staffing remained frozen at 480 positions. Meanwhile, since 1974, many of the industries the CPSC regulates have experienced explosive growth. One example is home improvement equipment (e.g., lighting fixtures, power sanders, vises, gardening supplies, etc.) sold in superstores like Home Depot.[110] The first Home Depot, opened in Atlanta in 1979, stocked 25,000 products.[111] Today there are more than 900 Home Depot stores, each offering between 40,000 and 50,000 products.[112] The market for recreational equipment, from snowmobiles to scooters, has mushroomed as well. In 1992, U. S.

snowmobile sales were $356 million; by 2000 sales had more than doubled, to $821 million.[113] In September 2000, the CPSC issued a consumer warning on scooters, reporting that the new product had been associated with four thousand injuries in August, ninety percent of them to children under fifteen years of age.[114] High chairs, strollers, bath seats, and cradles are just a few of the scores of products under the CPSC's jurisdiction; in 2000, the agency's budget was a mere one percent of the size of the infant products industry's sales.[115]

Better funding is crucial to enable the agency to stand up to industry. With more money in its legal war chest, for instance, the CPSC would have credible bargaining power when negotiating recall remedies, press release language, and civil penalty settlements with manufacturers. How much does the agency need? "If I could double our budget," says a CPSC regulator, "the agency would be stronger."[116] At the top of the wish list: funds to hire more engineers and lawyers and to build more sophisticated testing labs. [117]

Congressional Action: Congress should increase the CPSC's annual budget to $100 million.

Consumer Action: Contact your representatives in Congress and tell them you want the CPSC's budget to be significantly increased, in the interest of child safety.

Unsafe in Any Nursery

In his eye-opening 1965 exposé, *Unsafe at Any Speed*, Ralph Nader revealed the U.S. automotive industry's proclivity for profits over safety. "The American automobile is produced exclusively to the standards which the manufacturer decides to establish," Nader wrote. "It comes to the marketplace unchecked."[118] The similarities between the American automobile industry of the 1960s and the infant products industry in

2000 are uncanny. Of course, far more injuries and deaths are associated with motor vehicles than are linked to baby products. But while most parents now understand the importance of vehicle safety, few have any idea of the risks associated with products like portable cribs and infant swings. The fact that America's regulatory, legislative, and judicial systems have left families in the dark about the juvenile products industry's abysmal safety record is a national disgrace.

Documenting the automobile industry's inadequate pre-market testing, Nader exposed case after case of manufacturers blaming drivers for "accidents" in which they were injured, maimed, and killed. Driver "failure" and inadequate maintenance caused automotive deaths, the industry claimed, not unsafe cars. At the same time, Nader pointed out, the auto manufacturers' advertising experts were building corporate images of engineering excellence and reliability. Consumers bought into their claims, wrongly assuming that an automobile wouldn't be on the market if it were not completely safe. Thirty–five years later, infant product manufacturers play the same dangerous game, making bold claims about their safety reputations at one moment (even naming their company "Safety 1st"), and blaming parents for a succession of product-related "accidents" the next. Decades after their own parents were educated about auto safety, today's American parents maintain the same false sense of security about their babies' cradles and cribs.

Back in 1965, the Society of Automotive Engineers (SAE), an industry trade group, set safety standards for motor vehicles. "Membership on these [standard-setting] committees is held mostly by engineer-employees of the motor vehicle manufacturers," wrote Nader.[119] The result: SAE failed to address major automotive hazards, including passenger-side crash tests, front glare levels, and impact criteria for the steering assembly. American cars were being manufactured with "faulty features" that the industry was well aware existed. Thirty–five years later, the infant products industry utterly controls its own standard-setting process. As a result, insufficiently tested, shoddy brand-name products hit the marketplace each and every day, causing untold pain and suffering to American families.

During 1965 Senate hearings on automobile safety, manufacturers testified that when they became aware of product defects, they notified their dealers, but not necessarily their customers, by mail. Neither manufacturers nor their dealers kept records of how many defective cars were corrected. Thirty–five years later, infant product manufacturers follow a similarly careless approach to customer notification of potentially fatal hazards. Demonstrating greater concern for their corporate image than with preventing further death and injury, they tolerate low recall response rates, blaming the problem on everyone but themselves.

Unsafe at Any Speed was an impetus for change. In 1970, five years after it was published, the Highway Safety Act established a new regulatory agency, The National Highway Traffic Safety Administration (NHTSA).[120] NHTSA's mandate: to reduce deaths, injuries, and economic losses resulting from motor vehicle crashes. On the surface, the agency's goals are similar to the CPSC's, but there are a few profound differences. NHTSA has promulgated mandatory safety standards for most motor vehicles; manufacturers must demonstrate to the agency that their products meet these standards before they appear in dealers' showrooms. The agency's New Car Assessment Program evaluates the "crashworthiness" of passenger vehicles and searches for ways to motivate manufacturers "to provide higher levels of occupant protection."[121] The CPSC, by contrast, has promulgated relatively few mandatory standards, and manufacturers rarely have to demonstrate that their products are safe before consumers buy them. NHTSA's Consumer Information Program disseminates the agency's crash-test data to consumers through various media, "to assist in the purchase of safer vehicles."[122] The CPSC, on the other hand, is prohibited from disseminating much of its product-specific safety information to the public. NHTSA's 1999 budget was $361 million; the CPSC's was $47 million.[123] The result: Consumers can trust the government to help them buy a safe car, yet they have nowhere to turn for credible safety advice on infant products. Surely, the time has come for the government to take control of the infant products industry, as it did with the auto industry more than thirty years ago.

Great strides in nutrition and health care have decreased infant mortality and increased life expectancy in this country to record levels.[124] We are living longer, healthier lives than ever before. Yet, somehow, we have allowed our government to overlook a crucial component of childhood safety. It is shameful that the U.S. government does not require companies to test their baby products before selling them. It is shameful that the U.S. government cannot mandate manufacturers to do everything within their power to get deadly products out of consumers' homes. It is shameful that the government permits corporate censorship of life-and-death safety information. The auto industry was shamed into reforming itself. How many more babies need to suffer senseless, unnecessary deaths before infant product manufacturers reform? It is time for parents and the politicians they've elected to say: Enough. Figure out how to make baby products that are truly safe, or get out of the business.

"The Safe Nursery," a CPSC Pamphlet, Shows How Toddlers Were Killed by Portable Cribs

Between 1991 and 1998, at least thirteen toddlers were asphyxiated when their portable cribs collapsed. As the death toll mounted, manufacturers denied that their product design was defective (top rails with a hinge in the center), choosing instead to blame parents and caregivers for the babies' deaths.

2000 ASTM Committee Meeting Attendance Roster: Hand Held Carriers February 28–March 2, 2000

Manufacturers significantly outnumber consumer advocates in the voluntary safety standard-setting meetings. Industry consultants and representatives of product testing labs tend to vote with the manufacturers as a bloc, making it difficult for the consumer advocates to win votes that would lead to safer baby products.

Registrant	*Company*
Russ Butson	Evenflo[a]
Margie Cowan	Consumer[b]
Robert C. Craig	B&R Consulting, Inc.[c]
Dave Dart	ACTS Testing Labs, Inc.[d]
Paul Doppelt	PD Consultant, Inc.[c]
Jerry Drobrinski	Revmark[c]
Tim Edwards	Regalo International[a]
Terry Emerson	Cosco, Inc.[a]
Hector Ewing	Health Canada[b]
Marla Felcher	Consumer[b]
Mary Ellen Fise	Consumer Federation of America[b]
Werner Freitag	Consumers Union[b]
Steve Gerhart	Graco Children's Products[a]
Richard Glover	Cosco, Inc.[a]
Lindsay Harris	Intertek Testing Service[d]
Ron Hoffman	Graco Children's Products[a]
Owen Jones	J. C. Penney[e]
Arthur Kazianis	Playskool, Inc.[a]

A. Wayne Keller	ACTS Testing Labs[d]
Al Kozak	ACTS Testing Labs[d]
Mark Kumagai	CPSC Engineering Sciences
Jeffrey Lipko	Intertek Testing Services[d]
Rick Locker	Locker, Greenberg and Brainin[a]
Donald Mays	Good Housekeeping Institute[b]
Kandi Mell	JPMA[a]
Kitty Pilarz	Fisher-Price[a]
John Preston	John Preston Consulting[c]
Al Rapella	Intertek Testing Services[d]
Jon Robinson	Evenflo Co., Inc.[a]
Charlie Roos	Evenflo Co., Inc.[a]
Nate Saint	Graco Children's Products[a]
Tim Snyder	Fisher-Price[a]
Paul Terronez	Kolcraft Enterprises, Inc.[a]
Robert Waller	JPMA[a]
Jack Walsh	The Danny Foundation[b]
Paul Ware	Safety 1st, Inc.[a]
Tony Zeszut	Century Products[a]

[a] = manufacturers, manufacturers' lawyer, JPMA (industry trade group) staff

[b] = consumer advocate

[c] = industry consultant

[d] = testing lab hired by manufacturers

[e] = retailer

Baby Bath Seats—Deaths Only
1/11/83 to 2/25/00

Since bath seats hit the U.S. market in 1981, about 70 babies have drowned while using this product. As the death toll continues to rise, manufacturers like Safety 1st deny that their product is hazardous, choosing to focus instead on the fact that most children who drown are left unattended by caregivers. What these manufacturers refuse to explain is why they continue to keep the product on the market, in light of ample research that demonstrates the product increases the chances a parent will leave a child unattended in a bathtub, and that child will subsequently drown.

Appendix 2–3: BABY BATH SEATS—DEATHS ONLY 1/11/83 to 2/25/00

	Document	Date (Year/Month/Day)	City and State	Age/Sex (Age In Months)	Narrative
1	830826DALS118 D83801 11 A	830818	Unknown, KS	16 M	Entrapped under water in tub by an infant's bathing device.
2	851016CBB3004 H85AO026A	850906	Unknown, AL	07 F	Placed in plastic hoop for bathing and suction cups came undone. Overturned with victim and she drowned.
3	880413CDB0292 H8846891A	861106	Grand Rapids, MI	08 F	Left unattended for about 1 hour in a bathing ring. Baby was found floating in the tub.
4	891129CCC2074 C89A5008A	890812	Norton Shores, MI	11 F	Placed in tub on a plastic support seat anchored by 3 suction cups. Baby-sitter left room and child was found lying on back with support seat attached by only one cup. Child was drowned.
5	900305CCNl 140 G9020309A	900215	Eau Claire, WI	10 F	Drowned when left unattended in bathtub ring.

	Document	Date (Year/Month/Day)	City and State	Age/Sex (Age In Months)	Narrative
6	F9135015A 910315CWE5015 9135001979	910217	Albuquerque, NM	08 F	Died after being left unattended in a bath ring seat in a tub with more than recommended amount of water.
7	930312CCC3272 9106037899	910307	Hemet, CA	09 F	Placed in bathtub seat and mother left room. Victim climbed out of the seat and was face down in water.
8	G9140197A	910419	Council Bluffs, IA	07 M	Drowned in tub after being left unattended in a bath seat.
9	C9240012A 910429CCN1 151	910612	Unknown	12 F	Drowned in tub when left in a bath seat.
10	N9230119A 920731CCC1532	920213	West Palm Beach, FL	05 M	Left alone in infant bath seat in sink.
11	921105CCC3049 C9375022A U92B0728A C92C5005A	920529	Broken Arrow, OK	08 F	Found face down in water in tub during use of swivel bath seat.
12	94t104CBB 1051 X9284656A	920709	Philadelphia, PA	05 M	Sitting in bath chair and left unattended. Discovered upright in chair with face in water.

Document	Date (Year/Month/Day)	City and State	Age/Sex (Age In Months)	Narrative
13 921013CCC1010 X92AO267A F92BOO36A	920810	Alexandria, VA	06 F	In a bath seat in tub and bath seat tipped over. Child suffered cardiac arrest and died 8 days later.
14 921130CWE4015 F928401OA	921027	San Diego, CA	07 F	Victim was in bath ring and mother left. Ring tipped over and victim was lying on side in water.
15 941104CAA2050 X93B1077A	931003	East Cleveland, OH	08 M	Victim in bath seat in tub when left and then found face down in water.
16 961129CCC5084 9304028035	931027	Phoenix, AZ	06 F	Placed in infant seat in tub then father left room and connections became loose. Seat turned over and child was drowned.
17 X9530641A	940300	Unknown	07 M	Drowned when left in a bath seat in tub.
18 940602CNE5147 N9460077A	940507	Miami, FL	08 F	Left unattended in bath seat with 2 suction cup legs missing and seat tipped over causing child to drown.
19 950413HB83087 X94BO437A	940611	West Covina, CA	08 M	Sitting in bath seat child was left unattended and child was

Document	Date (Year/Month/Day)	City and State	Age/Sex (Age In Months)	Narrative
20 950918CCC2998 9426046238	940711	Dearborn, MI	06 M	found submerged under water. Drowned in tub when a bath aid was used, but it was in an upright position and still adhering when victim was found.
21 950412HEP9017	940716	Ft. Benning, GA	07 F	Child sitting in bath seat and was left. Father returned to find victim face down in water still sitting in bath seat.
22 X9485612A 940830CBB3723	940818	Bakersfield, CA	10 M	Drowned during a bath in seat in tub.
23 950601HAA4050 X955113 iA 9406130125	940826	Blue Jay, CA	07 F	Found floating face down in tub after being left unattended in bath seat.
24 X94AO017A 941012CAA1008	941010	Baltimore, MD	09 F	Drowned using bath seat in tub left unattended.
25 950504HB84014 X9551131A	9411026	Joshua Tree, CA	07 F	Found floating face down in tub after being left unattended in bath seat. Guard on seat was found open.
26 950207HWE7020 F9527007A	950113	Russellville, AR	07 F	Left unattended in bath seat in tub. Found lying in water

	Document	Date (Year/Month/Day)	City and State	Age/Sex (Age In Months)	Narrative
27	960910CCC5610 9518001675	950129	Mitchell, IN	06 M	drowned. Left sitting in a bath seat in a tub and drowned.
28	950308CCNI422 G9530`129A	950215	Hammond, IN	07 M	Submersion death with bath seat involvement.
29	950621HCC1144 X9561596A	950228	Danbury, CT	09 F	Drowned after mother left infant in tub seat in tub with 2 yr old sibling.
30	X9561647A 9506211HAA21153 X9572080A	9506119	White Lake, MI	07 F	Drowned in tub when left unattended in a bath ring seat.
31	950926CBB2034 G9590064A	950614	Newport, IN	09 M	Victim left in bath seat in tub and was found lying on his back under water.
32	950830CBB1943 X9582566A	950821	Orlando, FL	09 M	Drowned in tub using a bath seat and left unattended.
33	960603CCC5215 X9652562A	950906	Naples, FL	10 M	Left victim in bathtub aid/ring in tub and returned to find the victim out of ring and face down in water.
34	960719CCC5365 9506196492 960816CCC5520 X9683572A	951003 Dup IDI	Bell Gardens. CA	09 F	Sitting in bath seat in tub and father left room. Returned to find seat on its side and child face down in water.

Document	Date (Year/Month/Day)	City and State	Age/Sex (Age In Months)	Narrative
35 970418CCC2121 X9741439A	951027	Des Moines, IA	14 F	Mother left child unattended in bath seat returned to find baby had fallen out and face down in water.
36 96091gCCC5628 9534072190	951030	Garfield, NJ	10 M	Died 38 days after near drowning when he was in a baby bath ring in a tub and toppled over.
37 970131CCC5287 9513054196	951207	Moultrie, GA	09 F	Found in bathtub face down. Bath ring was involved.
38 970213CCC5317 9606037381	960404	Yucca Valley, CA	10 F	Sitting in bath ring and was left alone. Child was found out of the bath seat and floating face down.
39 960924CCC5643 9612067808	960518	Lynn Haven, FL	12 M	Drowned in tub when he tipped over his bath seat.
40 F9677029A 960712HWE7166	960618	Baytown, TX	06 M	Drowned in tub when infant bath seat fell over when hugged by sibling.
41 960708CAA5323 X9673047A	960702	Grandview, KS	07 F	Child left alone sitting in a used bath seat in tub. Found with bath seat turned over and victim face down in water.

Document	Date (Year/Month/Day)	City and State	Age/Sex (Age In Months)	Narrative
42 97011 OCCC5217 9619019286	960818	Cedar Rapids, IA	10 F	Placed in tub in infant bath seat and left unattended. Found submerged in water.
43 970626CCC3238 9606139780	960928	Bakersfield, CA	05 M	Sitting in a baby bath seat left unattended. Victim found under water and out of seat.
44 961213CCC514i X96C0724A	961016	Greensboro, NC	09 F	Placed in bath seat in tub and left alone. Found face down in water.
45 9704i8CC3103 9622039489	961112	Leesville, LA	09 F	Placed in bath seat in tub by drunken mother who left. Water overflowed the tub and victim drowned. Mother charged.
46 G9710237A 970129CCN0298	961222	Huntington, IN	09 M	Drowned in bathtub when he wriggled out of bathtub seat.
47 97032OCCN0375 G9730224A	970116	Cicero, IL	07 M	Left alone in bath ring in tub and found face down in water.
48 X9762059A 9706iICCC1300	970309	Philadelphia, PA	06 F	Died after nearly drowning in tub during use of a bath seat when left unattended.
49 N9820027A 980217CNE5086	970415	Bronx, NY	05 M	Died almost a month after tipping over in a bath seat during a bath and nearly drowned.

Document	Date (Year/Month/Day)	City and State	Age/Sex (Age In Months)	Narrative
50 980529CCCO458 9766030998	970624	Bronx, NY	20 F	Child drowned when whe was left unattended in a bath seat in a bathtub.
51 980116CCC1997 9745017310	970704	Greer, SC	07 F	Child left unattended in bath seat/ring. When mom returned, child had slipped through the ring and was lying on her side with face partially submerged.
52 980219CCC3611	970713	Tyler, TX	06 F	Child left unattended in bath seat/ring. When adult returned, child found face down unresponsive in bath tub.
53 970717CBB2337 X972410A X9782617A	970715	Cicero, IL	08 F	In bath seat left unattended. Seat and baby found tipped on side with baby's head underwater.
54 9W513CCC5555 9739MS276	970729	Monroe, Ml	11 F	Child left unattended in bath seat in tub with 2 year old sibling. Child found face down in tub when father returned.

Document	Date (Year/Month/Day)	City and State	Age/Sex (Age In Months)	Narrative
55 99D415CCCO429 9725045435	970920	Lynn, MA	09 M	Child left unattended in bath ring while in tub with 3 year old sister; pronounced dead from drowning.
56 X9832416A 980319CCCi2O8	970930	Brattleboro, VT	07 F	Drowned in bathtub when left unattended in an infant tubseat.
57 98081iCCCO643 N850169A	980324	Media, PA	08 M	Left alone in tub in a bath seat with a 6 inch incline. Child reportedly rolled off seat, found face down in water.
58 981228CCC6099 9835004882	980512	Albuquerque, NV	08 M	Child left alone in bath seat in tub. When mom returned, child was found outside of the seat, resulting in drowning.
59 000112CCC2198 C99B5016A	980603	Unk City, MI	07 F	Child drowned in bathtub while using a swivel bath seat that had no safety belt.
60 990312CCC3214 9848080152	980811	Austin, TX	11 M	Child left in tub with sibling in bath seat. Mom left, and upon return, found child face up in a foot of water.
61 980826CB83967	980821	Anchorage, AK	09 M	Left alone in a bath seat in 6

Document	Date (Year/Month/Day)	City and State	Age/Sex (Age In Months)	Narrative
H9880216A 9802001508				inches of water in tub. Child found face down in water when father returned.
62 990401CCC2372 9847047346	981012	Cedar Bluff, AL	11 F	Child left in bath seat in tub with 3–year–old sibling. When she returned, child was found submerged.
63 991026CCNOOOS G99AO141A	991022	Kansas City, KS	24 F	Child left in bath seat, with a seat belt. Mom left room and returned to find child sitting up but slumped over the seat, which was still secured in the tub.
64 990405CWE7189 F9947182A	981209	Fayetteville, AR	10 M	Child left in bath seat prior to drowning; 2 year old sister pulled him from the seat when the mother left the bathroom.
65 000202CCCO355 XOOiOO04A	991215	Syracuse, NY	05 F	Child drowned when left unattended in a bath seat.
66 000131CCN0078 G0010381A	000204	Grand Rapids, MI	07 M	While in a bath seat, child left in bathtub with 2 year old brother; child drowned. Children were in care of a 15 year old baby sitter.

Source: CPSC data

Original Instructions Included in Brandon Dorian's Crib

The assembly instructions included with Brandon's crib did not explicitly warn parents not to mix up the side and bottom crib rails, nor did they address the consequences of doing so.

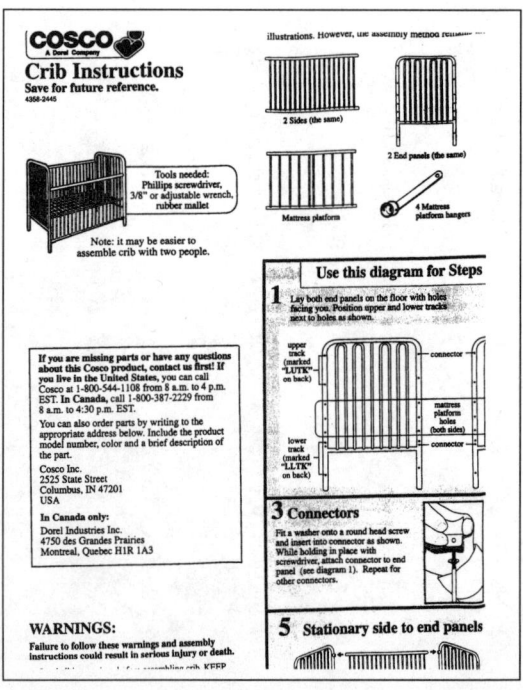

Revised Crib Instructions Sent to the Police by Cosco

While investigating Brandon Dorian's death, the police asked Cosco for the assembly instructions that had come with Brandon's crib. Cosco did not send these original instructions. Rather, the company sent revised instructions that contained a warning statement that was not part of Brandon's crib's instruction sheet: "Important: Tubing on mattress platform is spaced farther apart than on side rails. Do not use platform as a side rail." This additional warning may have saved Brandon's life.

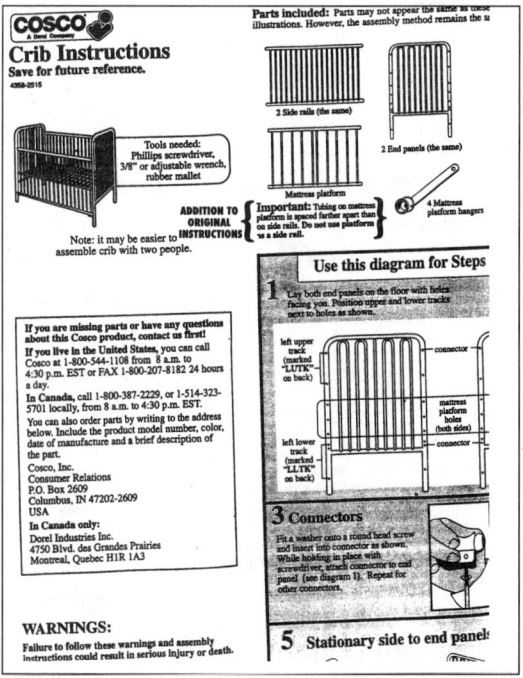

APPENDIX 3–1

Recall Press Releases Often Play Down a Product's Dangers

NEWS from CPSC

U.S. Consumer Product Safety Commission

Office of Information and Public Affairs   Washington, DC 20207

FOR IMMEDIATE RELEASE
October 17, 1995
Release # 96-005

CONTACT: Kathleen Begala
(301) 504-0580 Ext. 1193

CPSC, Playskool Announce Recall To Repair The 1-2-3 High Chair

WASHINGTON, D.C. - The U.S. Consumer Product Safety Commission and Playskool today announced a voluntary recall to repair program for all of Playskool's 1-2-3 High Chairs. Playskool has learned that plastic joints on some of its 1-2-3 High Chairs have cracked. These cracks may cause the high chair to collapse. Playskool has received ten reports of injuries, including bumps, bruises and one concussion.

Approximately 300,000 1-2-3 High Chairs were sold between May 1994 and October 1995. Playskool estimates that consumers have reported cracks in 1.5 percent of the high chairs sold. The high chairs were distributed nationally through wholesale and retail outlets for approximately $74.99. Playskool has asked all wholesale and retail outlets to stop selling the high chairs until a repair kit that will prevent the cracking can be included with each chair.

Cracks in the chair have appeared on the pivot joints at the top of the chair legs. The repair kit features a nylon strap that will stabilize the high chair's legs and prevent any stress cracks in the pivot joints. The strap attaches easily between the high chair's front and back base.

Consumers with a Playskool 1-2-3 High Chair should inspect it carefully for cracks at the pivot joints or elsewhere. If there are no cracks, the consumer should contact Playskool for a free repair kit. If consumers find any cracks in their 1-2-3 High Chair, they should stop using the chair immediately, and contact Playskool for a free replacement chair.

Consumers should call Playskool's toll free number (800) 752-9755 to receive the repair kit or to obtain further information. Consumers can also write to Playskool 1-2-3 Repair Program, 200 Narrangansett Park Drive, P.O. Box 200, Pawtucket RI 02860-0200. Media inquiries for Playskool should be directed to Wayne Charness, (401) 727-5983.

###

Because recall press releases are negotiated between manufacturers' lawyers and the CPSC, it is often difficult for caregivers and the media to decipher a product's true danger. This press release, announcing the recall of Playskool's 1–2–3 High Chair, is not titled, "Recall," but rather the less-alarming, "Recall to Repair." By the time this press release was issued, Playskool had logged more than 10,000 consumer complaints about the high chair; at least 4,500 concerning chairs that had cracked while in use. Playskool did not reveal all of this information in the press release. And the information that is reported is presented in a way that masks the magnitude of the problem; a percentage (1.5%) is given, rather than an absolute number (4,500 reports of cracked high chairs).

A Second Recall Notice for the Playskool 1–2–3 High Chair

NEWS from CPSC

U.S. Consumer Product Safety Commission

Office of Information and Public Affairs   Washington, DC 20207

FOR IMMEDIATE RELEASE   CONTACT: Jane Francis
January 13, 1997   (301) 504-0580 Ext. 1187
Release # 97-056

CPSC, Playskool Announce Recall to Repair Restraint Bar of the 1-2-3 High Chair

WASHINGTON, D.C. - In cooperation with the U.S. Consumer Product Safety Commission (CPSC), Playskool of Pawtucket, R.I., is offering free replacement restraint bars for about 287,000 of its 1-2-3 High Chairs. The restraint bar can crack or break off, which may allow a child who is not secured with the high chair's seat belt to fall from the chair and be injured.

Playskool has received hundreds of complaints of cracking and breaking restraint bars and 40 reports of injuries to children falling from the high chairs. Injuries primarily involve bumps and bruises; one child sustained a broken collarbone.

The plastic restraint bar of the 1-2-3 High Chair is located at the center of the front of the seat. The high chair's tray attaches to the restraint bar. Only restraint bars on Playskool 1-2-3 High Chairs made between May 1995 and May 1996 require replacement. These high chairs have serial numbers between TX51321 and TX61442. The serial number is on a label on the back of the seat of the high chair.

A second recall press release for the Playskool 1–2–3 High Chair, issued fourteen months after the first one, didn't mention that the chair had already been recalled for a different problem. By the time this press release was issued, thirty more children had been injured. Again, this notice does not reveal that the company had received more than 10,000 consumer complaints about the chair. Nor does it mention that at least 4,500 chairs had cracked while in use, or that a child had suffered a concussion in addition to the reported bumps, bruises and broken collarbone.

The Hazardous Cosco Toddler Bed

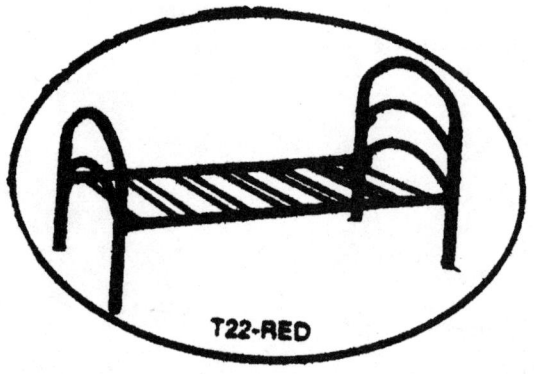

Dozens of parents called the Cosco consumer hotline to report that their children had been entrapped by the rails in the toddler bed's head- and foot-boards.

APPENDIX 4–2

Letter Written By Parent to Cosco, Warning of the Bed's Danger

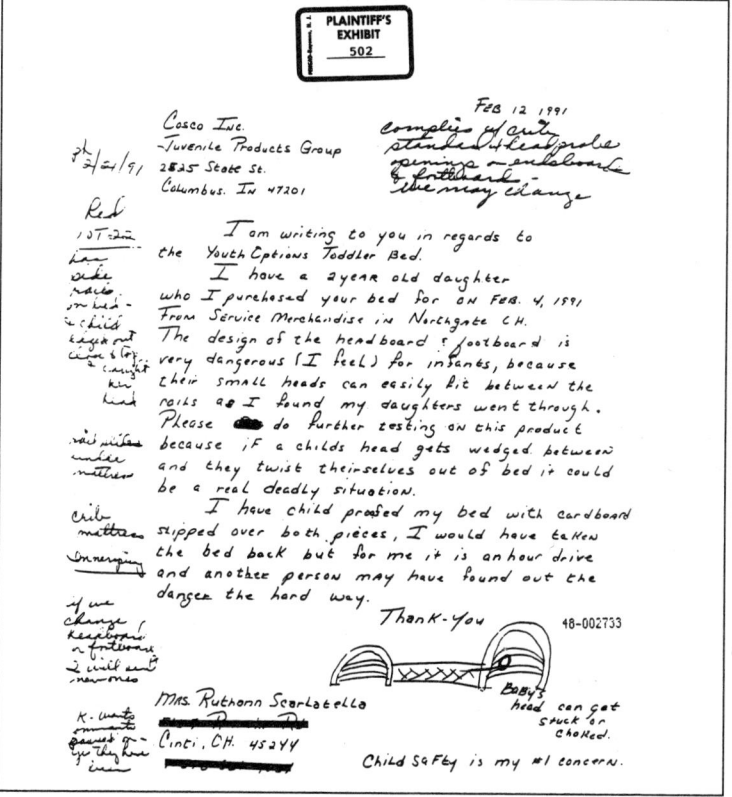

Mrs. Ruthann Scarlatella warned Cosco that its bed was dangerous, but the company took no action. Dozens of children were entrapped in the bed, and one child was killed, after the company received this letter.

How to File a Freedom of Information Act (FOIA) Request for Safety Information on Juvenile Products

If you need data on specific brands:

Use the following sample letter to request information on specific brands of products (i.e., Century 'Lil Napper Swing, Cosco toddler bed, etc.). In response to this request, the CPSC will send you very detailed files on all reported incidents. If you want information on more than one brand, send a separate letter for each brand (e.g., if you want to know about Cosco, Century, and Baby Trend strollers, send three separate letters). This will expedite your request.

Be prepared to wait at least a few months for this data. Before the CPSC can release it to you, the agency must send it to the manufacturers for approval (see Chapter 5). Also, be prepared for what you may see when it arrives; the contents of these files can be disturbing (see Chapter 5).

[date]

Mr. Todd Stevenson
FOIA Officer
U. S. Consumer Product Safety Commission
Washington, D. C. 20207

Dear Mr. Stevenson,

This is a request under the Freedom of Information Act.

I request all CPSC Compliance files, In-Depth Investigation files and consumer complaints associated with [insert name of brand and product here]. I would like information between 1995 and 2000 [be sure to specify dates].

I am seeking this information for personal, not commercial, use. I will use it to assess the safety of juvenile products for use by my family. Therefore, I request that you waive the fees as permitted under the FOIA.

Thank you,

Your Name
Your address
Your telephone number
Your email address

If you do not need data on specific brands:

Use the following sample letter to request information on a product category, such as strollers, cradles, high chairs or cribs. In response to this request, the CPSC will send you a computer printout that summarizes all reported incidents (injuries, "near-misses," and deaths) for the entire category. You will not receive any information on specific brands.

[date]

Mr. Todd Stevenson
FOIA Officer
U. S. Consumer Product Safety Commission
Washington, D. C. 20207

Dear Mr. Stevenson,

This is a request under the Freedom of Information Act.

I request all CPSC accident investigations for [insert name of product category here] from the National Injury Information Clearinghouse file. I do not request the names of specific manufacturers. I would like information between 1995 and 2000 [be sure to specify dates].

I am seeking this information for personal, not commercial, use. I will use it to assess the safety of juvenile products for use by my family. Therefore, I request that you waive the fees as permitted under the FOIA.

Thank you,

Your Name
Your address
Your telephone number
Your email address

Resources: Safety Organization Contact Information

Consumer Safety Organizations That Participate in Voluntary Standards Committees

Consumer Federation of America
1424 16th Street, N.W.
Suite #604
Washington, D.C. 20036
(202)462–6262
www.consumerfederation.org

The Danny Foundation
1451 Danville Boulevard
Suite #202
Alamo, California 94507
1–800–83DANNY
www.dannyfoundation.org

Kids In Danger
P.O. Box 146608
Chicago, Illinois 60614–6608
www.kidsindanger.org

Consumers Union
Office of Public Information
101 Truman Avenue
Yonkers, NY 10703
(914)378–2000
www.consumersunion.org

How to Contact the Industry Trade Group:

Juvenile Products Manufacturers Association, Inc.
236 Route 38 West, Suite 100
Moorestown, NJ 08057
(856)231–8500
www.jpma.org
(To access the "industry" portion of the website, type in the following user name and password: **User name:** industry **Password:** baby)

CPSC Press Releases, June 1998

The CPSC issues dozens of press releases each year, some more urgent than others. News directors and reporters complain that the sheeer volume and muddled language of these notices makes it difficult for them to quickly assess the severity of the product hazard. This decreases the probability that they will report the recall news.

In June 1998, a month after Danny Keysar became the Playskool Travel-Lite's fifth victim (and the twelfth portable crib victim), the CPSC issued a press release urging parents and caregivers to search once again for the recalled cribs. This same month, the agency issued eighteen other press releases, urging parents and caregivers to search once again.

Press Release Headline and Date	Hazard	# Injuries
1. "CPSC, Electronic Resources Ltd. Announce Recall of Power Strip Surge Protectors," June 2.	fire, shock, electrocution	0
2. "CPSC, Oscar Mayer Announce Recall to Replace Decals on Pedal Cars Because of Lead Hazard," June 2.	lead poisoning	0
3. "CPSC, RJS Inc. Announce the Recall of Ralph Lauren Thoroughbred Candles," June 3.	high flames	1 fire
4. "CPSC, GapKids Announce Voluntary Recall of Kids' Anoraks," June 3.	lead poisoning from zipper	0
5. "CPSC Chairman Awards Safety Commendation to the National SAFE KIDS Campaign," June 5.	N/A	N/A
6. "CPSC, K-B Toys Announce Recall of Bubble Beauties Floating Balls," June 8.	kerosene poisoning	0

Press Release Headline and Date	Hazard	# Injuries
7. "CPSC, Specialized Bicycle Components Inc. Announce Recall to Repair Bicycle Chains," June 9.	fall	0
8. "CPSC Reminds Residential Pool Owners and Parents of Precautions to Prevent Drownings of Young Children," June 11.	drowning	350 deaths/ year
9. "CPSC and Safety 1st Announce Recall to Replace Bouncing Buggy Toys," June 11.	sharp edge cut	700 incidents/ 33 injuries
10. "CPSC Announces Study Results Showing Soft Bedding Link to Infant Deaths," June 15.	SIDS/suffocation	N/A
11. "CPSC, Durapro Systems Announce Recall of Scuba Bouyancy Compensator Devices (BCDs)," June 16.	drowning	0
12. "CPSC Urges Search for Previously Recalled Portable Cribs and Play Yards," June 18.	suffocation	12 deaths

Press Release Headline and Date	Hazard	# Injuries
13. "CPSC, Payless ShoeSource Announce Recall of Children's Sneakers," June 23.	choking	2 incidents
14. "CPSC, Rite Aid Corp. Announce Recall of Butane Gas Lighters," June 23.	burns/fires	0
15. "CPSC, STK International Announce Recall of Baby Rattles," June 24.	choking	0
16. "CPSC, Davidson Ladder Inc. Announce Recall of Attic Stairways," June 24.	fall	5 incidents
17. "CPSC, EKCO Housewares Inc. Announce Recall of Skillets," June 25.	burn	0
18. "CPSC, Michael Friedman Corp. Announce Recall of Rattles," June 29.	choking	1 incident
19. "CPSC, Laiko International Announce Recall of Knock-A-Block Wooden Toy," June 29.	choking	0

Source: CPSC press releases #98-117 through 98-135, www.cpsc.gov.

Product Registration Card

If you buy a baby product and it does not come with a warranty card or a product registration card, make up your own, and send it to the manufacturer (see Appendix 7–4 for contact information). The CPSC has been working to require manufacturers to enclose mandatory registration cards in products like portable cribs, high chairs, cradles, etc., but so far, the industry has successfully resisted the agency's efforts. It is time for parents and caregivers to take this situation into their own hands. Photocopy these cards, keep some on hand for yourself, and give them to friends who have small children, to your daycare provider, and to friends and relatives who are expecting a baby soon (insert them along with baby showere gifts!). Fill in the contact and product information. Don't forget to photocopy your filled-out form, and keep a copy in your files.

PRODUCT REGISTRATION FORM
FOR MY CHILD'S CONTINUED SAFETY

Dear **(Name of Manufacturer)**,

I have just purchased a children's product marketed by your company. I would like to be notified, in a timely manner, of any recalls regarding this product. Do not use the information I have provided below for marketing purposes. You are to use it only to notify me of a product recall. If I am not notified directly of a recall, and my child is injured by this product, I will take legal action against your company. In the future, I urge you to include safety registration cards in all equipment intended to be used by children.

SAMPLE PRODUCT REGISTRATION CARD

YOUR NAME: _____

YOUR TELEPHONE NUMBER: _____

YOUR ADDRESS: _____

_____

CITY: _____STATE: _____

ZIP CODE: _____

IMPORTANT: **The following is essential and can be found on the product.**

PRODUCT BRAND/MANUFACTURER: _____

PRODUCT MODEL NUMBER: _____

SIGNATURE: _____

DATE: _____

Appendix 7–4: Baby Products Manufacturers' Contact Information

These are the leading manufacturers of baby products. When you make your own product registration card (see Appendix 7–3), send it to the manufacturer at the address listed here. Also use this list to contact a company if your child is injured by a baby product. Don't forget to notify the CPSC, as well.

Baby Björn
1990 Delk Industrial Blvd., Suite 105
Marietta, GA 30067
(800)593–5522
www.babybjorn.com

Baby Trend
2019 Business Parkway
Ontario, CA 91760
(800)328–7363
www.babytrend.com

Bassett Furniture
Main Street
Bassett, VA 24055
(540)629–6000
www.bassettfurniture.com

Century Products
9600 Valley View Road
Macedonia, OH 44056
(800)837–4044
www.centuryproducts.com

Cosco
2525 State Street
Columbus, IN 47201
(800)544–1108
www.coscoinc.com

Delta Enterprise Corp.
175 Liberty Avenue
Brooklyn, NY 11212
(718)385–1000
www.deltaenterprise.com

Evenflo
707 Crossroads Court
Vandalia, OH 45377
(800)837–9201
www.evenflo.com

The First Years
One Kiddie Drive
Avon, MA 02322
(800)225–0382
www.thefirstyears.com

Fisher-Price
636 Girard Avenue
East Aurora, NY 14052
(800)432–5437
www.fisher-price.com

Generation 2 Worldwide
113 Anderson Court, Suite 1
Dothan, AL 36301
(334)792–1144
www.childesigns.com

Graco Children's Products
Rt. 23, Main Street
Elverson, PA 19520
(800)345–4109
www.gracobaby.com

Infantino/Cosco
9404 Cabot Drive
San Diego, CA 92126
(800)365–8182
www.coscoinc.com

J. Mason Products
19401 Business Center Drive
Northridge, CA 91324
(800)242–1922
www.Jmason.com

Kelty K.I.D.S.
6235 Lookout Road
Boulder, CO 80301
(800)423–2320
www.kelty.com

Kids II
1015 Windward Ridge Parkway
Alpharetta, GA 30005
(770)751–0442

Kolcraft
3455 West 31st Place
Chicago, IL 60623
(800)453–7673
www.kolcraft.com

Peg Perego U.S.A.
3625 Independence Drive
Ft. Wayne, IN 46808
(800)671–1701
www.perego.com

Primo
149 Shaw Avenue
Irvington, NJ 07111
(973)926–5900
www.primobaby.com

Regalo International
5740 Wayzata Blvd.
Minneapolis, MN 55416
(800)521–1186

Safety 1ˢᵗ
45 Dan Road
Canton, MA 02021
(800)723–3065
www.safety1st.com

Endnotes

Chapter 1

1 Kevin Cullen, "Deaths in Cradles Haunt Families: Concerns Raised on Design, Testing," *Boston Globe*, August 4, 1994.

2 Details of Connor's death from CPSC Epidemiologic Investigation Report, Case # 920303CAA3265, November 25, 1991.

3 Details of Malika's son's death from CPSC Epidemiologic Investigation Report, Case # 920103HCC1513, September 1, 1992.

4 Ibid.

5 "Woman Loses Kids After Baby Dies in Defective Cradle," *Associated Press*, March 9, 1992.

6 Letter from Marc Schoem, CPSC regulator, division of corrective actions to Derial Sanders, president, Graco Children's Products, September 10, 1991.

7 "Rockabye Baby," *Dateline NBC Transcript*, NBC News, May 23, 1995.

8 CPSC Epidemiologic Investigation Report, Case # 920303CAA3265, November 25, 1991; CPSC Epidemiologic Investigation Report, Case # 920103HCC1513, September 1, 1992; Cullen, "Deaths in Cradles Haunt Families: Concerns Raised on Design, Testing"; Kevin Cullen, "'91 Case Exposes Holes in Recall System: Mother in Cradle Death Remained Unaware," *Boston Globe*, August 30, 1994.

9 CPSC press release #92-054, www.cpsc.gov.

10 Kevin Cullen, "Couple Says Baby's Death is Linked to Faulty Cradle," *Boston Globe*, October 6, 1994.

11 "Rockabye Baby," *Dateline NBC Transcript*, May 23, 1995.

12 Jeanne Brokaw, "The Hand That Rocks the Cradle," *Mother Jones*, September/October 1996.

13 CPSC Epidemiologic Investigation Report #920618CCC2458, June 29, 1992.

14 CPSC Epidemiologic Investigation Report #920311CAA2284, March 16, 1992.

15 CPSC Epidemiologic Investigation Report #920228CWE7022, February 28, 1992.

16 CPSC Epidemiologic Investigation Report #920302CNE5086, March 3, 1992 (Glenn Farland); Kevin Cullen, "Families, Cradle Company Settle Suit Terms Undisclosed; Graco Denies Blame," *Boston Globe*, April 23, 1996.

17 CPSC Epidemiologic Investigation Report #920424CAA3354, May 14, 1992.

18 CPSC Epidemiologic Investigation Report #920313CNE5098, March

24, 1992.

19 CPSC Epidemiologic Investigation Report #910813CAA2681, August 13, 1991.

20 "Rockabye Baby," *Dateline NBC Transcript*, May 23, 1995.

21 Ibid.

22 Kevin Cullen, "Parents File Suit, Say Cradle-Maker Knew of Danger," *Boston Globe*, September 13, 1994.

23 "Rockabye Baby," *Dateline NBC Transcript*, May 23, 1995.

24 Cullen, "Deaths in Cradles Haunt Families: Concerns Raised on Design, Testing."

25 Ibid.

26 Ibid.

27 E. Patrick McGuire, "Learning From Others-Proactively; Pre-Market Safety Audits Can Cut Costs and Litigation," *Product Liability Law & Strategy*, February 1997.

28 "Rockabye Baby," *Dateline NBC Transcript*, May 23, 1995.

29 Robert S. Adler, "From 'Model Agency' to Basket Case-Can the Consumer Product Safety Commission Be Redeemed?" *Administrative Law Review, 61,* Winter 1989.

30 Sandy Jones and Wener Freitag, *Consumer Reports Guide to Baby Products*, Consumer Reports Books, New York, 1996, p. 2.

31 "Office of Compliance-Section 15(b) Internet Report," www.cpsc.gov.

32 Brokaw, "The Hand That Rocks the Cradle."

33 Cullen, "Deaths in Cradles Haunt Families: Concerns Raised on Design, Testing."

34 CPSC press release #92-054, February 24, 1992, www.cpsc.gov.

35 Ibid.

36 Cullen, "'91 Case Exposes Holes in Recall System: Mother in Cradle Death Remained Unaware."

37 Descriptions of Graco's recall notification tactics by CPSC Chairman Ann Brown did not suggest the company paid to advertise the recall. Nor did the CPSC's Graco Converta-Cradle file, sent to the author in response to a FOIA request, indicate that the company paid to advertise the recall. Calls made by the author to Graco to confirm this finding were not returned.

38 Cullen, "'91 Case Exposes Holes in Recall System: Mother in Cradle Death Remained Unaware."

39 N. J. Scheers, "Evaluation of the Fast-Track Product Recall Program of the U. S. Consumer Product Safety Commission," October 13,

1998.

40 Valerie Reitman, "Firm Owes Its Boom to Babies and God," *Philadelphia Enquirer*, March 5, 1990.

41 Cullen, "Deaths in Cradles Haunt Families: Concerns Raised on Design, Testing."

42 CPSC press release #90-157, October 9, 1990, www.cpsc.gov.

43 CPSC press release #91-036, February 6, 1991, www.cpsc.gov.

44 CPSC press release #92-033, December 20, 1991, www.cpsc.gov.

45 CPSC press release #94-012, November 17, 1993, www.cpsc.gov.

46 CPSC press release #97-015, October 30, 1996, www.cpsc.gov.

47 CPSC press release #97-126, May 19, 1997, www.cpsc.gov.

48 CPSC press release #98-048, December 19, 1997, www.cpsc.gov.

49 CPSC press release #98-171, September 28, 1998, www.cpsc.gov.

50 CPSC press release #99-020, November 12, 1998, www.cpsc.gov.

51 CPSC press release #99-026, November 24, 1998, www.cpsc.gov.

52 CPSC press release #00-098, April 13, 2000, www.cpsc.gov.

53 CPSC press release #00-124, June 14, 2000, www.cpsc.gov.

54 Cullen, "'91 Case Exposes Holes in Recall System: Mother in Cradle Death Remained Unaware."

55 Adler, "From 'Model Agency' to Basket Case-Can the Consumer Product Safety Commission Be Redeemed?"

56 "The Impact of Restrictive Disclosure Provisions on Freedom of Information Act Requests: An Analysis of Section 6(b)(1) of the Consumer Product Safety Act," *Minnesota Law Review*, Vol. 64:1021, 1980.

57 Kevin Cullen, "31 Infant Deaths, Injuries Linked to Cradle Manufacturer, U.S. Refuses to Release Information," *Boston Globe*, August 26, 1994.

58 Cullen, "Couple Says Baby's Death is Linked to Faulty Cradle."

59 "Watchdog Agency Reportedly Understated Crib Deaths," *The Legal Intelligencer*, August 29, 1994.

60 CPSC FOIA officer Todd Stevenson. Correspondence with author, January 31, 2000.

61 Cullen, "Deaths in Cradles Haunt Families: Concerns Raised on Design, Testing."

62 Juvenile Products Manufacturers Association website, www.jpma.org; Mitch Lipka, "Safety Agency Survived Many Incarnations," *South Florida Sun-Sentinel*, November 28–30 1999.

Chapter 2

1 CPSC *2001 Budget Request to Congress*, September 1999.

2 Robert S. Adler, "From 'Model Agency' To Basket Case—Can the Consumer Product Safety Commission Be Redeemed?" *Administrative Law Review*, 61, Winter 1989, pp. 63–64. Adler cites the 1968 National Commission on Product Safety Report, which estimated that 20 million Americans were injured and 30,000 were killed each year by consumer products.

3 Safe Kids Foundation, www.safekids.org.

4 Dawn D'Aries, "JPMA Spring Meeting: Organization Focus on Growth," *Home Textiles Today*, May/June 1999, p. 24.

5 Adler, "From 'Model Agency' To Basket Case—Can the Consumer Product Safety Commission Be Redeemed?"

6 Nixon favored a "voluntary and educational approach" to reducing product hazards, rather than the establishment of a federal agency. "Regulation Processes and Politics," *Congressional Quarterly Inc.*, Washington, D.C., 1983, p. 52.

7 "Consumer Product Safety Commission: Better Data Needed to Help Identify and Analyze Potential Hazards," GAO *Report to the Chairmen, Committee on Commerce, Science, and Transportation, U. S. Senate, and Committee on Commerce, House of Representatives, #* HEHS-97-147, September 1997, p. 4.

8 "Regulation Process and Politics," *Congressional Quarterly Inc.*, Washington, D.C., 1983, pp. 52–53 provides an overview of the history of the CPSC; Robert Adler, interview with author, August 11, 1999.

9 Adler. August 11, 1999.

10 "Regulation Process and Politics," *Congressional Quarterly Inc.*, pp. 52–53.

11 Andrew McGuire, executive director of the Trauma Foundation at San Francisco General Hospital. Interview with author, August 1998.

12 Adler, "From 'Model Agency' To Basket Case—Can the Consumer Product Safety Commission Be Redeemed?" p. 98.

13 Sandy Jones and Werner Freitag, *Consumer Reports Guide to Baby Products*, Consumer Reports Books, New York, 1996, p. 2. Toys are regulated by the CPSC as well.

14 Kathie Morgan, Director Technical Committee Operations, American Society for Testing and Materials. E-mail to author, April

26, 2000.

15 CPSC recall press releases #94-106, 96-175, 98-037, 98-048, 98-076, 99-138, 00-034; www.cpsc.gov. The following manufacturers recalled hard-handled carriers between 1994 and 2000: Gerry, Playskool, J. Mason, Graco, Evenflo, Kolcraft, and Cosco.

16 Adler, "From 'Model Agency' To Basket Case—Can the Consumer Product Safety Commission Be Redeemed?" p. 98.

17 Mary Ellen Fise, general counsel, Consumer Federation of America. Interview with author, August 15, 1998.

18 Coalition for Consumer Rights study, Chicago, IL, released October 29, 1999.

19 CPSC press release #98-128, June 18, 1998, www.cpsc.gov.

20 CPSC "Consumer Product Incident Report," Task #941115CAA1092, October 19, 1994.

21 Gary L. Smith, All Our Kids/Draco. Letter to Marc Schoem, CPSC Division of Corrective Actions, November 14, 1994.

22 Ibid.

23 State of Michigan Standard Crime Report, Incident #172994, August 30, 1994 (Baby Trend death); Sue Lindsay, "Playpen Maker Won't Recall Product in Death of Baby," *Denver Rocky Mountain News*, April 4, 1994, 28A.

24 John Preston, CPSC engineer. Memo to Zuma Soto and William Moore, April 22, 1996.

25 Century never publicly announced that the cribs were manufactured by Draco, and the recall announcements did not acknowledge this relationship between the two companies. Yet CPSC documents indicate that Draco did indeed make Century's portable cribs. Specifically, the April 22, 1996 memo written by CPSC engineer John Preston to his colleagues states that the All Our Kids Model #741JT "appears to be the same as the Century model 10.810JGF playpen, sample T-793-0223." Then, on November 21, 1996, an internal CPSC memo announcing the Draco All Our Kids crib recall reads, "The text has been negotiated with Century Products. Any changes must be conveyed to compliance."

26 John Preston, CPSC Engineering Sciences. Memo to Zulma Soto and William Moore, Jr., April 22, 1996, p. 3.

27 Ibid. Preston wrote of this Century crib model: "The low torque (minimum of 5 lbf-in), coupled with the early collapse (35 cycles) of a top rail when the product was retested using an air cylinder to apply the cyclic force, leads us to believe that this product may col-

lapse during use."

28 Ibid. Preston wrote of the All Our Kids crib: "The minimum torque (3 lbf-in) is the lowest value recorded for any brand or model of playpen featuring rotating top rail latches that has been tested to date."

29 Zulm Soto, CPSC staff. "Memo to the files—All Our Kids, CA940087," June 7, 1996.

30 Ibid.

31 CPSC press release #98-128, June 17, 1998, www.cpsc.gov. Century Products recalled its portable crib the same day.

32 On November 4, 1996, Marc Schoem sent a memo to CPSC regulators William Moore, Theresa Rogers, and Zulma Soto from California, where he had gone to look for All Our Kids. He wrote, "This afternoon I visited the last known address of All Our Kids/Draco... The place is now occupied by a firm called MBF Last Five Soccer, which has no tie with All Our Kids... As far as the Montebello Post Office is concerned All Our Kids is still located at the above address." The next day, Schoem wrote to his colleagues again, this time advising them that he had spoken with All Our Kids' lawyer, Todd Serota. "He said he, too, was looking for Mr. Jerry Teng, president of the firm (Draco). He said Mr. Teng owed his law firm a $250,000 legal fee. He believes Mr. Teng now lives in Taiwan."

33 Kolcraft: CPSC press release #93-043, March 10, 1993; Baby Trend: #95-056, January 1, 1995; Century: #97-026, November 21, 1996; Draco: #97-028, November 21, 1996; Evenflo: #97-146, June 25, 1997, www.cpsc.gov. Children continued to be killed after some of the cribs were recalled.

34 CPSC press release #93-043, March 10, 1993.

35 Sandy Jones and Werner Freitag, *Consumer Reports Guide to Baby Products*, Consumer Reports Books, New York, 1996, p. 3.

36 Recall consultants are often former manufacturers' employees. Independent recall consultant Bob Craig is a former Cosco employee, who was involved in Cosco's toddler bed and guard rail recall (Chapter 4) and consultant Jerry Dobrinski worked for Graco when the Converta-Cradle was recalled (Chapter 1).

37 Adler, "From 'Model Agency' To Basket Case—Can the Consumer Product Safety Commission Be Redeemed?" p. 98.

38 "ASTM: A Proven Partnership," and "What is ASTM?" ASTM promotional brochures, www.astm.org.

39 Ibid.

40 "2000 ASTM Committee Meetings Attendance Roster, Hand Held Carriers," February 28–March 2, 2000.

41 CPSC recall press releases: #94-106, 96-175, 98-037, 98-048, 98-076, 99-138, 00-034, www.cpsc.gov.

42 Ibid.

43 Oral communication with anonymous source, February 29, 2000.

44 Author notes of ASTM meeting, February 29, 2000.

45 ASTM official meeting notes, February 29, 2000.

46 The first ASTM organizational meeting for hard-handled carriers was held on November 7, 1997. Mark Kumagai, email communication to author, August 29, 2000.

47 Author notes of ASTM meeting, February 29, 2000.

48 ASTM official meeting notes, February 29, 2000.

49 Kandi Mell, JPMA, email communication to author, July 24, 2000.

50 Author notes of ASTM meeting, August 30, 1999.

51 Ibid.

52 ASTM official meeting notes, Hand Held Infant Carriers, February 29, 2000.

53 Renae Rauchschwalbe, Ruth Brenner, and Gordon Smith, "The Role of Bathtub Seats and Rings in Infant Drowning Deaths," *Pediatrics*, Vol. 100, No. 4, October 1997, pp. 1–5.

54 Anonymous CPSC regulator. Interview with author, October 26, 1999.

55 Rauchschwalbe et. al., "The Role of Bathtub Seats and Rings in Infant Drowning Deaths."

56 Plaintiff v. Safety 1st, Deposition of Paul Alan Ware, Jones, Fritz & Sheehan, Boston, MA, p. 17.

57 ASTM official minutes of meetings, February 24, 1999 and August 30, 1999.

58 "Petition of Consumer Federation of America, The Drowning Prevention Foundation, et al. To Ban Baby Bath Seats," petition filed with CPSC by Mary Ellen R. Fise, Attorney for Consumer Federation of America, July 25, 2000.

59 "Baby Bath Seats—Deaths Only, January 1, 1983 to February 25, 2000," CPSC files.

60 Notes taken by author at ASTM meeting, August 30, 1999.

61 Rauchschwalbe et. al, "The Role of Bathtub Seats and Rings in Infant Drowning Deaths," pp. 1–5.

62 "Petition of Consumer Federation of America, The Drowning

Prevention Foundation, et al., To Ban Baby Bath Seats," petition filed with CPSC by Mary Ellen R. Fise, Attorney for Consumer Federation of America, July 25, 2000.

63 Plaintiff v. Safety 1st, Inc., Deposition of Paul Alan Ware, Jones, Fritz & Sheehan, Boston, MA, June 1, 1999, pp. 13–19

64 Notes taken by author at ASTM meeting, August 30, 1999.

65 Anonymous CPSC regulator. Interview with author, October 26, 1999.

66 Kip Viscusi, *Regulating Product Safety*. Washington, D.C.: American Enterprise Institute for Public Policy Research, 1984.

67 Ken Giles, CPSC Office of Compliance. E-mail communication with author, July 13, 2000. Total number of recalls for 1998: 273; for 1999: 304. Total number of recalled children's products for 1998: 120; for 1999: 95.

68 "Plaintiff vs. K-Mart Corporation, Baby Trend, Inc., and Juvenile Products Manufacturers Association," Trial Brief, State of Michigan Circuit Court for the County of Macomb, Case #94-4557-NP, September 24, 1996.

69 CPSC press release #95-056, January 1, 1995, www.cpsc.gov.

70 "Plaintiff vs. K-Mart Corporation, Baby Trend, Inc., and Juvenile Products Manufacturers Association," September 24, 1996.

71 Jim Dodds' deposition, "Plaintiff vs. K-Mart Corporation, Baby Trend, Inc., and Juvenile Products Manufacturers Association," May 15, 1996, pp 33–34, 77–78.

72 Safety Sells Conference transcript, CPSC document #6001, March 28, 1995. Playskool 1–2–3 High Chair instruction sheet reads: "This model tested by an independent laboratory for compliance to ASTM F-404 safety standard for high chairs."

73 CPSC press release #96-005, October 17, 1995, www.cpsc.gov.

74 Hasbro interoffice correspondence, "#731 Playskool 1–2–3 High Chair—Field Test Results," April 1994.

75 Ibid.

76 "Plaintiff vs. Cosco, Inc., Montgomery Ward, and Juvenile Products Manufacturers Association," Summons and Complaint, State of Michigan Circuit Court for the County of Oakland, Case #97-547894-NP, July 16, 1997.

77 The Danny Foundation Safety Brochure, www.dannyfoundation.org.

78 CPSC press release #97-154, July 9, 1997, www.cpsc.gov.

79 Ven Johnson, attorney with Fieger, Fieger & Schwartz, Southfield, MI. Interview with author, December 28, 1999.

80 Ibid.

81 Ibid.

82 CPSC press release #97-154, July 9, 1997, www.cpsc.gov.

83 LaTrina Blair-Birden, "Baby's Death: Crib Was Recalled," *The Herald News*, August 5, 1998, A1.

84 Johnson, December 28, 1999.

85 Notes taken by author at ASTM meeting, February 1, 2000.

86 Ibid.

87 Ibid.

88 Ibid. Pilarz often breaks rank with the manufacturers and aligns herself with consumer advocates on votes.

89 Van Buren, Arkansas Police Department Death Investigation Report, CPSC IDI #931214CAA3145, November 30, 1993.

90 Ibid.

91 Kathie Morgan, American Society for Testing and Materials. Email to author, April 26, 2000.

92 Century Products Lil' Napper infant swing instructions.

93 Arkansas State Crime Laboratory Report, Case #ME-879-93.

94 CPSC National Injury Clearinghouse data, baby swing incidents, January 1990–April 2000.

95 "Infant Swings—Calendar Year 1990 to the Present, Accident Investigations," CPSC National Injury Information Clearinghouse, April 7, 2000.

96 Handout at February 2000 ASTM meeting, "Minutes of Meeting on Infant Swings Held September 1, 1999."

97 B. Jay Martin, "The Value of Explicit Hazard and Consequence Information in Warnings About Hidden Hazards," *Proceedings of Human Factors and Ergonomics Society 44th Annual Meeting*, San Diego, CA, August 2000.

98 Ibid.

99 ASTM meeting notes, February 2000.

100 "CPSC Advance Notice of Proposed Rulemaking," *Federal Register*, Vol. 59, No. 147, August 2, 1994. At the time, walkers accounted for more injuries than any other baby product. In 1998, strollers moved up to first place on this list, and walkers dropped to second place (see Chapter 7, Table 7–1).

101 Ibid.

102 CPSC National Injury Information Clearinghouse, baby walker incidents.

103 Karen M. Sheehan, Stacy Gordon, Robert Tanz, "Bilateral Fibula Fractures from Infant Walker Use," *Pediatric Emergency Care*, February 1995, pp. 27–29.

104 "CPSC Advance Notice of Proposed Rulemaking," August 2, 1994.

105 CPSC National Injury Information Clearinghouse, baby walker incidents.

106 Sandy Jones, *Consumer Reports Guide to Baby Products*. Yonkers, N.Y.: Consumer Reports Special Publications, 1999, p. 229.

107 Damien Cave, "Rolling Baby Killers," *Salon*, December 30, 1999, www.salon.com.

108 Jones, *Consumer Reports Guide to Baby Products*, pp 229–230.

109 Teresa M. Schwartz and Robert S. Adler, "Product Recalls: A Remedy in Need of Repair," *Case Western Reserve Law Review*, 34, 1984, p. 31.

110 CPSC Advance Notice of Proposed Rulemaking, *Federal Register*, Vol. 59, No. 147, August 2, 1994.

111 CPSC press release #93-063, April 15, 1993, www.cpsc.gov.

112 Jones, *Consumer Reports Guide to Baby Products*, p. 230.

113 The 1981 Consumer Product Safety Act amendments prohibited the CPSC from issuing mandatory safety standards that contained product design requirements, that is, standards that specified how a product should be made. Manufacturers argue against "design restrictive" voluntary standards as well, noting that such requirements are anti-competitive. Competition will thrive, the argument goes, only when manufacturers are left to their own devices to figure out how to approach a specific safety hazard.

114 Ibid.

115 CPSC Document #5086, "CPSC Gets New, Safer Baby Walkers on the Market," June 16, 2000, www.cpsc.gov.

116 CPSC National Injury Information Clearinghouse, baby walker incidents.

117 Jones, *Consumer Reports Guide to Baby Products*, p. 229.

118 Steven P. Shelov (editor), *Caring for Your Baby and Young Child: Birth to Age 5*, New York: Bantam Books, 1998, p. 230.

119 Damien Cave, "Rolling Baby Killers," *Mothers Who Think*, December 30, 1999, www.salon.com.

120 "Moving Toward the Millennium: The 1999 International Juvenile Products Show Directory," Juvenile Products Manufacturers Association.

121 CPSC Epidemiologic Investigation Report #980721HAA2713, July

27, 1998.

122 Author notes, ASTM meeting, August 31, 1999.

123 Ibid. Industry consultant Jerry Dobrinski was employed by Graco when it launched the Converta-Cradle and played a key role in the product's recall (see Chapter 1).

124 Cave, "Rolling Baby Killers."

125 Viscusi, *Regulating Product Safety*, American Enterprise Institute for Public Policy Research, Washington, D.C., 1984.

126 Warren Shoulberg, "Making the Case for a Mandatory Sentence," *Home Textiles Today*, Mar/April 1999, pp. 51–52.

127 Paula Markowitz, president of Patchcraft, Inc., interview with author, November 1, 1999.

Chapter 3

1 "Report and Proceedings: Safety Sells," Conference transcript, CPSC Document #6001, March 28, 1995.

2 Kathleen Day, "Sitting Pretty," *Washington Post*, August 3, 1994.

3 "Report and Proceedings: Safety Sells," Conference transcript, March 28, 1995.

4 "JPMA Product Competition Winners 1989–1999," Juvenile Products Manufacturers Association memo, December 17, 1999.

5 "Report and Proceedings: Safety Sells," Conference transcript, March 28, 1995.

6 Graph of 1–2–3 High Chair Defects, Hasbro Customer Affairs Department, May 1994–August 1995.

7 Ibid.

8 July 3, 1995–July 30, 1995 Summary of 1–2–3 Complaints, Hasbro Consumer Affairs Department.

9 Graph of 1–2–3 High Chair Defects, Hasbro Customer Affairs Department, May 1994–August 1995.

10 Dr. Stephen W. Boris, M.D. Correspondence with Hasbro, September 22, 1995.

11 CPSC Corrective Actions Division Report Sheet, October 18, 1995.

12 "Report and Proceedings: Safety Sells," Conference transcript, March 28, 1995.

13 Graph of 1–2–3 High Chair Defects, Hasbro Customer Affairs Department, May 1994–August 1995.

14 CPSC press release #96-005, October 17, 1995, www.cpsc.gov.

15 "CPSC Recall Effectiveness Forum Transcript," March 23, 1999.

16 "1998 Annual Report to Congress," Consumer Product Safety Commission.

17 CPSC press releases #00-034, #97-102, #97-110, #98-128, www.cpsc.gov.

18 "Regulated Products Handbook," CPSC Document #8001, February 1994.

19 N. J. Scheers, Ph.D., "Evaluation of the Fast-Track Product Recall Program of the U. S. Consumer Product Safety Commission," October 13, 1998.

20 "Office of Compliance—Section 15(b) Internet Report," www.cpsc.gov.

21 "Consumer Product Safety Commission 2000 Budget Request to Congress," September 1998, p. 23.

22 Ibid, p. 1.

23 CPSC 1998 Annual Report to Congress, p. 17.

24 Ibid, p. A-5.

25 "Consumer Product Incident Report," CPSC files, October 19, 1995.

26 John Fitch, CPSC compliance officer. Memo to March Schoem, CPSC compliance regulator, August 29, 1995.

27 "Consumer Product Safety Commission: Better Data Needed to Help Identify and Analyze Potential Hazards," United States General Accounting Office, GAO/HEHS-97-147, September 29, 1997.

28 Ibid, p. 16.

29 Kolcraft recall: CPSC press release #00-34, December 20, 1999; Cosco recall: CPSC press release #99-062, February 17, 1999; Safety 1st recall: CPSC press release #98-125, June 11, 1998; Graco recall: CPSC press release #97-126, May 19, 1997, www.cpsc.gov.

30 Marc Shoem, "CPSC Compliance Workshop," presentation given in Rosemont, Il., May 26, 1999.

31 "Consumer Product Safety Commission: Better Data Needed to Help Identify and Analyze Potential Hazards," United States General Accounting Office, GAO/HEHS-97-147, September 29, 1997.

32 Shoem, "CPSC Compliance Workshop," May 26, 1999.

33 "Regulated Products Handbook," CPSC Document #8001, February 1994.

34 Mary Ellen Fise, general counsel, Consumer Federation of America. Interview with author, August 10, 1999.

35 Anonymous CPSC regulator. Interview with author, July 19,1999.

36 Robert S. Adler, former CPSC lawyer. Interview with author, August 11, 1999.

37 "The First Years Announce Recall to Repair High Chair Gym Toys," CPSC press release #98-071, February 19, 1998; "Playskool Announces Repair Program For Playskool 1–2–3 Swing," CPSC press release #95-100, April 24, 1995; "Baby's Dream Furniture Announces Recall to Repair Cribs," CPSC press release #98-065, February 10, 1998, www.cpsc.gov.

38 Anonymous CPSC regulator. Interview with author, July 19,1999.

39 CPSC press release #98-156, August 21, 1998, www.cpsc.gov.

40 CPSC IDI #930415CAA1318, April 19, 1993.

41 Lawrence Ben, attorney. Letter to Jim Dodds of Baby Trend, May 25, 1993. CPSC files indicate that the child's mother, not his grandfather, administered CPR.

42 Ven Johnson, attorney with Fieger, Fieger & Schwartz. Interview with author, December 28, 1999.

43 CPSC IDI #930824CAA3518, August 26, 1998.

44 Correspondence from CPSC to Jim Dodds, September 1, 1993.

45 Johnson, December 28, 1999. CPSC press release #93-111a also notes "death of child," whose age was reported as one year old.

46 CPSC press release #93-111a, October 8, 1993, www.cpsc.gov.

47 CPSC IDI #940901CNN2282, September 2, 1994.

48 CPSC press release #96-005, October 17, 1995, www.cpsc.gov.

49 CPSC files held an early version of press release, stamped "Draft," which originally read: "Playskool Recalls Its 1–2–3 High Chair." This title was crossed and replaced with: "Playskool Announces Recall to Repair Its 1–2–3 High Chair." The following sentence was also crossed out: "Playskool has learned that plastic joints on more than 4,000 of its 1–2–3 High Chairs cracked." This sentence and the number "4,000" never appeared in the official press release.

50 CPSC press release #97-056, January 13, 1997, www.cpsc.gov.

51 Russ Rader, CPSC public affairs officer. Interview with author, August 1998.

52 CPSC Recall Handbook, Office of Compliance, May 1999.

53 Robert S. Adler, "From 'Model Agency' to Basket Case—Can the Consumer Product Safety Commission Be Redeemed?" *Administrative Law Review*, 61, Winter 1989. One CPSC regulator, who asked to remain anonymous, complained to the author that Section 6(b) of the Consumer Product Safety Act "doesn't allow us [CPSC] to do anything out in the sunshine."

54 John D. Donahue, "Fast Track Product Recall," *Making Washington Work: Tales of Innovation in the Federal Government*. Washington,

D.C.: Brookings Institution Press, 1999, p. 25.

55 Adler, interview with author, August 11, 1999.

56 CPSC press release #98-076, March 5, 1998, www.cpsc.gov.

57 "Firms Resisted Seat Recall, U.S. Says," *Los Angeles Times*, March 6, 1998, p. D3.

58 Mitch Lipka, "Company Pays, Takes No Blame," *Sun-Sentinel South Florida*, November 28–30, 1999.

59 Ibid.

60 Carol Dingledy, Cosco public relations. E-mail communication with author, September 2, 1999.

61 Cosco Annual Report, 1999.

62 *American Baby*, October 1999; *Childbirth*, Second Printing 1999.

63 *Baby Talk*, October 1999.

64 Hasbro sales information from Hasbro Annual Report 1998; Advertising statistics from Steff Gelston, "Hasbro Shifts Playskool Ad Account," *The Boston Herald*, April 1, 1997.

65 Mattel sales information from Mattel Annual Report 1998; Advertising statistics from Karen Benezra, "Category Wars: Fisher-Price, Little Tikes Defend Preschool Turf," *Brandweek*, February 9, 1998.

66 Anonymous CPSC regulator, July 19, 1999. According to this source, Fisher-Price did advertise its October 22, 1998 Power Wheels recall.

67 N.J. Scheers, Ph.D., "Evaluation of the Fast-Track Product Recall Program of the U. S. Consumer Product Safety Commission," CPSC internal report, October 13, 1998.

68 Barbara Finigan, Hasbro attorney. Letter to Theresa Rogers, CPSC office of complaince, October 27, 1995.

69 "Corrective Action Plan Progress Report," filed by Hasbro with CPSC, October 25, 1995.

70 "Corrective Action Plan Progress Report," filed by Hasbro with CPSC, August 31, 1996.

71 Morgan Hilliard, California consumer. E-mail message sent to Playskool Consumer Relations, February 12, 1996.

72 Rader, August 1998.

73 David Baker, lawyer with Thompson, Hine, and Flory, Washington, D.C. Interview with author, August 28, 1998.

74 Alison Golub, "Secrets of Success," *Small World*, October 1999, p. 58.

75 Ibid, p. 60.

76 CPSC Safety Sells transcript, CPSC Document #6001, March 28, 1995. Hasbro CEO Alan Hassenfeld said, "We made the decision to

become a major player in the juvenile furniture area as a result of many internal meetings in 1992. At the time, we were not really involved in the business. We did license our name out in a small number of categories within juvenile furniture, but, quite honestly, the result had been a disappointment in terms of both sales and the type of product that we were putting our name on." The company licensed its Playskool name to Kolcraft for use on the Travel-Lite cribs, which were shipped to customers between January 1990 and early 1992.

77 John Staas, Kolcraft executive V.P. of operations. Correspondence to Joel Friedman, CPSC, June 12, 1992.

78 "JPMA Product Competition Winners 1989–1999," Juvenile Products Manufacturers Association memo, December 17, 1999.

79 CPSC "Memo of Telecon with Judith Oldham re: Kolcraft/Playskool Recall," February 12, 1993.

80 CPSC IDI #910906HCC0239, October 8, 1991.

81 Donald M. Robbins, senior vice president/general counsel of Hasbro. Letter to Joel I. Friedman, CPSC, May 4, 1992.

82 John Staas, executive vice president of operations, Kolcraft. Letter to Joel Friedman, CPSC, June 12, 1992.

83 CPSC IDI # 930105HWE7003, January 13, 1993.

84 Gina M. Scott, "Baby Suffocates When Playpen Collapses," *Northwest Arkansas Morning News*, December 2, 1992.

85 CPSC IDI #930114HCC3083, January 14, 1993.

86 Marc Schoem. Letter to Bernard Greenberg, president of Kolcraft, February 1, 1993.

87 "Section 15(b) Full Report: Playskool Travel-Lite Portable Crib," submitted by John A. Staas, executive vice president, Kolcraft Enterprises, Inc., February 12, 1993.

88 Ibid.

89 Ibid.

90 Ibid. Initially, Kolcraft agreed to send a recall notification letter to the American Academy of Pediatrics and instruct the trade group to notify its members. Eventually the company agreed to notify the pediatrician members itself, and sent each a recall poster.

91 Notes written by CPSC attorney William Moore during phone conversation with Kolcraft attorney Kerrie Hook, March 10, 1993.

92 CPSC press release #93-043, March 10, 1993, www.cpsc.gov.

93 William Moore, CPSC attorney. Letter to Judith Oldham, Kolcraft

attorney, February 24, 1993.

94 Ibid.

95 Notes of meeting between Judith Oldham, Kerrie Hook, John Staas, Marc Schoem, Terri Rogers, and Bill Moore, March 1, 1993. Although the handwritten notes are not signed, they match other file notes and correspondence written by Terri Rogers.

96 Notes taken by William Moore of his telephone conversation with Kerri Hook, March 10, 1993.

97 Recall effectiveness report from Kolcraft to CPSC, March 29, 1993.

98 Notes taken by Marc Schoem of telephone conversation with Kerrie Hook, March 10, 1993.

99 Ibid.

100 Marc Schoem. Memo to Terri Rogers, June 7, 1993.

101 "Corrective Action Plan Progress Report" filed by Kolcraft with CPSC, July 12, 1993.

102 CPSC IDI #961015CAA6007, October 15, 1996.

103 CPSC IDI #980513CNN0280, May 13, 1998.

104 Thomas Koltun, Kolcraft president. Statement written to author, August 27, 1998.

105 CPSC IDI # 980820CNE5258, August 20, 1998.

106 Linda Ginzel and Boaz Keysar. Letter to Alan Hassenfeld, Hasbro CEO, September 15, 1998.

107 CPSC press release #99-021, November 17, 1998, www.cpsc.gov.

108 CPSC file notes, January 8, 1999. The number of cribs returned in response to this reward is still unknown. Both Kolcraft and Hasbro failed to return the author's calls to update this number.

109 Transcript, CPSC Recall Effectiveness Forum, March 23, 1999.

110 Ibid, pp. 25–26.

111 Ibid, p. 32. Alan Schoem is the brother of Marc Schoem, CPSC Regulator of Recalls and Compliance.

112 Jayne O'Donnell, "Tracking Buyers Critical to Product Recalls: Federal Policy Considered," USA Today, November 12, 1998, p. 6B.

113 Transcript, CPSC Recall Effectiveness Forum, March 23, 1999, p. 49.

114 Ibid, p. (on cost).

115 Ibid, pp. 157–158.

116 Fise, August 10, 1999.

117 Anonymous CPSC regulator. Interview with author, July 19, 1999.

118 Fise, August 10, 1999.

119 Transcript, CPSC Recall Effectiveness Forum, March 23, 1999, p. 5.

120 Jon Bigness, "Boy's Playpen Death Spurs Recall Efforts, Second-Hand Sales Also Targeted," *Chicago Tribune*, June 15, 1998.

121 "Report of the Recall Effectiveness Task Force of the Consumer Product Safety Commission," August 25, 1980.

122 Loren Lange, "Recall Effectiveness Study," Office of Strategic Planning, Consumer Product Safety Commission, May 1978. Also see: N. Craig Smith and John A. Quelch, "Managing Product Recalls," *Ethics in Business*, Homewood, Il.: Irwin, 1993, pp 359–385.

123 R. Dennis Murphy and Paul H. Rubin, "Determinants of Recall Success Rates," *Journal of Products Liability*, 11, 1988, pp 17–28.

124 "Firm Resisted Seat Recall, U. S. Says," *Los Angeles Times*, March 6, 1998, p. D3. Sue Lindsay, "Playpen Maker Won't Recall Product in Death of Baby," *Denver Rocky Mountain News*, November 4, 1994, p. 28A.

Chapter 4

1 Details of the Century crib case are found in the company's settlement agreement with the CPSC: CPSC Docket No. 98-C0003, December 24, 1997.

2 "Office of Compliance—Section 15(b) Internet Report," www.cpsc.gov.

3 CPSC press release #95-076, February 10, 1995, www.cpsc.gov.

4 CPSC Docket no. 91-C0004, January 11, 1991.

5 CPSC Docket no. 98-C0003, December 24, 1997.

6 CPSC press release #97-102, April 16, 1997, www.cpsc.gov.

7 CPSC press release #91-039, February 13, 1991, www.cpsc.gov.

8 CPSC press release #98-064, February 9, 1998, www.cpsc.gov.

9 *Cleveland Plain Dealer*, May 20, 1998.

10 Century settlement agreement with CPSC: CPSC Docket No. 98-C0003, December 24, 1997.

11 Russ Rader, CPSC public affairs officer. E-mail message to author, June 22, 2000.

12 CPSC Docket No. 98-C0003, December 24, 1997, p. 3.

13 Robert S. Adler, "From 'Model Agency' to Basket Case—Can the Consumer Product Safety Commission Be Redeemed?" *Administrative Law Review*, 61, Winter 1989, p. 120.

14 "Product Recalls: Less Than Meets the Eye," *Consumer Reports*, November, 1994, pp. 732–735.

15 Rader, e-mail message to author, August 27, 1999.

16 CPSC press release #96-187, September 5, 1996, www.cpsc.gov.

17 Cosco promotional literature.

18 Kathie Morgan, director, technical committee operations, American Society for Testing and Materials. E-mail communication to author, April 26, 2000.

19 Ruthann Scarlatella. Letter to Cosco, Inc., February 12, 1991.

20 "Records of Entrapment Incidents From Cosco Files," United States v. Cosco Inc., U. S. District Court Southern District of Indiana, Indianapolis Division, Case No. IP95-1648C-B/S, December 11, 1995, p. 1.

21 Ibid, p. 6.

22 Ibid, p. 6.

23 CPSC handwritten notes, "Incident re: T22," December 5, 1991. The notes document a telephone conversation between a CPSC regulator (no name identified) and New York State Police investigator Robert Fish of Plattsburg, New York. The memo was marked "Plaintiff's Exhibit 12," and was used in the government's case against Cosco, "Complaint for Civil Penalties," United States of America v. Cosco, Inc., U. S. District Court Southern District of Indiana, Indianapolis Division, Case No. IP95-1649-C B/S, December 11, 1995.

24 "Objections and Responses of the United States of America to Defendant's First Set of Interrogatories and Document Requests," Case No. IP 95-1648-C B/S, p. 26.

25 "Youth Beds" memo written by T. Emerson, December 11, 1991, Plaintiff's Exhibit 13, in the government's case against Cosco.

26 "Records of Entrapment Incidents From Cosco Files," United States v. Cosco Inc., Civil No. IP95-1648C-B/S.

27 "Complaint for Civil Penalties," United States of America v. Cosco, Inc., Case No. IP95-1649-C B/S, December 11, 1995, p. 4.

28 Ibid, p. 2.

29 "Records of Entrapment Incidents From Cosco Files," United States v. Cosco Inc., Case No. IP95-1648C-B/S.

30 Ibid.

31 Ibid.

32 Ibid.

33 "Complaint for Civil Penalties," United States of America v. Cosco, Inc., Case No. IP95-1649-C B/S, p. 2.

34 CPSC press release #94-088, June 7, 1994, www.cpsc.gov.

35 "Complaint for Civil Penalties," United States of America v. Cosco,

Inc., Case No. IP95-1648-C B/S; and "Complaint for Civil Penalties," United States of America v. Cosco, Inc., Case No. IP95-1649-C B/S.

36 "Case Management Plan," United States of America v. Cosco, Inc., Case No. IP 95-1649-C B/S, p. 3.

37 Ibid.

38 "Records of Entrapment Incidents From Cosco Files," United States v. Cosco Inc., Case No. IP95-1648C-B/S.

39 "Case Management Plan," United States of America v. Cosco, Inc., Case No. IP 95-1649-C B/S, May 1996, p. 6.

40 "Operating Results," Annual Report, Dorel Industries, 1997.

41 CPSC press release #96-187, September 5, 1996, www.cpsc.gov.

42 "Settlement Agreement" between CPSC, U. S. Department of Justice, and Cosco Inc. Case No. IP95-1648C-B/S, August 1996.

43 CPSC press releases #97-154, June 9, 1997; #96-034, December 6, 1995; #97-110, April 24, 1997; #96-059, January 16, 1996, www.cpsc.gov. The chifferobe and dresser press releases were titled "Warnings" rather than "Recalls."

44 Rader. E-mail message to author, June 15, 2000.

45 Marc Schoem, CPSC regulator of corrective actions and compliance. Author notes of presentation, International Consumer Product Health and Safety Organization (ICPHSO) seminar, Chicago, May 26, 1999.

46 CPSC Field Activity Investigation, #970513CEN1016, May 19, 1997.

47 Bengt Lager, president of Regal + Lager. Interview with author, August 30, 1999. Lager described the incident, but did not provide a date. A January 1, 1999 memo sent by CPSC regulator Marc Schoem to the agency's public affairs staff and field investigators Eric Ault and George Gayman indicates that this first incident occurred on May 28, 1995.

48 Letter from parent to Bengt Lager, September 26, 1996.

49 Mitch Lipka, "Consumers in Jeopardy," South Florida Sun-Sentinel, November 28–30.

50 CPSC Epidemiologic Investigation Report #961105CWE5001, October 24, 1996.

51 CPSC Epidemiologic Investigation Report #970507CNE5124, May 19, 1997.

52 CPSC Field Activity Investigation, #970513CEN1016, May 19, 1997.

53 Eric Ault, CPSC Director Central Regional Office. Letter to Lager, August 6, 1997.

54 Frederick B. Locker, attorney, Locker, Greenberg & Brainin. Letter to George Gayman, CPSC senior compliance officer, September 19, 1997.

55 CPSC Epidemiologic Investigation Report #980401CNE5119, April 2, 1998.

56 CPSC Epidemiologic Investigation Report #98113CWE5009, November 6, 1998.

57 Locker. Letter to Gayman, March 18, 1998.

58 CPSC Epidemiologic Investigation Report #980722CWE5007, July 24, 1998.

59 Gayman. Memo to Marc Schoem, October 13, 1998.

60 Ibid.

61 CPSC Consumer Product Incident Report (no case number assigned), January 29, 1999.

62 CPSC Epidemiologic Investigation Report #981005CMC9001, October 5, 1998.

63 Portia R. Moore. Letter to Ann Brown, CPSC chairman, October 8, 1998.

64 Lager. Interview with author, February 29, 2000.

65 Ibid.

66 Ibid.

67 CPSC Epidemiologic Investigation Report #981116CWE5012, November 16, 1998.

68 Gayman. Letter to Locker, November 17, 1998.

69 CPSC press release #99-053, January 21, 1999, www.cpsc.gov.

70 Lager. Interview with author, February 29, 2000.

71 "Matthew John Gordon and Portia Moore v. Regal Lager, Inc.," United States District Court for the Northern District of California, November 25, 1998.

72 CPSC Field Activity Investigation, #970513CEN1016, May 19, 1997.

73 Ibid.

74 Transcript, CPSC Recall Effectiveness Forum, March 23, 1999.

75 Transcript, CPSC Recall Effectiveness Forum, March 23, 1999.

76 Portia Moore. Interview with author, February 5, 2000.

77 Lager. Interview with author, February 29, 2000.

Chapter 5

1 Robert S. Adler, "From 'Model Agency' to Basket Case—Can the Consumer Product Safety Commission Be Redeemed?" *Administrative Law Review, 61*, 1981, p. 107.

2 The *New York Times* Information Bank Abstracts, November 26, 1970, p. 46.

3 The *New York Times* Information Bank Abstract, November 18, 1971, p. 94.

4 "The Impact of Restrictive Disclosure Provisions on Freedom of Information Act Requests: An Analysis of Section 6(b)(1) of the Consumer Product Safety Act," *Minnesota Law Review, 64*, 1021, 1980, p. 1024.

5 Frances E. Zollers, "Consumer Product Safety Act Section 6(b), The Freedom of Information Act, and Information Disclosure Patterns Within the Consumer Product Safety Commission: Lessons Learned," *Consumer Safety and Industry Compliance with the New Reporting Requirements of the Consumer Product Safety Commission: A Blueprint for Cooperation in the '90's*, American Bar Association, 1992.

6 Adler, "From 'Model Agency' to Basket Case—Can the Consumer Product Safety Commission Be Redeemed?" p. 114.

7 Ibid, p. 107.

8 Russ Rader, CPSC public affairs officer. E-mail message to author, March 6, 2000.

9 Mitch Lipka, "Law Requires Agency to Keep Data a Secret," *South Florida Sun-Sentinel,* November 28–30, 1999, p. 12.

10 Ibid.

11 Denise and Alan Fields, *Baby Bargains*. Denver: Windsor Peak Press, 1999, p. 247.

12 Sandy Jones, *Consumer Reports Guide to Baby Products*. Yonkers, N.Y.: Consumer Reports Special Publications, 1999, p. 136.

13 CPSC press release #00-098, April 13, 2000, www.cpsc.gov.

14 CPSC press releases #97-180, September 2, 1997; #94-037, February 8, 1994; #93-095, July 22, 1993; #95-121, May 16, 1995, #97-110, April 24, 1997, www.cpsc.gov.

15 "Infant Swings"—Accident Investigations, U. S. Consumer Product Safety Commission–National Injury Information Clearinghouse Report, 1990 to April 7, 2000.

16 Joliet, Illinois Police Department report, May 9, 1997; CPSC

Epidemiologic Investigation Report #931214CAA3145, December 15, 1993; report filed by grandmother with Ohio Attorney General, February 21, 1996; letter from mother to Century Products, addressed "To Whom it May Concern," December 6, 1993. The mother states in the letter: "Because of my stupidity I lost my son. I know I am a good mother but because I did not heed the warnings found in your direction book I lost [my son].... When I got up the next morning to check on him, I found him hanging from the swing with one of the straps of the belt around his neck. I knew he was dead right when I saw him because there was just no way he could be alive because he was hanging from the swing with the belt strap around his neck.... Let me say one more time that I am the one who made the mistake of putting an active unattended baby in that swing, but I can't change anything about what happened... I can only think that [my son] is with Jesus and is well taken care of... Thank you for listening."

17 Todd Stevenson, CPSC FOIA officer. Letter to author, "FOIA Request S-9120007," December 15, 1999.

18 "Regulation: Process and Politics," *Congressional Quarterly,* Washington, D. C., 1982, p. 23.

19 State of Michigan in the Circuit Court for the County of Macomb, Case #94-4557-NP, September 24, 1996.

20 Paula Mergenhagen, "Product Liability: Who Sues?" *American Demographics,* June 1995.

21 Francis H. Hare, Jr., James L. Gilbert, and Stuart A. Ollinak, *Full Disclosure: Combating Stonewalling and Other Discovery Abuses.* Washington, D.C.: ATLA Press, 1994.

22 Ralph Nader and Wesley J. Smith, *No Contest: Corporate Lawyers and the Perversion of Justice in America.* New York: Random House, 1996, p. 60.

23 Hare, Jr., Gilbert and Ollinak, *Full Disclosure: Combating Stonewalling and Other Discovery Abuses,* p. 81.

24 "Plaintiff's First Set of Interrogatories and First Requests for Production of Documents To Cosco, Inc.," United States of America V. Cosco, Inc., in the U. S. District Court of Southern District of Indiana, Indianapolis Division, Case No. IP95-1648-c-H/G, February 7, 1996.

25 Peter Winik, Latham & Watkins. Letter to William Zoffer, U. S. Department of Justice, March 5, 1996.

26 "Cosco, Inc.'s Response to Plaintiff's First Set of Interrogatories and

First Requests for Production of Documents," United States of America v. Cosco, Inc., in the U. S. District Court of Southern District of Indiana, Indianapolis Division, Case No. IP95-1648-c-H/G, April 10, 1996, p. 2.

27 Ibid, p. 6.

28 Ibid, p. 7.

29 Ibid.

30 William Zoffer. Letter to Peter L. Winik and Minh N. Vu, April 19, 1996.

31 Zoffer. Letter to Winik and Vu, June 3, 1996.

32 "Cosco, Inc.'s Supplemental Response to Plaintiff's First Set of Interrogatories and First Requests For Production of Documents," United States of America v. Cosco, Inc., in the U. S. District Court of Southern District of Indiana, Indianapolis Division, p. 2.

33 Ibid.

34 Ibid, p. 8.

35 Joseph C. Gergits, U. S. Department of Justice. Letter to Minh N. Vu, Latham & Watkins, June 20, 1996.

36 Ibid.

37 Mihn N. Vu. Letter to Joseph C. Gergits, June 28, 1996.

38 "Deposition Upon Oral Examination of David A. Zike," United States of America v. Cosco, Inc., in the U. S. District Court of Southern District of Indiana, Indianapolis Division Case. Nos. IP 95-1648-C-B/S and IP 95-1649-C-B/S, June 25, 1996.

39 "Settlement Agreement," U. S. Department of Justice and the Consumer Product Safety Commission and Cosco, Inc., August 30, 1996.

40 Don Dillman. Memo to Roy Schwartzkopf, May 7, 1992. Also copied on the memo were Ray Hall, Bob Craig, and Cosco customer service manager Brenda Smith.

41 Memo written by "T. Emerson" to distribution list with following initials: "DZ, JR, RS, BS, RH, RK, BC, TF, BS, JF," December 11, 1991.

42 Ibid. Bob Craig no longer works for Cosco, but continues to attend industry voluntary standard-setting meetings as an independent consultant. As of February 2000, Craig was the chair of the portable crib/play yard committee. Terry Emerson, still a Cosco employee, remains active in industry standard-setting as well; as of February 2000, he was the chair of the toddler bed rail safety standards committee.

43 Dick Dahl, "Strictly Confidential," *The Massachusetts Lawyers*

Weekly, January 11, 1993, p. 37.

44 Ibid, p. 45.

45 Ibid.

46 Ibid, p. 37.

47 Stephen J. Kiely, "Public Access to Private Lawsuits," *The Massachusetts Lawyers Weekly*, February 19, 1992, p. 18.

48 Attorney Ven Johnson. Interview with author, December 28, 1999. Apparently, Baby Trend's lawyer, Rick Locker (also counsel for the industry trade group, JPMA) successfully convinced the jury that Jared's mother was at least partially responsible for her son's death, as they awarded the Zaliniskis only $500,000. But the judge disagreed, and increased the award to $1.15 million. After post-trial hearings, Baby Trend ultimately agreed to pay the family $1 million. This was the limit on the company's insurance. ("Settlement Reported in Playpen Death," *The Chicago Tribune*, February 2, 1997).

49 Dahl, "Strictly Confidential," p. 37.

50 There is a dearth of data on the number of confidential settlements signed each year. A staff attorney with the plaintiffs' lawyers' trade group, ATLA, said, "Asking about the number of confidential settlements is like asking how many secrets there are. You just don't know." Personal communication with staff attorney, Association of Trial Lawyers of America, May 30, 2000.

51 Bob Gibbins, "Secrecy versus Safety," *ABA Journal*, December 1991, pp. 74–77; Arthur R. Miller, "The Debate Over Courthouse Confidentiality," *ABA Journal*, August 1991, pp. 65–68.

52 Richard A. Zitrin, "Legal Ethics: The Case Against Secret Settlements (Or, What You Don't Know Can Hurt You)," *Journal of the Institute for the Study of Legal Ethics*, 115, 1999, pp. 1–52.

53 Anonymous source. Interview with author, July 19, 1999.

54 Zitrin, "Legal Ethics: The Case Against Secret Settlements (Or, What You Don't Know Can Hurt You)."

55 Ibid.

56 Andrew D. Miller, "Federal Anti-Secrecy Legislation: A Model Act to Safeguard the Public From Court Sanctioned Hidden Hazards," *Boston College Environmental Affairs Law Review*, Winter 1993, p. 52.

57 Alison Golub, "Industry Insight," *Small World*, October 1999, p. 60–64. The top three manufacturers in each juvenile product category are listed. Cosco's rankings are as follows: Car seats—#2; Strollers—#3; Cribs/Bassinets/Cradles—#2; Play Yards—#3.

58 CPSC press release #92-076, April 9, 1992; #94-088, June 7, 1994;

#96-034, February 6, 1995; #96-059, February 16, 1996; #97-110, April 24, 1997; #97-154, July 9, 1997; #98-045, December 16, 1997; #99-062, February 17, 1999; #99-063, February 17, 1999; #99-138, July 8, 1999, www.cpsc.gov.; The "Youth Furniture" release announced a "warning" rather than a "recall."

Chapter 6

1 "The 1999 International Juvenile Products Show Directory: Moving Toward the Millenium," The Juvenile Products Manufacturers Association, www.jpma.org.
2 For industry sales statistics, 1980–1993, see: Loretta Roach, "Jumping Juvenile," *Discount Merchandiser*, November 1994, p. 28 and the Juvenile Products Manufacturers Association website, www.jpma.org. For birth statistics see: "National Vital Statistics Reports," Centers for Disease Control and Prevention, U. S. Department of Health and Human Services, 1998. For 2000 projections, see: Brad Edmondson, "Children in 2001," *American Demographics*, March 1997.
3 Stephanie J. Ventura, Joyce A. Martin, Sally Curtin, and T. J. Mathews, "Births: Final Data for 1997," *National Vital Statistics Reports*, Centers for Disease Control and Prevention, National Center for Health Statistics, April 29, 1999.
4 JoAnn Johnston, "Older, Wealthier Customers Spend $350B a Year, Feed Booming Industry," *The Boston Globe*, April 1, 1998, p. F1.
5 Vanessa Facer, "Billion Dollar Babies," *Discount Merchandiser*, October 1998, p. 46.
6 *Childbirth*, Second Printing 1999.
7 Cosco ad in *American Baby*, October 1999.
8 *American Baby*, November 1998.
9 CPSC press releases #00-098, April 13, 2000 (The swing incidents occurred over many years— Graco recalled all of its swings made before November 1997. The *American Baby* article reported that parents "couldn't live without" Graco's Open Top swing, but it did not recommend specific model numbers. The Open Top swings were among the models recalled in April 2000.; #99-053, January 21, 1999; #98-076, March 5, 1998, www.cpsc.gov. #99-053, #98-076.
10 Michael Jacobson and Laurie Ann Mazur, "The Impact of Commercialism: Affecting Our Minds, Pocketbooks, and Planet," *Marketing Madness: A Survival Guide for a Consumer Society*. Boulder:

Westview Press, 1995, p. 187.

11 Arlene Eisenberg, Heidi E. Murkoff, and Sandee E. Hathaway, *What to Expect: The Toddler Years*. New York: Workman Publishing, 1994; William Sears and Martha Sears, *The Baby Book*. Boston: Little, Brown and Company, 1993.

12 Benjamin Spock and Stephen Parker, *Dr. Spock's Baby and Child Care*. New York: Pocket Books, 1998, pp. 368–369.

13 Steven P. Shelov, *Caring For Your Baby and Young Child: Birth to Age 5*. New York: Bantam Books, 1998, p. 230.

14 Ibid, p. 395.

15 Sandy Jones, *Consumer Reports Guide to Baby Products*. Yonkers, NY: Consumer Reports Special Publications, 1999, p. 256.

16 See the Evenflo website: www.evenflo.com

17 www.safekids.org/study.html

18 Jones, *Consumer Reports Guide to Baby Products*, p. 80.

19 See CPSC website for details of the study: www.cpsc.gov/library/thrift.html.

Chapter 7

1 Melinda Beck, "The Tylenol Scare," *Newsweek*, October 11, 1982.

2 Rick Atkinson, "The Tylenol Nightmare: How a Corporate Giant Fought Back," *The Kansas City Times*, November 12, 1982.

3 "Report Clears Tylenol," *The Courier Post*, Camden, New Jersey, October 23, 1982.

4 Beck, "The Tylenol Scare."

5 Ibid.

6 Jerry Knight, "Tylenol's Maker Shows How to Respond to Crisis," *The Washington Post*, October 11, 1982.

7 Ibid.

8 See Beck, "The Tylenol Scare," and Thomas Moore, "The Fight to Save Tylenol," *Fortune*, November 29, 1982.

9 Atkinson, "The Tylenol Nightmare: How a Corporate Giant Fought Back."

10 Patricia McCormack, "Tylenol's Poison Rebound: A Study in Corporate Painkilling," *New Brunswick Home News*, October 13, 1985.

11 Ibid.

12 "Rockabye Baby," *Dateline NBC Transcript*, NBC News, May 23, 1995.

13 CPSC press release #99-021, November 17, 1998; #98-128, June 18, 1998, www.cpsc.gov.

14 CPSC report: "Bath Seats—Deaths Only 1/1/83–2/25/00," memo distributed by CPSC at September 1999 ASTM meeting.

15 Richard Bethea, Graco attorney. Interview with *Dateline NBC*. Transcript, May 23, 1995.

16 Christopher Smith, attorney with Arent Fox Kintner Plotkin & Kahn. Letter to CPSC regulator Marc Schoem, July 15, 1996.

17 CPSC press release #00-109, November 17, 1999, www.cpsc.gov.

18 Sue Lindsay, "Playpen Maker Won't Recall Product in Death of Baby," *Denver Rocky Mountain News*, November 4, 1994, p. 28A.

19 CPSC press release #97-146, June 25, 1997, www.cpsc.gov.

20 Dawn D'Aries, "JPMA Spring Meeting: Organization Focus on Growth," *Home Textiles Today*, May/June 1999, p. 24.

21 Adler

22 Ibid.

23 Paula Markowitz, president of Patchcraft. Interview with author, November 1, 1999.

24 ASTM letter to JPMA/ASTM Members of F15.11 & 16.21 "Subcommittees on Juvenile Products," August 21, 2000.

25 ASTM official meeting notes for all committees, February/March 2000.

26 Author's notes of ASTM meeting on bed rails, March 1, 2000.

27 After losing the vote, Ware added, "Why does it have to be toll-free?"

28 ASTM pays the meeting-related expenses of up to three consumer advocates. But the organization does not actively recruit consumers, nor does it provide any training. Often, a consumer will attend meetings at her own expense with no knowledge that ASTM may have paid for the trip if she had known to ask.

29 There are a few exceptions: Don Mays of the Good Housekeeping Institute and Werner Freitag of Consumers Union are frequent consumer-contributors to ASTM standards. Both Mays and Freitag are engineers.

30 "The most frequent injuries involve children falling either when the bottom of the bassinet or cradle breaks, or when the whole thing tips over and collapses," writes Sandy Jones in the *Consumer Reports Guide to Baby Products*, Consumer Reports Special Publications, New York, 1999, p. 56.

31 Fise. Author notes of ASTM standards meeting for cradles, February

28, 2000.

32 John Drengenberg, manager of global consumer affairs, Underwriters Laboratory. Interview with author, June 16, 2000.

33 Ibid.

34 "Detroit Testing Laboratory report of Play Yard testing," Report number 30873Z-Z, October 8, 1993.

35 Jack Walsh, executive director of the Danny Foundation. Interview with author, June 20, 2000.

36 Drengenberg, June 16, 2000.

37 ASTM meeting notes taken by author, August 31, 1999.

38 Steven P. Shelov, M.D. (Ed.), *Caring for Your Baby and Young Child: Birth to Age 5*. New York: Bantam Books, 1991, p. 14.

39 Robert Tanz, MD. Interview with author, January 22, 2000.

40 "Section on Injury and Poison Prevention," American Academy of Pediatrics website, www.aap.org.

41 For Deppa's recommended language, see Handout of February 2000 ASTM meeting, "Minutes of Meeting on Infant Swings Held September 1, 1999." For language adopted by ASTM committee, see ASTM meeting notes, February 2000.

42 ASTM official meeting notes, February 29, 2000.

43 CPSC Epidemiological Investigation Report #931214CAA3145, December 15, 1993; Written communication from Terri Rogers, CPSC senior compliance officer and Sharon Freimuth of Century Products, July 9, 1997; Letter from victim's grandmother to Century Products, addressed "Dear Sirs," February 15, 1996, describing grandson's "almost fatal accident."

44 "Consumer Product Safety Commission Product Safety Assessment Report," Case #CA960080, undated.

45 CPSC press release #97-180, September 2, 1997, www.cpsc.gov.

46 Markowitz. Interview with author, November 1, 1999.

47 "Bath Seat Incident Data," Enclosure B, ASTM official meeting notes, February 24, 1999.

48 CPSC ASTM notes.

49 Ibid.

50 Mary Ellen Fise, "In the Matter of the Petition of the Consumer Federation of America, The Drowning Prevention Foundation, et. al. to Ban Baby Bath Seats," submitted to the CPSC, July 25, 2000.

51 George Rutherford, CPSC project manager. Memo to John Preston, CPSC Directorate for Engineering Sciences. "Increase in Consumer Complaints Associated with Baby Strollers," August 24, 1999.

52 N. Craig Smith and John A. Quelch, "Managing Product Recalls," *Ethics in Marketing*. Homewood, Il.: Irwin, 1993, p. 361.

53 Ibid.

54 Russ Rader, CPSC public affairs officer. Interview with author, August 1998.

55 Internal Cosco memo, undated, included in Department of Justice file, marked "48-000662."

56 Atkinson, "The Tylenol Nightmare: How a Corporate Giant Fought Back."

57 Smith and Quelch, p. 358.

58 1997: 362 recalls (CPSC 1997 Annual Report to Congress); 1998: 273 recalls (Ken Giles, CPSC staff, email communication with author, July 13, 2000); 1999: 304 recalls (Giles).

59 Russ Rader, CPSC public affairs officer. Interview with author, August 1998.

60 "Recall Handbook," U.S. Consumer Product Safety Commission Office of Compliance, May 1999, pp. 12–13.

61 Ibid.

62 FOIA requests filed for information on multiple recalled products typically did not yield information about the CPSC's hazard rating. These are the only two products for which the CPSC released this information to the author.

63 Anonymous source, interview with author, July 19, 1999; Robert Adler, former CPSC laywer, interview with author, August 11, 1999.

64 Russ Rader, CPSC public affairs officer. Interview with author, August 1998.

65 Adler, August 11, 1999.

66 Ibid.

67 Fise, August 10, 1999.

68 "Report of the Recall Effectiveness Task Force of the Consumer Product Safety Commission," August 25, 1980.

69 Transcript of CPSC Recall Effectiveness Forum, March 23, 1999, p. 15.

70 Ibid, p. 49.

71 CPSC regulators claim that the agency does not have the authority to require manufacturers to enclose mandatory registration cards in products. However, this may not be the case. Law professor and former CPSC lawyer Bob Adler, posits that Section 27(e) of the CPSA may grant the CPSC this authority. "I'd say that there's a good argument to be made that the agency could require registration cards if it

could demonstrate a safety need," said Adler. Email communication from Adler to author, July 21, 2000.

72 "Recall Handbook," U.S. Consumer Product Safety Commission, May 1999, p. 15.

73 The Lane Furniture Company recalled its cedar chests in September 1996 after six children became locked inside them and suffocated, CPSC press release #96-186, September 4, 1996. In March 2000 Lane issued a second recall notice after learning of a seventh death and two "near fatalities," CPSC press release #00-084, March 30, 2000. Fisher-Price recalled 10 million Power Wheels battery-powered cars after 700 of the child-size vehicles overheated, causing 150 fires, CPSC press release #99-012, October 22, 1998.

74 Anonymous CPSC regulator. Interview with author, July 19, 1999.

75 Ibid.

76 William Moore, CPSC attorney. Notes taken during phone conversation with Kolcraft attorney Kerrie Hook, March 10, 1993.

77 CPSC press release #99-021, November 17, 1998.

78 CPSC press release #98-128, June 18, 1998. One crib manufacturer, Draco, offered consumers no remedy—after the crib recall, the company went out of business and its owners disappeared.

79 CPSC press release # 00-098, April 13, 2000.

80 On April 28, 2000, the author called the Graco hotline to request a swing repair kit. It arrived three weeks later, on May 17, 2000.

81 Graco repair instruction sheet.

82 A notable exception was the CPSC's lawsuit against Black & Decker. The CPSC alleged that the company's 1997 recall of its Spacemaker Horizontal Toaster "did not go far enough in notifying the public of the recall or the potential fire hazard associated with the toasters, and the consumer remedy was not adequate." Initially, the company had offered consumers only a coupon to be used toward the purchase of another Black & Decker product. The suit was settled in April 1998, when Black & Decker agreed to improve its consumer remedy by offering consumers their choice of a free toaster or another product replacement. CPSC press release #98-097, April 23, 1998.

83 "Report of the Recall Effectiveness Task Force of the Consumer Product Safety Commission," August 25, 1980, p. 3.

84 Jayne O'Donnell, "Child Dangers Ignored: 17 Firms Kept Quiet Problems Quiet," USA Today, April 3, 2000, p. 1A.

85 Michael R. Lemov, "Product Liability," The National Law Journal, August 10, 1998, p. 2.

86 Rader. Written communication with author, August 27, 1999.

87 CPSC Docket No. 98-C0003, December 24, 1997.

88 Lemov, "Product Liability," p. 3.

89 Ibid.

90 Robert S. Adler, "From 'Model Agency' to Basket Case—Can the Consumer Product Safety Commission Be Redeemed?" *Administrative Law Review*, 61, Winter 1989, p. 121.

91 CPSC Recall Handbook, CPSC Office of Compliance, May 1999, pp. 8–9.

92 CPSC press release #97-102, April 17, 1997, www.cpsc.gov.

93 Mary Ellen Fise, general counsel, Consumer Federation of America, interview with author, September 7, 2000.

94 CPSC press release #00-108, May 12, 2000, www.cpsc.gov.

95 Ibid.

96 Ibid.

97 Settlement agreement between U.S. Department of Justice, CPSC, and Cosco, Inc., August 30, 1996.

98 CPSC Docket No. 98-C0003, December 24, 1997.

99 Kip Viscusi, *Regulating Product Safety*, American Enterprise for Public Policy Research, Washington, D. C., 1994.

100 "The Consumer Product Safety Act as a Freedom of Information 'Withholding' Statute," *University of Pennsylvania Law Review*, 128, 1980, pp. 1166–1167.

101 "The Consumer Product Safety Act as a Freedom of Information 'Withholding' Statute," pp. 1167.

102 "Keeping Secrets: Justice on Trial," Report of the Conference on Courtroom Secrecy, Society of Professional Journalists and Association of Trial Lawyers of America, 1990, p. 1.

103 Ibid, pp. 39–40.

104 Dick Dahl, "Strictly Confidential," *The Massachusetts Lawyer Weekly*, January 11, 1993, p. 45.

105 Bill Heery, "Car Seat Suit Ends in $2 Million Settlement," *The Tampa Tribune*, March 10, 1995, pp. 1–2.

106 Historically, Kolcraft has had problems with its car seats. Between 1990 and June 2000, the company recalled some or all of the following models of the following car seats: Performa, Secure Fit, Travel About, Plus 4, Plus 5, Infant Rider, Carter Travel 5, Traveler 700, Automate, Perfect Fit, Dial-A-Fit, Rock-N-Ride, Infant Rider, Secura, Kolcraft Instant Restraint, and Kolcraft Infant Car Seat.

Kolcraft also manufactures car seats marketed under the Playskool brand name, several of which have been recalled (for complete list, see: www.nhtsa.gov). In 1995, a *Consumer Reports* test of car seats gave a failing grade to the Kolcraft 700 convertible seat (*The Baltimore Sun*, July 27, 1995, p. 3A) and urged the company to recall it. Four months later, NHTSA announced a recall of the seat (*Consumer Reports*, November 1995, p. 694), after the government determined that the car seat "failed" several crash tests. *Consumer Reports* applauded Kolcraft for recalling the seat so quickly. But a few months later, Kolcraft issued a press release quoting executive V.P. of operations John Staas as follows: "Recent news reports on the number of recalls of car safety seats have been misleading and potentially harmful to the public… Recalls are not all created equal. Many of the recalls do not involve performance issues related to crash situations… Kolcraft's goal is to go the extra mile for customers, particularly because our products help to protect children." ("Recall Coverage Misleading, Potentially Tragic," *PR Newswire*, September 21, 1995).

107 "Keeping Secrets: Justice on Trial," p. 63.

108 "Materials on Secrecy Practices in the Courts," 2000 Forum for State Court Judges, Roscoe Pound Institute, Washington, D.C., July 29, 2000.

109 "Better Data Needed to Help Identify and Analyze Potential Hazards," GAO/HEHS-97-147, September 1997, pp. 4–5.

110 NEISS Product Summary Report, Injury Estimates for Calendar Year 1998, CPSC.

111 www.homedepot.com

112 Ibid.

113 www.snowmobile.org

114 CPSC press release #00-178, September 5, 2000, www.cpsc.gov.

115 Infant equipment industry sales were $4.9 billion, see www.jpma.org; CPSC budget was $50 million, see CPSC 2001 Budget Request to Congress.

116 Anonymous CPSC regulator. Interview with author, July 19, 1999.

117 Ibid.

118 Ralph Nader, *Unsafe at Any Speed*. New York: Grossman Publishers, 1965, p. 42.

119 Ibid, p. 189.

120 www.nhtsa.gov.

121 Ibid.

122 Ibid.
123 NHTSA budget data: www.nhtsa.gov; CPSC budget data: CPSC 2001 Budget Request to Congress, p.1.
124 Kimberly M. Thompson, "Doing Our Best for Children: A Guide for Evaluating Hazard Claims and Setting Priorities," Harvard Center for Risk Analysis, 1999, www.kidsrisk.harvard.edu.

Index

Acknowledgments

Thanks to everyone who talked with me on and off the record. Without you, I couldn't have figured out the puzzle. (You know who you are).

To Ellen Liberman, my oldest friend, thanks for teaching me how to pitch a story, and for holding my hand as I wet my journalistic feet.

Thanks to my parents, Toby and Bernie Felcher, who listened to me rant for two years, then didn't complain (very much) when I got caller I.D. and stopped answering the phone.

To Aunt Shirley, my muse, you've gotten your pillow.

Thanks to my friends, who read portions of early manuscripts, offered wise criticism, and said, "Go Girl!": Christine Allred, Elizabeth Ames, Helen Campbell, Linda Carmichael, Jacki Isaacs, Jan Katz, Deborah Marlino, Judy Messick, Jackie Nicholson, Patti Polisar, Estelle Raiffa, Penny Savitz, Ruth Stern, Sandy Waxman and Marjorie Williams. To Michael Tushman (my fashion role-model), thanks for yelling at me.

Thanks to Dale Gody, for laying the foundation.

Thanks to the Mather House crew: Michelle Brown, Christina Farag and Joanna Holzman, for research support and for taking really, really long dog walks.

Thanks to Timber and Stowie for keeping my feet warm.

A huge thanks to Fred Shafer, for handing me the key to a world outside of Marketing 101. An equally huge thanks to my editors, Katherine Shonk (a woman who really knows her way around verbs) and Arthur Stamoulis, whose insights and suggestions significantly improved this book.

Thanks to Michael Curtis and *The Atlantic Monthly*, for believing in this story.

A bittersweet thanks to Linda Ginzel and Boaz Keysar. I wish I hadn't needed to write this book.

Thanks to Mary Ellen Fise, my hero. She should be President.